The Word
Enfleshed

The Word
Enfleshed

Exploring the Person and Work of Christ

Oliver D. Crisp

Baker Academic
a division of Baker Publishing Group
Grand Rapids, Michigan

© 2016 by Oliver D. Crisp

Published by Baker Academic
a division of Baker Publishing Group
P.O. Box 6287, Grand Rapids, MI 49516-6287
www.bakeracademic.com

Printed in the United States of America

All rights reserved. No part of this publication may be reproduced, stored in a retrieval system, or transmitted in any form or by any means—for example, electronic, photocopy, recording—without the prior written permission of the publisher. The only exception is brief quotations in printed reviews.

Library of Congress Cataloging-in-Publication Data
Names: Crisp, Oliver, author.
Title: The word enfleshed : exploring the person and work of Christ / Oliver D. Crisp.
Description: Grand Rapids : Baker Academic, 2016. | Includes bibliographical references and index.
Identifiers: LCCN 2016014914 | ISBN 9780801098093 (pbk.)
Subjects: LCSH: Jesus Christ—Person and offices.
Classification: LCC BT203 .C755 2016 | DDC 232/.8—dc23
LC record available at https://lccn.loc.gov/2016014914

Scripture quotations labeled ESV are from The Holy Bible, English Standard Version® (ESV®), copyright © 2001 by Crossway, a publishing ministry of Good News Publishers. Used by permission. All rights reserved. ESV Text Edition: 2011

Scripture quotations labeled NIV are from the Holy Bible, New International Version®. NIV®. Copyright © 1973, 1978, 1984, 2011 by Biblica, Inc.™ Used by permission of Zondervan. All rights reserved worldwide. www.zondervan.com

Scripture quotations labeled NKJV are from the New King James Version®. Copyright © 1982 by Thomas Nelson, Inc. Used by permission. All rights reserved.

Scripture quotations labeled NRSV are from the New Revised Standard Version of the Bible, copyright © 1989, by the Division of Christian Education of the National Council of the Churches of Christ in the United States of America. Used by permission. All rights reserved.

Chapter 3 is a revision of Oliver D. Crisp, "Incorporeality," in *The Routledge Companion to Philosophy of Religion*, ed. Chad Meister and Paul Copan (London: Routledge, 2012), 344–55. Used with permission from Taylor & Francis.

Chapter 4 is a revision of Oliver D. Crisp, "A Christological Model of the *Imago Dei*," in *The Ashgate Research Companion to Theological Anthropology*, ed. Joshua R. Farris and Charles Taliaferro (Farnham, UK: Ashgate, 2015), 217–29. Copyright © 2015.

In keeping with biblical principles of creation stewardship, Baker Publishing Group advocates the responsible use of our natural resources. As a member of the Green Press Initiative, our company uses recycled paper when possible. The text paper of this book is composed in part of post-consumer waste.

16 17 18 19 20 21 22   7 6 5 4 3 2 1

To Mike Rea,
Mensch

Contents

Preface ix
Acknowledgments xv

1. The Eternal Generation of the Son 1
2. Christ without Flesh 19
3. Incorporeality and Incarnation 33
4. The Christological Doctrine of the Image of God 51
5. Desiderata for Models of the Hypostatic Union 71
6. Compositional Christology 97
7. The Union Account of Atonement 119
8. The Spirit's Role in Union with Christ 145
9. The Nature and Scope of Union with Christ 165

Bibliography 173
Index 185

Preface

The great New England Puritan Jonathan Edwards once said that in Christ we find an "admirable conjunction of diverse excellencies." The more I think about it, the more his remark seems to capture something fundamental about my own fixation with the person and work of Christ. Edwards was speaking about the constitution of Christ himself when he wrote these words in a sermon entitled "The Excellency of Christ."[1] But it is not just that the incarnation instantiates *in one entity* an admirable conjunction of diverse excellencies: divinity and humanity, God Incarnate, and so on. It also provides the theologian—indeed, anyone with a stake in the Christian religion—with a compelling topic for investigation and intellectual engagement, for the very idea that a human being might also be divine is as riveting as it is scandalous.

My previous forays into this area have sought to tackle issues bearing upon the metaphysics of the incarnation, or what one might call the philosophical underpinnings of the theological claims made by historic, orthodox Christianity about the person of Christ. This has involved trying to get at what the traditional two-natures doctrine might entail. (Very roughly, the two-natures doctrine is the view that Christ is a divine person who takes on a human nature in addition to his divine one, in order to bring about the reconciliation or union of human beings with God.) It has also involved reflecting on christological method, as well as more

---

1. See Jonathan Edwards, *Sermons and Discourses, 1734–1738*, vol. 19 of *The Works of Jonathan Edwards*, ed. M. X. Lesser (New Haven: Yale University Press, 2001), 561–95.

unexpected questions about such things as whether Christ had a fallen human nature, or whether the virginal conception of Christ has any bearing on the medical-ethical quandary about the status of the embryo, or even whether there could be more than one incarnation. At the same time I have also developed an interest in the atonement as the culminating aspect of the work of Christ. To date, the results of my work in this area have been more scattered and occasional, but I hope to remedy that in a sequel to this volume, on the nature of the atonement.

This work is a further contribution to Christology. It is a study in systematic theology written from the perspective of analytic theology. On my way of thinking, analytic theology utilizes the tools and methods of contemporary analytic philosophy for the purposes of constructive Christian theology. Often, analytic philosophy is regarded as an enterprise that is not particularly interested in the origin or development of an idea, only in its utility, or its approximation to the truth of the matter. By contrast, Christian theology is usually thought to be deeply entangled with the genealogy of ideas. It is not just that for many theologians the origins and development of particular notions in the Christian tradition are as important as how we use such notions today. It is also that one cannot present theological arguments without paying attention to the ways in which the ideas contained in these arguments have been shaped by the Christian tradition. One cannot separate out the history from the concepts like the kernel from the husk without doing violence to the subject matter of theology.

Theologians have always been concerned to pass on the deposit of faith committed to them. Analytic theology can certainly be pursued in a way that seriously engages the Christian tradition. Indeed, this is how it is commonly practiced. Nevertheless, there is still a popular perception that analytic theology is an ahistorical project not interested in the genealogy of ideas or the ways in which ideas of the past influence our current thinking—an accusation that brings it under suspicion in the eyes of many systematic theologians. Work being done at the cutting edge of analytic theology shows this accusation is wide of the mark, though, as is often the case, these results take time to filter down to the popular imagination.[2]

2. See, e.g., Thomas H. McCall, *An Invitation to Analytic Christian Theology* (Downers Grove, IL: IVP Academic, 2015), recent volumes in *The Oxford Studies in Analytic Theology*

This project is a small contribution to that literature, providing one instance of analytic theology that (I hope) is historically and theologically engaged. It is also written from the perspective of the Reformed tradition, which inevitably shapes the work in important respects, though it addresses thinkers from other theological traditions as well.

One of the main aims of this work is to provide a "joined-up" account of the person and work of Christ. There are books on the incarnation and books on the atonement; this is a book that treats the incarnation and atonement as two parts or phases of one divine work—which is what I mean by a joined-up account. The atonement is the mediatorial work of Christ, but it is not the whole of the work of Christ. We might say that the atonement is a culminating moment of the work of Christ, a work that begins in eternity and is executed in time in the life and action of Christ in history.

With this in mind, the book begins with protological issues, matters pertaining to "first things"—that is, first things *as applied to the person and work of Christ*. To this end, chapters 1–3 deal with the eternal generation of the Son, the preexistence of Christ, and the relationship between divine incorporeality and incarnation. The first two of these topics have been the subject of some dispute in recent evangelical and systematic theology. The last involves an important cluster of issues about the relationship between God and the world that are much discussed in contemporary theology (viz., panentheism, emergence, and so on). I argue that the traditional, catholic notion that the Second Person of the Trinity is eternally generated by the Father should be upheld, contrary to some recent evangelical criticisms of that doctrine. I also argue that God the Son exists *asarkos*, or without flesh, prior to the incarnation. However, this raises worries about the relationship between God's incorporeality and Christ's corporeality. The third chapter addresses this concern, arguing that God is indeed incorporeal and that the assumption of human nature by the Second Person of the Trinity does not compromise this claim.

Chapter 4 addresses the vexed issue of the divine image, arguing that this should be understood protologically, in terms of humanity being made in the image of Christ, who is the image of God. This concept connects

---

series published by Oxford University Press, and *The Journal of Analytic Theology*, located at http://journalofanalytictheology.com.

up with the seventh and eighth chapters, in which a union account of the atonement is set out, and the relationship between the notion of union with Christ and the work of the Holy Spirit is spelled out. (The connection is something like this: Christ is the prototypical divine image in whose image we are fashioned in the expectation that we will be united to God through Christ by the power of the Holy Spirit. Thus, the fact that Christ is the image of God makes him a kind of hub or interface between human beings and God, enabling us to be united to God by the Holy Spirit, by means of the atoning work of Christ.) In between these chapters are two pieces (chs. 5–6), the first concerning desiderata for models of the hypostatic union, and the second giving an account of the hypostatic union set out in terms of compositionalism—one of the recent contributions made by analytic theologians to the doctrine of the incarnation. It is important to see what is meant by the hypostatic union if this union is the very means by which human beings are united to God.[3] So it is important to attend to the questions of desiderata for the hypostatic union and a model of that union between the chapters on the christological account of the divine image and the two chapters that spell out union with Christ in terms of atonement and the secret work of the Spirit.

In the final chapter, I turn to address the question of union with Christ more directly, tackling one recent internecine dispute among Reformed theologians about the nature and scope of union with Christ. Although this might be thought to be of little concern to those outside the Reformed community, I think that the issues raised are of wider interest. At any rate, clarifying the matter of the nature and scope of union with Christ as it bears upon this study is surely salient.

Taken together, these chapters present the outline of an account of the person and work of Christ, arguing that only when we see these as parts of one divine act do they make sense. In addition, the work makes a case for a particular way of thinking about the person and work of Christ, one that privileges the idea that God creates a world of human beings made in the image of Christ in order that they may participate in the divine life through

---

3. As will become clear in the following, by saying that the hypostatic union is the "very means by which human beings are united to God," I do not mean to suggest that the hypostatic union independent of Christ's atonement and the secret work of the Holy Spirit is *sufficient* to unite humans to God, only that it is one of the conditions *necessary* for this union that has been ordained by God. Since, in the purposes of God, no union with the divine can obtain without the incarnation, discussion of hypostatic union is an important consideration.

the agency of Christ's atoning work, by means of the union with Christ brought about by the person of the Holy Spirit. Although this is a work of contemporary systematic theology, it taps into notions of the divine image and union with Christ, alongside an exploration of participation in the divine life, that echo ancient theological themes found in the work of many other theologians of the past, from the early church onwards. The material on the hypostatic union and on matters of protology round out the whole, providing a conceptual snapshot, as it were, of how it is that the Word of God is enfleshed in Christ—hence the title of the work.[4]

There is a groundswell of interest among contemporary theologians, including theologians from my own Reformed tradition, in the notion of union with Christ and in ways of thinking about his mediatorial work that connects it to other aspects of his incarnation.[5] This is part of a growing awareness of the catholicity of Reformed thought, and a recovery of its deep connections with earlier phases of the Christian tradition. An important motif in much recent work concerned with the catholicity of Reformed theology is retrieval—of ideas from the ancient church as well as from medieval and Reformation theology.[6] Our concern about union

---

4. However, I should make it clear at the outset that I don't claim that the argument offered here is the *whole story* of the person and work of Christ, or of union with Christ, though I think it is an important aspect of that story. Hence, my claim that this is a "conceptual snapshot" and an "outline of an account" of the person and work of Christ.

5. Recent examples from Reformed thinkers include the work of Todd Billings, Julie Canlis, William B. Evans, Robert Grow and Myk Habets, Michael Horton, Marcus Peter Johnson, Mark Garcia, Robert Letham, and Kathryn Tanner. (References to the works of these theologians are given in ch. 8, footnote 18, and in the bibliography.) Michael J. Gorman's work is a good example of the wider theological interest in the topic of union with Christ. See, e.g., his recent monograph *The Death of the Messiah and the Birth of the New Covenant: A (Not So) New Model of the Atonement* (Eugene, OR: Cascade, 2014). Constantine R. Campbell's comprehensive study, *Paul and Union with Christ* (Grand Rapids: Zondervan, 2012), repays careful study. In addition to this there is the revival of interest in thinking about the work of Christ in terms of *theosis*, or divinization. (See, e.g., Michael J. Christensen and Jeffrey A. Wittung, eds., *Partakers of the Divine Nature: The History and Development of Deification in the Christian Traditions* [Grand Rapids: Baker Academic, 2008.]) Although I do not explore theosis in detail here, it should be clear that I am in sympathy with a version of it. Finally, there are participatory accounts of atonement that tap into similar themes, e.g., Tim Bayne and Greg Restall, "A Participatory Account of the Atonement," in *New Waves in Philosophy of Religion*, ed. Yujin Nagasawa and Eric J. Wielenberg (Houndmills, UK: Palgrave Macmillan, 2009), 150–66, which draws on the work of the New Testament scholar Douglas Campbell.

6. See, e.g., Michael Allen and Scott R. Swain, *Reformed Catholicity: The Promise of Retrieval for Theology and Biblical Interpretation* (Grand Rapids: Baker Academic, 2015), and W. David Buschart and Kent D. Eilers, *Theology as Retrieval: Retrieving the Past, Renewing the Church* (Downers Grove, IL: IVP Academic, 2015).

with Christ is hardly novel. Variations upon this theme can be found in the work of a host of historic theologians, such as Eusebius of Caesarea, St. Athanasius, St. Thomas Aquinas, John Calvin, John Owen, Jonathan Edwards, and John Williamson Nevin, as well as in the output of more recent divines such as Thomas F. Torrance and Kathryn Tanner. I am happy to acknowledge my debt to this "great cloud of witnesses" and to their writings. Even if they are not always footnoted in what follows, their influence stands behind much of what I have written. We do indeed stand on the shoulders of giants.

Acknowledgments

Theology is addictive. Theologians spend many of their waking hours thinking about something theological, some problem, some concern that they cannot seem to let go without resolution. Often, the results of these deliberations find their way to the press. But along the way there is usually reading, talking, reflection, note-taking, discussion, rumination, typing up draft after draft, the consumption of large amounts of caffeine-based products, and a lot of time in which the problem is left "on the back burner" while other, more pressing practical tasks are addressed. Writing is a large part of that process. Some of it occurs in one's head, some of it in notebooks and the margins of texts. Much of it finds its way onto the computer screen in various iterations of a paper or book manuscript. In a sense, the final published version of a work of theology is really only a record of the intellectual struggle that has gone into its resolution. Solving some theological worry is not the same as writing out the solution at which one has been aiming. And writing out the solution is not the same as arriving at the final published form of the text, which usually appears long after the process has ceased to be a live issue for its author. Yet *writing* is the activity that connects these various stages of the theological process.

So it is with this book. Working through the different parts of this study over the last seven or eight years has involved trying out earlier (and often inferior) iterations of most of the chapters as papers or articles published separately. These were stages along the way toward a greater understanding of the connections between person and work of Christ, or what I shall call a "joined-up" account of Christology—the results of which you now hold in your hands. But this result is really the product of a long, generative process with many false starts, several blind alleys, and more revisions than I care to recall. It is a kind of palimpsest, but one whose earlier, partially effaced markings are now (hopefully) only visible to its author.

A precursor to the first chapter was given in a panel on the eternal generation of the Son at the annual meeting of the Evangelical Theological Society, Milwaukee, November 2012. I am grateful for that invitation and the questions and discussion that followed. I thank Paul Helm and Jordan Wessling for reading and commenting on a version of that chapter.

An earlier version of the second chapter was read by Scott Swain, whose comments saved me from more than one serious oversight. Robert W. Jenson also provided trenchant feedback on an earlier iteration of this material that led me to rewrite the entire chapter. I am grateful to them both.

An earlier version of chapter 3 was published as "Incorporeality," in *The Routledge Companion to Philosophy of Religion*, edited by Chad Meister and Paul Copan (London: Routledge, 2012), 344–55.

A forerunner to chapter 4 first saw the light of day as an essay in Joshua R. Farris and Charles Taliaferro, eds., *The Ashgate Research Companion to Theological Anthropology* (Farnham, UK: Ashgate, 2015). I am grateful to the publisher and editors for permission to reuse much of that material here.

An earlier iteration of the fifth chapter was given as a plenary paper at the inaugural Los Angeles Theology Conference in 2013 at Biola University, and it was subsequently published in the proceedings of the conference: Oliver D. Crisp and Fred Sanders, eds., *Christology Ancient and Modern: Explorations in Constructive Dogmatics* (Grand Rapids: Zondervan Academic, 2013). I am grateful to the publisher for permission to reuse much of that material here.

A version of chapter 6 originally appeared in Anna Marmadoro and Jonathan Hill, eds., *The Metaphysics of the Incarnation* (Oxford: Oxford University Press, 2010). I thank the editors for permission to reproduce much of that material here, with some important changes that reflect developments in my own thinking since its original publication.

Much of the material contained in the seventh chapter was published in an earlier essay that can be found in Thomas P. Flint and Michael C. Rea, eds., *The Oxford Handbook of Philosophical Theology* (Oxford: Oxford University Press, 2009), 430–51. I thank the press and editors for permission to reuse the material contained in this volume.

An earlier version of chapter 8 was first given as a plenary address at the Wheaton Theology Conference in 2014 and published in the proceedings of that conference: Jeffrey W. Barbeau and Beth Felker Jones, eds., *Spirit of God: Christian Renewal in the Community of Faith* (Downers Grove, IL: IVP Academic, 2015). I am grateful to the organizers of the conference for the invitation, and to the editors for permission to reuse the material in this volume.

I would also like to thank Mark Hamilton and Joshua Farris for reading through and commenting on drafts of the chapters, and Bob Hosack, my editor at Baker Academic, who was willing to take the project on. Thanks also to Darian Lockett and Matt Jenson for their encouragement of the work and for their advice at an important stage of development. Derek Rishmawy provided me with a copy of the paper by Kevin Vanhoozer that helped me in framing the final chapter; my thanks to him for this kindness. Finally, I would like to acknowledge my family for their unstinting support, and in particular my wife, Claire. As with all my previous work, she has made it possible for me to write, giving me the space, time, and encouragement to do so. She has also made me think hard about the craft of writing in the last two years, and I am sure that her help has made this a better work as a consequence.

This volume is dedicated to my analytic-theological collaborator Michael C. Rea, who, in addition to his many intellectual accomplishments, is without doubt one of the finest human beings I have had the privilege to call my friend.

Let us now readily attend, with the whole consideration of our mind, to understanding and treating those things which pertain to the mystery of the Word made flesh, so that, with God revealing, we may be able to utter some thing on these ineffable matters.

—Peter Lombard, *The Sentences*, book II

1

The Eternal Generation of the Son

> We believe in one Lord, Jesus Christ, the only Son of God, Eternally begotten of the Father.
>
> —Nicene-Constantinopolitan Creed, AD 381

Is the Second Person of the Trinity eternally begotten by the First Person? If he is, what might this *mean*? And what of dogmatic significance follows from such an affirmation or its denial? In this chapter, I will defend the view that the Father eternally generates the Son, which is the historic position of the Christian church. I will also show that the affirmation or denial of the doctrine has important dogmatic implications. I begin by setting out what is at stake in the doctrine. I will then offer some theological considerations in favor of the doctrine. Finally, I will consider several problems entailed in its denial, focusing on the treatment of eternal generation by the British philosophical theologian Paul Helm. I close with a brief restatement of the doctrine.

What Is at Stake in the Doctrine

The doctrine of the eternal generation of the Son provides the traditional dogmatic means by which to differentiate the First from the Second Person of the Trinity. It is the relation of origin that (so it is said) distinguishes the Second from the First Person of the Trinity as a particular subsistent relation within the Godhead. It is also a dogmatic safeguard against the error of *ontologically* subordinating the Son to the Father. This is not the same as the *economic* subordination of the Son to the Father. We will come to the economic subordination of the Son in a moment. Before doing so, let us briefly consider the question of self-differentiation in the Godhead.

The classic doctrine of divine self-differentiation, at which the creedal statements of the eternal generation of the Son take aim, is Arianism. According to the Arians, God is timeless. Yet there was a moment at which God the Son was not. In commenting on this aspect of Arian theology, Lewis Ayres writes, "Arius insists that the Father is alone God, simple and immutable. The Son is born from the Father before the creation and although we cannot describe the Son's birth in temporal categories, we should not say that the Son is coeternal."[1] For if the Son were coeternal in an unqualified sense, he could not be said to be *born* of the Father, a central tenet of Arianism. This can be seen in the confession sent by Arius and his followers to Bishop Alexander of Alexandria during the fourth-century christological controversy. In it, they write:

> And God, being the cause of all things, is without beginning and supremely unique [*monōtatos*], while the Son, *timelessly* [*achronōs*] begotten by the Father, created and established before all ages, did not exist prior to his beginning, but *was timelessly begotten before all things*; he alone was given existence [directly] by the Father. For he is not eternal or co-eternal or equally self-sufficient [*sunagennētos*] with the Father, nor does he have his being alongside the Father, [in virtue] as some say, [of] his relation with him [*ta pros ti*], thus postulating two self-sufficient first principles. But it is God [only], as monad and first principle of all things, who exists in this way before all things. That is why he exists before the Son [*pro tou huiou*]. . . . Accordingly then, since he has his existence, his glories and his life from the Father, and all things are delivered to him, it is in this sense that God is his principle and source [*archē*].[2]

---

1. Lewis Ayres, *Nicaea and Its Legacy: An Approach to Fourth-Century Trinitarian Theology* (Oxford: Oxford University Press, 2004), 54–55.
2. Athanasius, *De Synodis* [On the Synods], translated by Rowan Williams in his study *Arius*, 2nd ed. (London: SCM, 2001), 271 (emphasis added). An older, more cumbersome translation of the whole of Athanasius's *De Synodis* can be found in Philip Schaff and Henry Wace, eds.,

In patristic formulations of Arianism, the language used can sometimes be confusing—for example, phrases like the infamous line "There was [a time] when he was not," which might suggest temporal succession in the divine life. In which case there is a time at which there is only God the Father. Then there is a later time at which God the Father generates God the Son. Non-Arian theologians that defend a doctrine of divine temporality may well have a problem on their hands in making sense of this claim, although I shall not deal with that particular difficulty here.[3] For our purposes it is important to note that the historic Arians did not think of the eternal generation of the Son in this manner, though their language is sometimes unguarded in this respect.[4] Instead, as Athanasius makes clear in his reporting of Arius's views in *De Synodis*, they thought that the Son is somehow timelessly eternally generated such that he is not of the same substance as the Father, but only of *like* substance (that is, *homoiousios*, not *homoousios*). One plausible way of understanding this Arian claim is as a causal thesis about the Son's eternal generation. If God the Father is the eternal cause of the existence of God the Son, then the two are not of the same substance. For if the existence of God the Son is logically but not temporally consequent or dependent upon the action of God the Father, then the Father and Son have different individual essences. But this implies two different deities, not two divine persons.

At the heart of the Arian doctrine as I have characterized it is a mistake about the nature of the divine self-differentiation between the Father and the Son. The divine nature or essence is shared between the divine persons. It does not have its source in the Father, who gives it to the Son in eternally generating/causing him. Nor does the Father impart some of his essence to the Son, because, as God, he is indivisible. This must be the

---

Nicene and Post-Nicene Fathers, Second Series, vol. 4 (Peabody, MA: Hendrickson, 1994), 458. Hereafter cited as *NPNF*[2] 4.

3. For recent discussion of this matter see Paul Helm, "Eternal Creation," *Tyndale Bulletin* 45, no. 2 (1994): 321–38, and Richard Swinburne, "God and Time," in *Reasoned Faith*, ed. Eleonore Stump (Ithaca, NY: Cornell University Press, 1993), and Swinburne, *The Christian God* (Oxford: Oxford University Press, 1994), ch. 4. See also Thomas H. McCall, *Which Trinity? Whose Monotheism? Philosophical and Systematic Theologians on the Metaphysics of Trinitarian Theology* (Grand Rapids: Eerdmans, 2008), ch. 6.

4. For instance, "We worship him as eternal because of him who was born in the order of time [*en chronois*]" (Williams's translation of the relevant part of *De Synodis*, in *Arius*, 102). Newman's translation in *NPNF*[2] 4 reads, "We praise him as without beginning because of Him who has a beginning" (457). I take this to be consistent with the claim that Christ has a beginning in time in his human nature, which is not unorthodox.

case, otherwise not only would the Son have his existence from the Father, he would also have his nature from the Father. But then he could not have all the attributes of deity. For not only would he be caused rather than uncaused, he would also lack aseity, being dependent upon the Father for his existence. But since aseity is a divine attribute, this is tantamount to saying the Son does not have the divine essence without qualification or modification. This is made abundantly clear in the second canon of the Fourth Lateran Council of AD 1215, which states,

> For the Father begetting the Son from eternity imparted to Him His own substance, as He Himself testifies: "That which my father hath given me, is greater than all" (John 10:29). And it cannot be said that He gave to Him a part of His substance and retained a part for Himself, since the substance of the Father is indivisible, that is, absolutely simple. But neither can it be said that the Father in begetting transferred His substance to the Son, as if He gave it to the Son without retaining it for Himself, otherwise He would cease to be a substance. It is evident, therefore, that the Son in being begotten received without any diminution the substance of the Father and thus the Father and Son as well as the Holy Ghost proceeding from both are the same entity.[5]

In sum: if the Son is eternally caused by the Father as the Arians claimed, then his nature is derived, and he cannot have the complete complement of divine attributes because he does not exist *a se* (from himself, independent of other entities) but *per aliud* (from or by means of another).

This way of understanding the Arian account of eternal generation presumes some meaning can be given to the notion of atemporal causation. Some contemporary philosophical theologians dispute this. For instance, Richard Swinburne thinks that causation requires some temporal metric.[6]

---

5. This translation of the canon can be found at: http://www.fordham.edu/halsall/basis/lateran4.asp (last retrieved November 11, 2012). Cf. Richard Muller, who writes,
> In the traditional western model, as argued by Peter Lombard and ratified by the Fourth Lateran Council, the divine essence neither generates nor is generated; rather the person of the Father generates the person of the Son—with the result that the Son, considered as to his sonship, is generated, but considered as to his essence is not. Or, to put the point another way, there is no essential difference between the Father and the Son, the only difference being the relation of opposition, namely, the begottenness of the Son. The Son, therefore, has all of the attributes of the divine essence, including aseity.

See Richard A. Muller, *Post-Reformation Reformed Dogmatics*, vol. 4, *The Triunity of God* (Grand Rapids: Baker Academic, 2003), 88.

6. Swinburne, *Christian God*, 75, 79, 137–38. He sets out his claim that there are irreducibly tensed facts in "Tensed Facts," *American Philosophical Quarterly* 27 (1990): 117–30. Helm

On his view, to cause a thing to happen is to be logically and temporally prior to the thing that is caused.[7] But according to many classical Christian theologians, this is not the case. Take St. Augustine, for instance, who in his *Confessions*, book 11, argues that God creates the world with time, not in time. God causes the world to be; he brings it into existence. But he does not do so at a particular moment in time, for there is no first moment in time until God creates the world with time.[8] God's action "prior" to creating the world in this context refers to something that is logically or conceptually, but not temporally, prior to creation. If God the Father eternally causes the existence of God the Son, then his existence is logically dependent on the eternal causal action of the Father. But the Son is not temporally dependent on the action of the Father on this traditional Arian way of thinking about the matter.

The orthodox declared that the Arians were mistaken, and this view won the day, being codified in the symbol of the First Ecumenical Council in AD 325 and again in the Nicene-Constantinopolitan Creed of AD 381, according to which Christ is "begotten, not made" and "of one essence with the Father" (γεννηθέντα, οὐ ποιηθέντα, ὁμοούσιον τῷ Πατρί). In other words, God the Son is eternally generated by God the Father but is not eternally caused to exist by the Father. This is captured in the creed by distinction between *being begotten* (*gennēthenta*) and *being made* (*poiēthenta*). It should be clear from the context that the referent here is God the Son, not Christ's human nature, since his human nature is made in the womb of the Virgin and has a beginning in time. What is at stake here is not the moment at which the human nature of the Son began to exist. Rather, the issue concerns the origin of the divine nature of Christ. Specifically,

---

discusses Swinburne's view at length in *Eternal God: A Study of God without Time*, 2nd ed. (Oxford: Oxford University Press, 2010), ch. 15.

7. So as not to complicate the present argument unnecessarily, I shall ignore the doctrine of backwards causation, which is controversial and runs counter to this deep-seated intuition about the priority of causes over their effects.

8. Augustine says things like the following: "However, no physical entity existed before heaven and earth; at least if any such existed, you had made it without using a transient utterance, which could then be used as the basis for another transient utterance, declaring the heaven and earth be made." Later he says this: "You created all times and you exist before all times. Nor was there any time when time did not exist. There was therefore no time when you had not made something, because you made time itself. No times are coeternal with you because you are permanent" (*Confessions* 11.6; 11.13–14, trans. Henry Chadwick [Oxford: Oxford University Press, 1992], 230). See also the discussion of this by Paul Helm in *Faith and Understanding* (Edinburgh: Edinburgh University Press, 1997), ch. 4.

the issue turns on whether, in being eternally generated, God the Son is also caused by God the Father. The creed underlines the fact that the Son is not *made* like other creatures are made; he is not brought into being. He is of the same substance (*homoousios*) as the Father. But it is true to say that he is begotten—that is (on my reading of the anti-Arian animus of the pro-Nicene theologians, at least), eternally generated by the Father.

The doctrine of the eternal generation of the Son also has some dogmatic bearing on the question of the functional subordination of the Son in the economy of salvation. Typically, this is understood to be a temporary subordination accompanying Christ's state of humiliation in the incarnation (as intimated in Phil. 2). I take this to mean *God the Son is subordinate to God the Father in his human nature during his state of humiliation.*[9] Note that this is consistent with divine timelessness. It is the human nature of the Son that is functionally subordinate as a creature to the Father; it is not his divine nature that is subordinate. How could this be if the Son is "of one essence with the Father," as the creed states? But it is eternally true that the Son is functionally subordinate to the Father in his human nature for the purposes of the state of humiliation. There is no theological problem with this statement, since if God is eternal, becoming incarnate (with all that entails) is an eternal act of God the Son. Clearly this does not imply any subordination of the Son to the Father that would imperil his deity or that suggests a sort of eternal subordination of one divine person to another *qua* divine person. That way leads back to Arianism.

Theological Considerations in Favor of the Eternal Generation of the Son

In recent times a number of theologians—including, perhaps surprisingly, some evangelicals—have distanced themselves from the doctrine of the eternal generation of the Son. Others have even asserted an eternal subordination of the Son to the Father.[10] I have already given reasons for

---

9. Cf. Thomas Aquinas: "We are to understand that Christ is subject to the Father not simply but in his human nature even if this qualification be not added; and yet it is better to add this qualification in order to avoid the error of Arius, who held the Son to be less than the Father" (*Summa Theologiae* III, q. 20, a. 1; translation from *Summa Theologica*, trans. Brothers of the English Dominican Province [New York: Benziger Brothers, 1948]).

10. McCall deals with these matters in some detail in *Which Trinity? Whose Monotheism?*, ch. 6. Many of the important articles on this topic among evangelicals in the recent literature

thinking it is unorthodox to claim that the Son is eternally subordinate to the Father either ontologically or functionally, *qua* divine. Rather than spending further time on those who straightforwardly deny the doctrine, I will deal with a subtler objection raised in the literature by the British philosophical theologian Paul Helm. However, prior to doing that let me say something in favor of the doctrine. There are, it seems to me, three reasons for retaining it. The first is that it is implied in Scripture. The second is that it was canonized in the ecumenical symbols of the church catholic. The third reason is that it is a means by which to preserve an important claim about the individuation of the divine persons in the Trinity.

Suppose a doctrine is plainly taught in Scripture. Then, I say, a Christian has good reason to hold it. After all, Scripture is the norming norm that norms all other theological authority this side of the grave (*norma normans non normata*). But what if a doctrine is implied in Scripture but clearly taught by an ecumenical council? Then, I would say, a Christian also has good reason to hold it. For I take it that ecumenical councils of the church are a second tier of theological norm or authority under Scripture, wherein the mind of the church (guided by the Holy Spirit) is expressed on matters pertaining to Christian doctrine.[11] That is just the situation that obtains with the doctrine of the eternal generation of the Son. It is implied by certain biblical passages (e.g., John 3:16–17; 4:34; 8:42; Rom. 8:29; 1 Cor. 8:6; Gal. 4:4; Eph. 1; Heb. 1:2; Rev. 13:8), but it is not explicitly taught in Scripture, just as the doctrine of the Trinity is implied by certain biblical passages but is not explicitly taught in Scripture. No Christian theologian would seriously entertain the proposal that we

---

have been collected together in Dennis W. Jowers and H. Wayne House, eds., *The New Evangelical Subordinationism? Perspectives on the Equality of God the Father and God the Son* (Eugene, OR: Pickwick, 2012). There are no biblical passages that *unambiguously* demonstrate the eternal subordination of the Son to the Father. First Corinthians 15:28 might be thought an exception. It says, "When he has done this [i.e., conquered death in the eschaton], then the Son himself will be made subject to him who put everything under him, so that God may be all in all" (NIV). But the context makes clear that the referent here is Christ, or God the Son Incarnate, not God the Son *simpliciter*. In which case it is not at all obvious that the apostle is claiming that God the Son *simpliciter* is eternally subordinate to God the Father. What he seems to be saying is that God the Son Incarnate (i.e., in his human nature) subordinates himself to the Father in the eschaton. But that requires no significant change to God the Son, who eternally subordinates himself to the Father in his human nature in this manner.

11. I set out my own views on this matter in more detail in *God Incarnate: Explorations in Christology* (London: T&T Clark, 2009), ch. 1.

excise the doctrine of the Trinity from Christianity, because it is codified by an ecumenical council on the basis of the implicit testimony of Scripture and apostolic witness. So no one should deny the doctrine of the eternal generation of the Son if it too is implicit in Scripture and canonized by an ecumenical council.[12] As the Westminster Confession puts it, "The whole counsel of God concerning all things necessary for His own glory, man's salvation, faith and life, is either expressly set down in Scripture, or by good and necessary consequence may be deduced from Scripture" (1.6). I say we can "deduce" the eternal generation of the Son, like the Trinity, as a "good and necessary consequence" of Scripture.

The doctrine is also clearly taught by key Reformation confessions, which usually closely follow the wording of the ecumenical symbols.[13] (These represent a third tier of theological authority standing under ecumenical symbols.) Three examples will suffice to illustrate this. The second of the Thirty-Nine Articles reads, "The Son, which is the Word of the Father, begotten from everlasting of the Father, and very and eternal God [is] of one substance with the Father." The tenth article of the Belgic Confession, one of the three forms of unity in Continental Reformed churches, says, "We believe that Jesus Christ, according to his divine nature, is the only begotten Son of God, begotten from eternity, not made nor created (for then he should be a creature), but coessential and coeternal with the Father, the express image of his person, and the brightness of his glory, equal unto him in all things."[14] Likewise, the second chapter of the Westminster Confession, entitled "Of God, and of the Holy Trinity," says bluntly, "The Son is eternally begotten of the Father."[15] So it seems that those who wish to distance themselves from or abandon the doctrine must face the fact that they stand against the implicit teaching of Scripture as well as the explicit teaching of the ecumenical symbols and the

---

12. See Kevin Giles, *The Eternal Generation of the Son: Maintaining Orthodoxy in Trinitarian Theology* (Downers Grove, IL: IVP Academic, 2012), who offers a helpful survey of the biblical and historical reasons for maintaining the doctrine.

13. The Lutheran forms of unity simply reassert the ecumenical symbols, e.g., the *Epitome* of the Formula of Concord.

14. Cf. the Heidelberg Catechism, another of the three forms of unity. Question 33 asks, "Why is Christ called the 'only begotten Son' of God, since we are also the children of God?" The answer given is "Because Christ alone is the eternal and natural Son of God; but we are children adopted of God, by grace, for his sake."

15. This is echoed by the Baptist Confession of 1689, which largely follows the Westminster Confession apart from matters of ecclesiology and sacramental theology.

confessions of the Reformation churches—which, when taken together, represent quite a united theological front.

This leaves us with the matter of the dogmatic import of the doctrine. It seems clear (to me, at least) that the eternal generation of the Son offers a bulwark against mere monotheism. Traditionally, Augustinian theologians have invoked the basic trinitarian law that *in God all is one where there is no opposition of relations*.[16] This serves to distinguish the unity and perfection of the divine essence from the subsistent relations that differentiate the divine persons and that are the only distinctions within the Godhead (on the presumption that God is metaphysically simple). But, as I have already indicated, the eternal generation of the Son is one of those relations, a relation of origin. These are relations that distinguish or individuate divine persons in the Godhead. So the doctrine plays a vital—indeed, a fundamental—dogmatic role in Augustinian trinitarianism. For those who reject the doctrine of divine simplicity and/or think that there are real distinctions in the Godhead other than the relations of origin, the doctrine of the eternal generation of the Son may still serve as a bulwark against mere monotheism, but in this case as part of a richer or "thicker" understanding of those features that distinguish particular divine persons in the Trinity.

Paul Helm's Objection to the Eternal Generation of the Son

We come to Paul Helm's objection to the eternal generation of the Son. Suppose God the Son is eternally generated by God the Father. That is, suppose the divine Trinity exists eternally, without time. And suppose that it is eternally true that the Father generates the Son. What would this *mean*? What content can we give the claim that one divine person *eternally generates* another beyond the bald affirmation of this claim given in the creed? Taking up this concern, Helm writes:

> The residual problem is not, how can the Son be co-divine when there was a time when the Father was and the Son was not, but, how could the

---

16. See Ludwig Ott, *Fundamentals of Catholic Dogma*, trans. Patrick Lynch (Rockford, IL: Tan Books, 1955), 70. Cf. Anselm of Canterbury, *On the Procession of the Holy Spirit*, §2 in *Anselm of Canterbury: The Major Works*, ed. Brian Davies and Gillian Evans (Oxford: Oxford University Press, 1998).

Son have a timeless relation of begottenness while being equally divine with the Father? Perhaps the solution to this may be found in expunging the language of subordination entirely from the account of the Trinity, in asserting the co-equality of the Father and the Son, not their equality in every respect, but their equality in respect of divinity. The puzzle (at least to me) is why a satisfactory doctrine may not rest content with saying that God exists in three persons co-eternal and equally divine persons. Is the language of begottenness and procession not a reading back into the doctrine of the Trinity per se of those roles which according to the New Testament each person of the Trinity adopts in order to ensure human salvation?[17]

Some relations of logical or conceptual priority do not require temporal priority. For example, the priority of the monarch over her subjects, or the priority of the major premise over the minor premise in a syllogism—neither requires a temporal priority of one thing over another. As we have already noted, if God is eternal, then the notion of temporal priority (of one event before another, say) has no purchase in the divine life. Eternal generation cannot mean there is a first moment at which God the Son begins to exist, because there is no first moment in God's life. Indeed, there are no "moments" in the life of an eternal being, according to the classical, Boethian account of God's eternity, which is the account of divine eternity Helm favors. God lives in an eternal present.[18] No part of God's life recedes from him into the past and no part of his life comes to him from the future. Since the divine persons of the Trinity just are instantiations of the divine nature, there can be no first moment of the life of a divine person either. An illustration will help make the point: if the Trinity is like an eternal, mereological whole of which the divine persons of the Trinity are the only proper parts, no proper part of the whole exists temporally prior to the whole.[19]

---

17. Helm, *Eternal God*, 286. See also Helm's short article "Of God, and of the Holy Trinity" (*Churchman* 115, no. 4 [2001]: 350–57), in which he makes substantially the same case.

18. The classical, Boethian account of divine eternity is not the only possibility, however. Brian Leftow traces several different ways of construing the doctrine in *Time and Eternity* (Ithaca, NY: Cornell University Press, 1991). The locus classicus of a non-Boethian account of divine eternity in the modern literature is Eleonore Stump and Norman Kretzmann, "Eternity," *Journal of Philosophy* 78, no. 8 (1981): 429–58. See also Paul Helm, "Eternity," in *Stanford Encyclopedia of Philosophy*, http://plato.stanford.edu/entries/eternity/.

19. I am not claiming that God has proper parts, only that this picture may be a useful analogue that helps explain the worry about parts existing independent of wholes.

This brings us to the heart of Helm's worry. The Son's being begotten and the Spirit's proceeding from the Father (and the Son, for those Western Christians enamored of the *filioque*) seem to be ways of distinguishing the divine persons that pertain to their economic, not their ontological, functions. (This is how I understand his concern about "reading back" into the Trinity roles that each divine person takes on for the purpose of securing human salvation.)[20] In which case we might want to deny that these economic functions are necessarily true of the ontological Trinity. For if God is free to create or refrain from creating, then it would appear that he is free not to create. In which case we cannot say that "being eternally begotten" is *intrinsic* to the life of the Son. For it is not a predicate he has independent of the contingent relation he bears to the world that is created.

Let us be clear: Helm is not saying God the Son is *not* eternally begotten of the Father. What he is saying is that *possibly* God the Son was not eternally begotten of the Father, because possibly God does not create a world that requires him to take on the economic role of being the Son in relation to the Father. In which case "being eternally begotten" is an extrinsic predicate of the Son. In other words, Helm's objection to the doctrine amounts to the claim that the predicate "eternally begotten of the Father" expresses an economic function of the Son that does not capture the ontological relation that subsists between Father and Son independent of any world God deigns to create. On his view, we can rid our trinitarianism of such economic language without losing what is essential to the doctrine. That is, we can do away with the language of eternal generation without thereby collapsing the Son into the Father or removing any reason for thinking the Son and the Father are eternally distinct divine persons in the Godhead.

An example may help illustrate the point. Consider Bruce Wayne. He *is*—that is, he is identical to—Batman. They are one and the same person. But it is possible that Bruce Wayne fails to be Batman. If he had not been orphaned and vowed to take revenge on the villainous scum of Gotham City, then Bruce Wayne would not have become the Dark Knight. Yet he would still have been Bruce Wayne. We might say, Bruce Wayne is contingently Batman. (There are possible worlds in which Bruce Wayne exists,

---

20. Elsewhere he says, "Is it not more in keeping with the New Testament revelation to reserve the concepts of divine Sonship and Spirithood to the economy of redemption?" (Helm, "Of God, and of the Holy Trinity," 355).

but Batman does not.) Nevertheless, Batman cannot exist without Bruce Wayne because he just is Bruce Wayne in those states of affairs in which Bruce Wayne becomes Batman. (I presume there are no possible worlds in which Batman exists but Bruce Wayne does not exist.) A similar sort of modal distinction is being made here between the economic and ontological Trinity. If God had refrained from creating the world, then, so Helm thinks, God the Son would not necessarily have been eternally begotten of the Father, though he would still have been the Second Person of the Trinity. His being eternally begotten is an economic function of the Second Person that might have been different had God refrained from creating. For this, according to Helm, is "a reading back into the doctrine of the Trinity per se of those roles which according to the New Testament each person of the Trinity adopts in order to ensure human salvation."[21]

There are at least three problems with Helm's line of argument. In the first place, eternal generation is an ontological procession in God, not an economic action that devolves upon one of the divine persons. A second, related concern is that Helm appears to have conflated the missions of God with the eternal generation of the Son as one of the divine processions. Finally, a third possible objection is that Helm's worry concerns the imputing of generation to the eternal Son, which I take to be a concern with the apparently paradoxical language implied by the doctrine. Let us take these objections in order.

First of all, eternal generation is not an economic function of the Second Person of the Trinity. It is the relation of origin by means of which the Second Person of the Trinity is distinguished from the First and Third Persons—at least according to those Augustinian versions of the doctrine of the Trinity in which divine persons are subsistent relations within the Godhead. On this way of thinking, a divine person is individuated by the particular relation of origin (i.e., the subsistent relation) he bears in relation to the other two divine persons. Indeed, the eternal generation of the Son is a metaphysically necessary eternal divine action by means of which the personal subsistence of the Son is expressed. It is not tantamount to the eternal generation of a distinct divine essence.[22] In fact, on this Augustinian way of thinking, the divine essence is shared between

---

21. Helm, *Eternal God*, 286.
22. A similar point is made by Louis Berkhof in his *Systematic Theology* (Edinburgh: Banner of Truth, 1988), 93–94.

the divine persons. Yet the divine persons as instantiations of the divine essence exist *a se*, not *per aliud*—that is, independent of any other divine person, not from another divine person. After all, that is what it means to say these divine relations are subsistent. As St. Anselm of Canterbury puts it in the *Monologion* 44,

> For it is in no way contradictory that the Son both subsists through himself and has being from the Father. For just as the Father has essence and wisdom and life in himself, so that it is not through someone else's but through his own essence that he exists, through his own wisdom that he is wise, and through his own life that he lives, so by begetting the Son he grants the Son to have essence and wisdom and life in himself, so that it is not through someone else's essence, wisdom and life but through his own that he subsists, is wise, and lives. Otherwise the being of the Father and the Son would not be the same, nor would the Son be equal to the Father.[23]

In other words, the divine persons share numerically the same essence, on pain of tritheism. They both possess aseity (they do not exist "through someone else's essence") because they have the divine essence essentially. Yet the Son is eternally generated by the Father through whom he is said to have his being. To this we may add the warning of Aquinas, to the effect that "it clearly does not follow" from this affirmation "that what serves as principle of individuation is *in* some other [i.e., some other divine person], because the divine essence is not in another god, nor is the paternity in the Son."[24] Aquinas makes it absolutely clear that the procession of the Son cannot yield the generation of another deity *outside* the Godhead, so to speak. Like the generation of an idea within a mind, the Son is eternally generated *within* the Godhead by the Father—it is like an intellectual procession in that it is an eternal divine act of *internal* self-differentiation.[25]

From this it should be clear that the sort of Augustinianism espoused by Anselm and Aquinas requires eternal generation as the means by which two of the divine persons are individuated within the Godhead. Helm is

---

23. Anselm, *Monologion*, in *Anselm: Basic Writings*, trans. Thomas Williams (Indianapolis: Hackett, 2007), 50–51.

24. Thomas Aquinas, *Summa Contra Gentiles* IV.14.7, trans. Charles J. O'Neil (Notre Dame, IN: University of Notre Dame Press, 1975), 99 (emphasis added).

25. See *Summa Theologiae* I, q. 27, a. 1, ad. 2, and the very helpful discussion in Gilles Emory, *The Trinitarian Theology of Thomas Aquinas*, trans. Francesca Murphy (Oxford: Oxford University Press, 2007), ch. 4, esp. 58–59.

an Augustinian about the doctrine of the Trinity, like our two medieval authors. So it is strange that he speaks about what is an eternal subsistent relation within the Godhead (that is, the Son's being eternally begotten by the Father) as if this were merely an economic function of the Second Person of the Trinity.

But perhaps Helm will reply, far from exposing a flaw in the argument, this only underlines the point at issue. To make this clear, let us refer to the divine persons as G1, G2, and G3. These placeholders avoid confusing divine persons with their relations of origin, which is the point at issue. Now, suppose that G1, G2, and G3 are three instantiations of the one eternal divine life. We might put it like this:

1. G1 is God.
2. G2 is God.
3. G3 is God.
4. "And yet there are not three gods, but one God" (Athanasian Creed).

Now, imagine a state of affairs in which God eternally refrains from creating. He remains the one God subsisting in G1, G2, and G3. So none of these divine persons acquire economic roles, because there is no reason for them to have such roles where there is no act of creation. In a similar fashion, in a world where Bruce Wayne's parents survive and he is brought up in their loving care, there is no reason for him to become the Batman. How do we distinguish these divine persons independent of their economic functions? By their eternal processions: there is the *generatio activa*, by means of which the Son "proceeds" (i.e., is eternally generated) by the Father, just as there is the *generatio passiva*, by means of which the Spirit "proceeds" (i.e., is spirated) from the Father (and the Son). But here is the rub: according to Augustinian theologians like Anselm and Aquinas, the eternal procession that individuates the Second Person of the Trinity just is his eternal generation by the Father. If we ask the Augustinian, "What distinguishes the Father from the Son in the ontological Trinity?," the answer is, "Being eternally begotten by the Father."

This brings us to our second objection to Helm's reasoning: in claiming that the eternal generation of the Son reads back into the ontological Trinity an aspect of the economic Trinity, he appears to have conflated the missions of God with the divine processions. Whereas the divine missions are usually thought to be economic in nature, the processions are ontological. That is, the divine missions obtain, provided God creates a world in which the divine persons are active in bringing about human salvation. But the divine processions are *de re* necessary relations within the divine life. There is no possible world in which God exists without this sort of internal self-differentiation. The eternal generation of the Son expresses the procession of the Second from the First Person of the Trinity. His mission as the mediator of salvation in Christ is distinct from but reflects the eternal self-differentiation of the First and Second divine Persons. Put slightly differently,

> "Mission" and "giving" have only a temporal significance in God; but "generation" and "spiration" are exclusively eternal; whereas "procession" and "giving," in God, have both an eternal and a temporal signification: for the Son may proceed eternally as God; but temporally, by becoming man, according to His visible mission, or likewise by dwelling in man according to His invisible mission.[26]

It is possible to inappropriately "read" the missions of particular divine persons "back into" the life of God. This would be to conflate the work of God *ad extra*, in the creation, from his work *ad intra*, within the divine life. On one plausible understanding of Helm's worry, it is this that he is concerned about, not the eternal generation of the Son per se.

Finally, and briefly, we touch upon our third objection to Helm. It may be that the juxtaposition of "eternal" with "begotten" or "generation" is what is at issue (as Helm hints, at points). How can the eternal Son be said to be generated or begotten without the implication that he is *caused* by the Father? Surely this is monstrous, something that no orthodox Christian would want to affirm, a return to the Arian heresy of old. But, as should be clear from even the cursory overview of the Arian controversy in fourth-century Christology outlined earlier in the first section of the chapter, this is not merely to misrepresent the nature of that controversy; it is to invert the very point at issue. Those fathers who framed the Creed of Nicaea in AD 325 and reaffirmed it in the Nicene-Constantinopolitan Creed of AD 381 were withstanding the Arians in their stipulations about the Son being eternally generated. Far from being incipient Arianism, the

---

26. Aquinas, *Summa Theologiae* I.43.2.

claim that God the Son is eternally begotten of the Father is one of the fundamental tenets of catholic trinitarianism that stands as a dogmatic bulwark against the Arian heresy.

Conclusion

The moral of the story, so it seems to me, is this: we tamper with the deliverances of ecumenical councils on these matters at our peril. There were very good and important dogmatic reasons for distinguishing between generation or begetting and making, as applied to the procession of the Son from the Father. It is indeed strange to say that a divine person is eternally begotten or even eternally generated by another. If we rephrase this as "God the Son proceeds from God the Father in an eternal act of active procession," some of the heat surrounding the doctrine might be dissipated. In addition to clarifying the dogmatic scope of eternal generation, care must also be taken to distinguish it from the mission of the Son. This is an economic act of God, but one that is distinct from the eternal active procession of the Son. To drive this point home, I propose the following constructive theological glosses on the dogmatic affirmation of the eternal generation of the Son. In endorsing them, evangelicals would be affirming what I take to be the conceptual hardcore of traditional, orthodox Christology:

> Thesis 1. The Second Person of the Trinity eternally, actively proceeds from the First Person of the Trinity.
>
> Thesis 2. This eternal active procession is expressed in the ecumenical symbols, as well as in the confessions of the Reformation churches, as the eternal generation of the Son.
>
> Thesis 3. The eternal active procession of the Second Person from the First Person of the Trinity is the relation of origin that individuates the Second Person of the Trinity.

Those non-Augustinian trinitarians who deny that the relations of origin are sufficient to individuate divine persons might substitute the following thesis:

> Thesis 3.1. The eternal, active procession of the Second Person from the First Person of the Trinity is a necessary but not sufficient condition

for the differentiation of the Second Person of the Trinity from the First Person of the Trinity.

This leaves the theses about functional subordinationism, mentioned earlier:

> Thesis 4. The eternal active procession of the Second Person of the Trinity should be distinguished from the mission of the Second Person of the Trinity in the economy of salvation. Whereas the procession is a *de re* necessary act of self-differentiation within the divine life, the mission is an economic act that obtains in time as a consequence of the act of creating the world.
>
> Thesis 5. The Second Person of the Trinity is subordinate to the First Person in his human nature during his state of humiliation.

I do not suppose these theses will resolve the current unhappiness about this doctrine within the evangelical constituency. But (I submit) they do underline the importance of attending to both the historical development of doctrine as well as its canonical form in the task of doing constructive theology, including constructive analytic theology. They also offer a way of making sense of the eternal generation of the Son that expresses the difference between procession and mission, as well as between subordination and equality of persons, consistent with the catholic creeds and Reformation symbols. Given that these topics have been the subject of such debate in recent evangelical discussion of the topic, these theses may provide a means by which to deflate some of the concerns of such authors without departing from creedal and confessional orthodoxy.

2

Christ without Flesh

> According to Barth . . . God is so unmitigatedly personal that his free decision is not limited even by his "divine nature": what he is, he himself chooses. But that must be to say, God *is* the act of his decision. . . . If we then ask what is chosen, in the act of choice that is the eternal being of God, Barth's answer is, he chose to unite himself in the person of Christ, with humankind. . . . But since God *is* his act of choice, God in making this actual choice not only chooses that he *will be* the man Jesus; as the event of the choice, he *is* the man Jesus.
>
> —Robert W. Jenson[1]

In the previous chapter we considered the case for the eternal generation of the Son. If the eternal generation of the Son is a kind of dogmatic starting point for thinking about the Second Person of the Trinity, how we understand his existence independent of his human nature, as an eternal divine person, is a second, closely related matter. Can we speak in a meaningful way about God the Son's existence *without his flesh*? Does such a claim have dogmatic content? It is to this matter that we turn in the present chapter.

---

1. Robert W. Jenson, *Systematic Theology*, vol. 1, *The Triune God* (New York: Oxford University Press, 1991), 140.

In recent systematic theology, one of the most creative and influential attempts to address this question can be seen in the work of the American Lutheran theologian Robert W. Jenson. In a recent article, Jenson has offered a clarification of his views on the *Logos asarkos*.[2] It provides readers of Jenson's work with a helpful addendum to, though not a retraction of, his previously published works on the matter. This, put somewhat roughly, is the idea that the Word of God, the Second Person of the Trinity, in some sense preexists his incarnate, or creaturely, state—that he exists in some sense "without flesh," or *asarkos*, as well as "enfleshed," or *ensarkos*.[3]

Jenson is implacably opposed to the idea that there is some state prior to his being incarnate in which the Word of God exists *without flesh*. In his article, he explains that his previous work does not constitute crypto-Arianism, as some critics have claimed, because he does not hold to the idea that the Word *begins to exist* at the first moment of the incarnation, nor that Christ *begins to exist* at the first moment of the incarnation—provided we are careful about what we mean by such phrases. What Jenson means, it seems, is that Christ eternally exists as the Second Person of the Trinity. Christ is identical to the Second Person of the Trinity so that there is nothing above and beyond the Word Incarnate's relation to the Father as an incarnate divine person to distinguish him from the Father. Because God does not bear relations to time in the same way that creatures do, Christ cannot be said to "preexist" his incarnate state as God the Son. For in "the divine life there is . . . no line on which the relation describable as God's sending and Jesus' obedience could occupy a position 'after' anything. And again we must remember that antecedent to God's life, there is no realm in which the Son/Logos might 'pre'-exist, or not."[4] For

---

2. Robert W. Jenson, "Once More the *Logos asarkos*," *International Journal of Systematic Theology* 13, no. 2 (2011): 130–33. As with his other writings, this short article bears careful scrutiny. He tackled this question in his earlier *Systematic Theology*, vol. 1, 141–44. I responded to this earlier account in terms of the doctrine of Christ's preexistence in *God Incarnate*, ch. 3. This chapter represents an attempt to reply to Jenson's clarification of his position in "Once More the *Logos asarkos*" as a means by which to get clearer the dogmatic content of the claim that God the Son exists without (i.e., independent of) his human nature.

3. See especially Jenson, *Systematic Theology*, vol. 1, 141–44, as noted by Jenson himself in "Once More."

4. Jenson, "Once More," 133. Jenson's account of the relation of time to the divine life is notoriously difficult to grasp. For an illuminating and charitable interpretation, see Scott R. Swain, *The God of the Gospel: Robert Jenson's Trinitarian Theology* (Downers Grove, IL: IVP Academic, 2013). Swain is particularly helpful in plotting Jenson's account of divine eternity, which I am unable to do here.

Jenson there is a monarchy of the Father's relation to the Son within the eternal divine life, and this might be said to be conceptually prior to the relation Christ bears to the Father. But there is no divine life apart from these person-constituting relations.[5]

In this chapter, I shall argue that although Jenson's clarification of his position does have its roots in classical Christology and does avoid Arianism, it has two important theological costs that those sympathetic to Jenson's disambiguated doctrine of Christ's preexistence may want to resist. These are, first, that in identifying God the Son with his human nature, Jenson commits himself to the view that God Incarnate is, in some important sense, composite (a notion that he wants to avoid). In addition, Jenson's position means God the Son cannot be immutable or impassible.[6] I begin by recapitulating and extrapolating the central issues in Jenson's recent article relevant to the present concern. I then offer an argument for the conclusion that Jenson's identification of Christ with the Word implies composition in the Second Person of the Trinity. Finally, I turn to the matter of divine impassibility, showing that Jenson cannot hold his model of the hypostatic union and uphold the ancient theological notion that "the impassible suffers."

The Question of Composition

Like Thomas Aquinas before him, Jenson maintains that the divine persons of the Trinity are individuated as subsistent relations.[7] That is, the Word of God is distinguishable as a divine person in virtue of his possessing a particular relation of origin, which can be expressed as his "being

---

5. Jenson, "Once More," 133.
6. This is a little complicated, and some commentators maintain that Jenson denies divine impassibility, e.g., Thomas Weinandy, "God and Human Suffering: His Act of Creation and His Acts in History," in *Divine Impassibility and the Mystery of Human Suffering*, ed. James F. Keating and Thomas Joseph White (Grand Rapids: Eerdmans, 2009), 99–116. In the same volume Jenson responds to Weinandy directly; see Jenson, "*Ipse Pater Non Est Impassibilis*," 117–26. He does not seem to entirely reject impassibility, but the form of his doctrine is rather difficult to discern. We shall return to the issue presently.
7. "Now distinction in God is only by relation of origin . . . while relation in God is not as an accident in a subject, but is the divine essence itself; and so it is subsistent, for the divine essence subsists. Therefore, as the Godhead is God so the divine paternity is God the Father, Who is a divine person. Therefore a divine person signifies a relation as subsisting" (*Summa Theologiae* I, q. 29, a. 4, trans. Brothers of the English Dominican Province).

eternally generated by the Father"—which was precisely the point at issue in the previous chapter. Recall that this relational predicate, which applies only to the Word, distinguishes him from the other two divine persons. Indeed it is, as Richard Cross has recently pointed out, the *only* distinguishing feature of particular divine persons in the Godhead in the vast majority of Western Christian theology.[8] We might say that in this respect God is unique. It is not that he belongs to a class of entities that possess such subsistent relations that are person-constituting. Rather, he is the only entity for whom this is true because he is the only entity that is tripersonal.

This has bearing upon the question of the putative preexistence of Christ because, according to Jenson, it is only as a subsistent relation within the Godhead that the Word exists. There is nothing more to his "preexistence" because there can be nothing more primitive standing "behind" the Word in this respect. God just *is* Father, Son, and Spirit, and the Son as the Word of God is distinguished from the Father by being eternally generated—and nothing more.[9] This encapsulates an important deliverance of what is sometimes referred to as the Latin model of the Trinity, which provides for a rather austere account of divine personhood over and against the so-called social or relational models of the Trinity, which typically have conceptually richer accounts of the "distinctions" that apply to the divine persons of the immanent Trinity.[10]

Thus far, Jenson's comments represent a helpful clarification (perhaps even development) of his previous views. To this disambiguation, Jenson

---

8. "The vast consensus in the West is inclined to hold, that the *only* distinguishing features of the persons are their relations—that, in the standard terminology, they are subsistent relations" (Richard Cross, "Two Models of the Trinity?," *Heythrop Journal* 43, no. 3 [2002]: 287).

9. But what work is the copula "is" doing here? How is God just Father, Son, and Spirit? This is an important theological matter as well. Jenson does not say exactly what he means by it, but what he says is consistent with the "is" of Latin trinitarianism, according to which the divine persons are subsistent relations within the Godhead, and he does affirm that much in the article and his other works. These divine subsistent relations do not "compose" the Godhead when taken together. Rather, they are said to be subsistent relations "in" God.

10. It is Cross's contention (among others) that the Latin and social models are really not two distinct models, as is often thought (see "Two Models of the Trinity?"). Whether that is true historically speaking, it is certainly the case that one can find instances of "Latin" and "social" models in the contemporary literature that are distinct and incommensurable. For present purposes, I mean by the Latin account of the Trinity the notion that the relations of origin are subsistent, person-constituting relations within the Godhead. I make no further claims about the Latin account, its historicity, or its relation to other distinct doctrines of the Trinity.

adds the claim that when we speak of Christ we are speaking of that which is identical to the Word. He writes, "We must not posit the Son's antecedent subsistence in such a fashion as to make the incarnation the addition of the human Jesus to a Son who was himself without him," and later, "It is not as an individual instance of humanity as such, not as one among many who have the same human nature, that Jesus is the second hypostasis of the Trinity."[11] What is more, "it is Jesus' relation to the Father—and not Jesus as a specimen of humanity—which is the second hypostasis of Trinity. The Father's sending and Jesus' obedience are the second hypostasis in God."[12]

It appears that the copula "is" stands in for the relation of identity in these passages. Christ just *is* the Word enfleshed (i.e., *ensarkos*); there is no meaning to be had in the claim that there is a state of affairs in which Christ is also *asarkos* (i.e., without flesh). Or rather, as Jenson repeats at the end of this article, if there is a meaning to it, it remains obscure, "a *Vorstellung* in search of a *Begriff*."[13] Christ's "preexistence" (if we may use such a locution) just is his trinitarian state as the Second Person of the Trinity, nothing more; that much is simply classical orthodoxy. Nevertheless, it seems that there may be problems for Jenson's account when one sets his claims about what I am calling Latin trinitarianism against what he says regarding the identity of Jesus with God the Son.

Several distinctions will help make the matter clearer. In his latest article, Jenson does not identify Christ's human nature with God the Son; he identifies Jesus with God the Son. The referents are Jesus and God the Son. That seems right. We want to say that there is only one person involved in the incarnation—namely, the Second Person of the Trinity. Jesus is not an additional person, a sort of human person adopted or assumed by God the Son. Conceding that would involve embracing unorthodoxy in the guise of adoptionism and Nestorianism, and Jenson is not enamored of either. So perhaps what Jenson can say is that at the incarnation the person of God the Son either (a) begins to exemplify the property of human nature, or (b) acquires a new relationship to a particular hunk of matter he did not have previously, one of metaphysical ownership. Note that in each of these scenarios, one and the same person is involved. The claim is not about

---

11. Jenson, "Once More," 130 and 133, respectively.
12. Ibid., 133.
13. Ibid. In other words, the *Logos asarkos* doctrine is an idea that still requires explanation.

whether God the Son is identical *to his human nature* but whether God the Son is identical *to Jesus*. Suppose we think that incarnation involves some sort of transformation in God the Son.[14] He begins to exemplify human nature. He has the properties necessary and sufficient to be human in addition to his divine nature. Then, on one way of construing things, it looks like Jesus is identical to God the Son because the incarnation is a matter of God the Son being transformed into a human—without ceasing to be a divine person, which is of course nonnegotiable for the two-natures doctrine of ancient orthodoxy. He instantiates humanity, expanding, as it were, so as to encompass a particular human life in addition to his divine life. In some respects this may be akin to the transformation from caterpillar to butterfly: the caterpillar begins to exemplify the properties necessary and sufficient for being a butterfly. Perhaps the insect does this without losing his essential "caterpillar nature," whatever that might entail. Something similar could be said regarding the incarnation, the relevant changes having been made.

Alternatively, the incarnation is about coming into a particular relation with another entity. The assumption of human flesh involves the assumption of a concrete thing that comprises human nature. Suppose that concrete thing is a human body and human soul, rightly configured. Then, in becoming incarnate, God the Son acquires a particular relation to a concrete particular—that is, his human nature. On this view the human nature is not another person but the natural endowment that would normally form a human person absent incarnation. (It cannot be another *person*, on pain of Nestorianism.)[15]

Now, in the case of the transformation model, it looks like Christ is identical to God the Son, who "expands" himself to include a human nature within his life, so that he has a phase of his life that is without human nature and a phase that includes a human nature. These two phases need not be chronological; they could be merely conceptual or logical, like the conceptual distinction between the morning star and the evening star, which both refer to the same thing at different times of the day—that is,

---

14. I owe the distinction between transformational and relational models of the incarnation to Jonathan Hill. See his introduction to Anna Marmadoro and Jonathan Hill, eds., *The Metaphysics of the Incarnation* (Oxford: Oxford University Press, 2011).

15. Brian Leftow elaborates upon this point in "A Timeless God Incarnate," in *The Incarnation*, ed. Steven Davis, Daniel Kendall, and Gerald O'Collins (Oxford: Oxford University Press, 2002), 273–99.

Venus. This certainly seems to fit better with what Jenson says about the identity of Christ and God the Son, though he doesn't align himself with a transformational model of incarnation. But, in any case, this view comes with a theological cost attached: it requires that God the Son has parts, including physical parts. If one wants to retain a Latin account of the Trinity according to which there are no real distinctions in the Godhead and no parts in God because he is metaphysically simple, then this looks like this cost could be significant. Jenson does endorse the key claim of Latin trinitarianism when he says that the eternal existence of God the Son is predicated upon the relation of origin he bears to the Father. But then what should be said about the parts God the Son acquires in becoming incarnate, including human parts?

Alternatively, on the relational model, God the Son is not necessarily identical to Christ. On one way of construing this model, Christ has God the Son as a component—in fact, the most fundamental component because God the Son is the person who becomes incarnate. But in addition to God the Son there is his human nature, a concrete thing comprising a human body and soul, rightly configured. In which case God the Son is not identical to his human nature, nor is he identical to Christ, strictly speaking. Rather, God the Son taken together with his human nature composes Christ. The idea seems to be that at the moment of incarnation the metaphysically simple Second Person of the Trinity comes to have metaphysical ownership of his human nature so that his human nature and he, taken together, constitute God Incarnate. The composite whole is Christ. But, clearly, God the Son is only one component part of that whole, so God the Son is not identical to Christ, just as I am not identical to my hand, though my hand is a part of the mereological whole that is me. Let us call this view *christological compositionalism*, since it is a view about the composition of Christ (i.e., mereology), in which the component "parts" of Christ—that is, God the Son, his human body, and human soul—are said to be "concrete" things like artifacts in the world around us, not merely "abstract" objects, like properties. (We shall return to this matter in chs. 5–6.)

Such christological compositionalism will not appeal to Jenson precisely because it cannot accommodate his central christological claim that God the Son and Christ are identical. At one point, almost in anticipation of such a view, he says that the Apologists' creation of the "*Logos* Christology," which presumes the *Logos* as a religious/metaphysical entity and then asserts its union with Jesus, was an historic mistake, if perhaps an inevitable one. Great genius has subsequently been devoted to the task of conceptually pasting together God and the Son/*Logos* and Jesus the Son/*Logos* of God, and we may be thankful for many of the ideas posted along the way. But the task itself is wrongly set and finally hopeless.[16]

However, there is an alternative version of christological compositionalism that goes back at least as far as Aquinas. It is also a concretist model of the hypostatic union. But unlike the first version of compositionalism just outlined, it can accommodate Jenson's claim that God the Son and Christ are identical.[17] The idea goes something like this. At the incarnation, God the Son "expands" or "grows" to include his human nature as a proper part of himself, so that from the first moment of incarnation onwards, God the Son is composed by his divine nature and his human nature. The idea is intuitive even if there are not many cases of persons that expand in this manner. We can conceive of scenarios in which a patient has a new limb graft that acquires the right neurological connections to become a working addition to the rest of her body. According to this second version of compositionalism, something akin to this happens at the incarnation. God the Son has a human nature grafted onto himself, so to speak. Thereafter, he has his human nature as a proper part of himself. In which case, unlike the first version of compositionalism, this version does imply that Christ and God the Son are identical. God the Son acquires a human nature (that is, a human body and soul rightly related) that becomes part of his divine life; he owns this nature; he grows into it, as it were, to include it as part of his life in a way analogous to the addition of a new limb grafted onto a living organism.

However, this second version of compositionalism has other drawbacks that make it a poor candidate for Jenson's Christology. Although it satisfies his desiderata that God the Son be identical to Christ, it comes at the cost of imputing parts to God the Son, which sits ill with his claim that the only distinctions in the Godhead are the relations of origin. For

16. Jenson, "Once More," 130.
17. For a recent outline and defense of the Thomist account, see Jonathan Hill, "Aquinas and the Unity of Christ: A Defense of Compositionalism," *International Journal of Philosophy of Religion* 71, no. 2 (2012): 117–35.

if this second version of compositionalism is right, then God the Son is also distinguished from the other divine persons by having a human body and soul, and, therefore, by being a composite entity.

The Question of Impassibility

To this point, the advocate of a Jensonian position might simply shrug her shoulders. Jenson is clear that his own position is not compositional.[18] So, attempting to repair or extend Jenson's account with a version of compositional Christology is unlikely to make much headway. In any case, compositional Christology has its own not insignificant problems and is often thought to be Nestorian, given its strong division between the Word and the human nature he assumes.[19] At the very least, it appears that the defender of compositional Christology exchanges one set of problems—namely, how to speak of the Word Incarnate without implying he has parts, while also upholding a traditional Latin Trinity—for another set of problems pertaining to the orthodoxy of one's Christology. The cure may well be worse than the disease, so to speak. Such are the vicissitudes of dogmatic theology.

However, the christological question is a pressing one for Jenson. Not only does his identification of Christ with the Word raise problems with respect to composition and divine simplicity. It also generates problems with the traditional doctrine of the impassibility of the Son. In another recent essay, "*Ipse Pater Non Est Impassibilis*," he argues (among other things) that the notion of divine impassibility is a paradox. If the phrase "one of the Trinity suffers in the flesh" is true, then, he contends, this must mean what it says: God suffers in the flesh. Since God the Son is identical to Christ, this can only mean that God the Son suffers. Yet the biblical God is not passible, avers Jenson. "What are we to do? We are of course dealing with paradox," he replies.[20] "Perhaps, *in divinis*, '*x est passibilis*' is not the

---

18. Personal communication to the author in 2010.
19. Objections to compositional Christology can be found in, e.g., Thomas Senor, "The Compositional Account of the Incarnation," *Faith and Philosophy* 24, no. 1 (2007): 52–71, and Robin Le Poidevin, "Identity and the Composite Christ: An Incarnational Dilemma," *Religious Studies* 45, no. 2 (2009): 167–86. We shall consider some of these worries in ch. 6.
20. Robert W. Jenson, "*Ipse Pater Non Est Impassibilis*," in *Divine Impassibility and the Mystery of Human Suffering*, ed. James F. Keating and Thomas Joseph White (Grand Rapids: Eerdmans, 2009), 120.

right contradictory to '*x est impassibilis*.'" He goes on to say, "Perhaps '*x non est impassibilis*' with the double negative is, *in divinis*, the precisely right stipulation."[21] This is very puzzling. Let us put it in plain language. If some entity is capable of suffering, then it cannot be said to be incapable of suffering; an entity cannot be both passible and impassible at one and the same time, on pain of contradiction. If an entity is not incapable of suffering, then it is possible for it to suffer, which is just to say that it is in principle passible. So if God is said to be not incapable of suffering (i.e., *non est impassibilis*), then possibly he suffers; he is capable of suffering.

Now, a paradox is a contradiction.[22] Plainly, several central Christian doctrines are *apparently* paradoxical. However, that is not the same as claiming that these doctrines are *actually* or *really* paradoxical. No *real* paradox can be true, because no contradiction can be true. Yet Jenson is clear that the doctrine of divine impassibility is a paradox (he does not qualify this as an apparent paradox but simply restates that "It is a paradox").[23] Yet when he comes to explain what he means by his use of paradox here, he ends up not with a paradox at all but with the admission that God is in principle passible.

This lines up with what we have already seen of his doctrine of the incarnation. If Christ is identical to God the Son, then it is very difficult to see how Jenson can insulate the divine person of the Son from the significant metaphysical changes his human nature undergoes. For if God the Son is identical to his human nature, as Jenson supposes, then God the Son cries, suffers, and dies. In other words, he is passible.

One common strategy deployed in order to avoid this implication is to claim via the doctrine of reduplication that when Christ suffers, we should understand by this that Christ's human nature suffers. His divine nature cannot suffer, because it is impassible. Nevertheless, Christ suffers *qua* human. But Jenson cannot avail himself of this strategy if he affirms

21. Ibid., 120–21.
22. I discuss paradox in Christian theology more fully in "Donald Baillie, Paradox and Christology," in *Revisioning Christology: Theology in the Reformed Tradition* (Aldershot, UK: Ashgate, 2011), ch. 1. The most substantial (and helpful) recent treatment of this topic is found in James Anderson, *Paradox in Christian Theology: An Analysis of Its Presence, Character, and Epistemic Status* (Milton Keynes, UK: Paternoster, 2007).
23. Jenson, "*Ipse Pater Non Est Impassibilis*," 120. Things get even more complicated later in this essay when Jenson attempts once more to clarify his doctrine of divine eternity, with (in my view) no greater clarity than his previous attempts.

that (a) God the Son is identical to Christ in the way he does in his "Once More the *Logos asarkos*" article, as well as claiming that (b) God is capable of suffering, which is the upshot of his "*Ipse Pater Non Est Impassibilis*" essay. In the first of these pieces he writes that it "is not as an individual instance of humanity as such, not as one among many who have the same human nature, that Jesus is the second hypostasis of the Trinity." Rather, "a divine hypostasis is 'a subsisting relation,' that is, a relation that is its own term, and so is not an instance of anything at all." What is more, "it is Jesus' relation to the Father—and not Jesus as a specimen of humanity—which is the second hypostasis of Trinity. The Father's sending and Jesus' obedience are the second hypostasis in God."[24] There is not a *Logos* independent of, logically prior to, the human nature of Christ, according to Jenson. For what could such an entity be? There is just Jesus who is (identical to) the Word Incarnate. To put this rather starkly, it appears that he believes Jesus is a subsisting, person-constituting relation within the Godhead. But he also clearly affirms the notion that God is capable of suffering, that "*non est impassibilis*" applies to the divine life. So reduplicative language isn't going to do much work for Jenson because there is no Word independent of Jesus, no divine person distinct from his humanity, and, in any case, God is capable of suffering.

So, in addition to the problem about composition generated as a consequence of Jenson's strong account of the identity of Jesus with the Second Person of the Trinity, we have a problem regarding impassibility. Here a brief analogy might be helpful. Suppose one thinks humans are composed of bodies and souls, rightly related, which has been the traditional view among Christians. Now, Jones is weeping on account of some terrible news he has just received. If a bystander were to ask, "Who is weeping, Jones's body or Jones's soul?," we might be forgiven for thinking that an odd question. Clearly, Jones's body is doing the weeping; his soul cannot weep because his soul is not physical, has no tear ducts, and so on. However, if pressed, we would surely say Jones is crying. Jones is sad. Not Jones's body, but Jones himself, the person. Why would we say this? Surely because we think Jones is identical to the person, Jones. Yes, it is by means of his body that he expresses his sadness in tears. But it is not his body that is sad; he is. Transpose this onto Jenson's account of the incarnation.

---

24. Jenson, "Once More," 133.

If Christ is identical to God the Son, then when he weeps in the Garden of Gethsemane, or at Lazarus's tomb, it is the person "in" Christ that is sad. Certainly he weeps in his body; his human soul and divine nature cannot weep because they are not physical objects. Nevertheless, it would be strange to say that Christ is sad in his human nature and not in his divine nature, given Jenson's account of the incarnation and his willingness to countenance the prospect of divine passibility. It might be argued that some version of this problem is common to all those who hold to the two-natures doctrine of the incarnation, because anyone who believes this must explain how it is that Christ suffers in his human nature and not his divine nature (if one thinks that he doesn't suffer in his divine nature, which is the traditional view). But, as I shall elaborate in chapter 6 when we consider the compositional account of the incarnation in more detail, that is not that case. If one is willing to allow that Christ is a composite that includes his human nature and God the Son, then this problem does not arise in quite the same way, for God the Son, the person "in" Christ, is not identical to his human nature. It is precisely because Jenson refuses this option, insisting that Christ is identical to his human nature, that he lands himself with this problem concerning Christ's suffering.

This, I think, is a serious problem for Jenson. It raises other worries about the Cyrillian tenor of his Christology. But, for now, this seems problematic enough.[25]

The Upshot

In summary, Jenson's clarification of his own position is helpful. He demonstrates that his view is compatible with an ancient model of the Trinity that has the weight of the Augustinian tradition behind it. However, when he affirms that Christ and the Word are identical, he generates particular problems for his own position, problems that (I think) are not easily resolved. Chief among these are implications this has for a doctrine of divine simplicity, which is normally thought to be a corollary of the subsistent-relation account of the individuation of the divine persons of the Trinity.

---

25. I should add that Jenson is not eccentric in his view that Christ is identical to God the Son. If anything, it is the compositional account of the incarnation that seems odd because it denies that Christ is God the Son. However, we shall postpone further discussion of this until ch. 6.

The worry is this: if God is essentially metaphysically simple, then he cannot have any parts. This is normally thought to be a constituent of subsistent-relation accounts of the Trinity common to Augustinianism—which, as we have seen, is the sort of view with which Jenson explicitly aligns himself in his recent work. Yet, on Jenson's account, Christ is identical to God the Son. However, if Christ is identical to God the Son, then God the Son has parts, for his human nature has parts. Naturally, Jenson could deny that God is simple in a strong sense—the sense that is often thought to be a constituent of the Latin trinitarianism which he espouses—but then his appeal to the tradition in order to shore up his account of the preexistence of Christ looks rather hollow, for it transpires that his doctrine is not equivalent to Latin trinitarianism. This worry isn't fatal for his position, but it does reveal a hidden cost that Jenson, and those enamored of his position, will need to address.

Jenson's position also means that there appears to be no way of insulating Christ's divine nature from the substantive changes incurred in the incarnation. So it would appear that Jenson has to give up divine impassibility and immutability if he is serious about his Christology. There is an irony here. Jenson's latest foray into the issue of the *Logos asarkos* is largely about showing how his position is of a piece with orthodoxy. His doctrine of the eternal existence of Christ is Augustinian alright. But it does not imply a species of *Logos asarkos* doctrine because he refuses to distinguish between the Word and the Christ in such a way that, on his rendition of the doctrine, it seems that Christ *just is* a subsistent divine relation.[26] However, this insistence upon identifying the Word with his human nature means he ends up committed to a position contrary to the doctrine of divine simplicity and/or divine immutability and impassibility (at least as they have often been understood in the tradition). Thus, rather surprisingly perhaps, Jenson's Christology requires a substantive revision to traditional ways of conceiving the hypostatic union and, by implication, the eternal existence of Christ.

---

26. A further worry: if Christ is identical to God the Son, and Christ, not God the Son, is a subsistent relation (as Jenson avers) then we might wonder how an entity that includes a corporeal part (Christ's human body) and a human soul can be a subsistent relation.

3

Incorporeality and Incarnation

πνεῦμα ὁ θεός
—John 4:24

Thus far we have considered two fundamental matters for Christology. These are the question of the eternal generation of the Son, which we tackled in the first chapter, and the issue of the existence of God the Son in abstraction, as it were, from his fleshly existence, which was the subject of the previous chapter. In both cases, we analyzed these topics in dialogue with modern interlocutors as well as with the Christian tradition. A natural next step is to turn to the consideration of the human and divine aspects of Christ in order to get clearer what it is that we are talking about when we ask whether Christ is eternally generated, or whether Christ preexists his earthly existence. I have considered elsewhere some of the important matters that arise when focusing upon the human nature of Christ, and I do not propose to repeat those arguments here.[1] Nevertheless, in discussing the eternal generation of the Son and the preexistence of Christ, another natural question concerns the incorporeality of God in relation to the incarnation. That is the focus of this chapter.

---

1. See, e.g., Oliver D. Crisp, *Divinity and Humanity: The Incarnation Reconsidered* (Cambridge: Cambridge University Press, 2007); Crisp, *God Incarnate*; Crisp, *Revisioning Christology*.

After a short preamble concerning the scope of incorporeality, we shall consider in some detail what this notion does and does not imply for an understanding of the doctrine of God, focusing on challenges to the doctrine from a number of perspectives concerning the God-world relationship. These include versions of global monism, pantheism, and panentheism. Then, having given some theological shape to incorporeality and its challenges, we shall apply the doctrine to the matter of the incarnation. I shall argue that although the incarnation complicates the doctrine of divine incorporeality, it is consistent with divine incorporeality. This is the case despite the fact that the exact relationship between incarnation and incorporeality is contested in contemporary accounts of the God-world relationship, as we shall see.

Preamble

According to the author of the Fourth Gospel, "God is spirit" (John 4:24; cf. 2 Cor. 3:17). Does that mean he *necessarily* lacks a body, that he is incorporeal? Certainly this is a claim of orthodox, classical theism and of orthodox, classical Christian theology in particular. Incorporeality is often thought to be an incommunicable divine attribute—that is, an attribute that God does not share with his creatures, other examples of which are immutability and impassibility. Like these other attributes, incorporeality is not so much a positive affirmation of something true of God as it is a denial that something applies to God: he is *without* a body; he is *not* a physical or material entity. It might be thought that the biblical tradition offers conflicting data on the question of whether God is incorporeal, for anthropomorphisms abound in both Old and New Testaments. Yet when we read of the "arm of the LORD" (e.g., Deut. 4:34; Isa. 53:1) or his "eyes" that "run to and fro throughout the whole earth" (2 Chron. 16:9 ESV), a moment's reflection is enough to see that these are tropes. They are not indications that God possesses a body; the language is metaphorical or poetic. Similarly, it would be hermeneutically naive to think that the line in Alfred Noyes's poem "The Highwayman" that says "The moon was a ghostly galleon tossed upon cloudy seas" means that our nearest celestial neighbor really is a spectral ship, or that it is actually tossed around in a sea of clouds in its trajectory across the heavens. In this chapter I shall understand divine incorporeality to be the doctrine that God is nonmaterial or nonphysical. These terms are used interchangeably. We shall see that "being without a body" is one application of the more general claim that God is nonmaterial/nonphysical. For if God is nonphysical, then he cannot have a body. But the reverse does not necessarily hold true. That is, God could possess a body and yet be nonmaterial. This is exactly what traditional, orthodox Christian theology teaches concerning the incarnation.

In addition to the biblical witness that God is spirit, both the Fourth Lateran Council and the First Vatican Council teach that God is "absolutely simple" (*substantia seu natura simplex omnino*)—a matter that is *de fide*, that is, a dogma of the faith.[2] An absolutely simple entity cannot be an entity that has a body, since bodies are composite. Hence, if God is absolutely metaphysically simple, he is also essentially incorporeal. This might be thought to provide an additional theological reason for thinking that God must be incorporeal. It certainly has that function in traditional Roman Catholic theology.

The traditional doctrine of divine simplicity is contested in contemporary systematic and philosophical theology. But we need not appeal to it in order to retain a doctrine of divine incorporeality. A more modest account of divine noncomposition might yield the same result for the purposes of offering dogmatic support for the doctrine without raising some of the more egregious problems that are often said to beset the traditional version of divine simplicity.[3] Here is a sketch of one such account. Suppose God is not absolutely noncomposite, as the traditional doctrine of divine simplicity supposes, but is nevertheless a metaphysical primitive or mereologically simple substance, like a soul. Whereas the doctrine of God's absolute simplicity states that there is no composition in God whatsoever (so that each of his attributes implies the others and implies the divine essence), this more modest doctrine of metaphysical simplicity makes the weaker claim that God is not a composite substance, like a body. Whereas my body can be divided, a soul cannot. It is immaterial and lacks extension, so it is indivisible. But it may be the subject of

---

2. See Ott, *Fundamentals of Catholic Dogma*, 31–32. We have already encountered this doctrine in passing in the earlier chapters of this volume.

3. For a recent attempt to set out a doctrine of divine unity without commitment to the traditional doctrine of divine simplicity, see Jay Wesley Richards, *The Untamed God: A Philosophical Exploration of Divine Perfection, Immutability, and Simplicity* (Downers Grove, IL: InterVarsity, 2003).

distinct mental states and properties. If God is like this, then he is not absolutely simple. Nonetheless, he is a mereological simple, or a simple substance. And this is clearly incompatible with the notion that God is a material entity, since material entities are normally composite and/or extended. (Electrons, quarks, and the like may be noncomposite physical primitives and yet compose entities that are extended. I take it that a simple immaterial substance is unlike this. It cannot compose a proper physical part of a larger whole—though it may have extrinsic relations with such wholes—because it lacks extension.)[4]

Charles Taliaferro argues that there are additional reasons for holding to divine incorporeality that depend on appeals to other divine attributes.[5] We might think of this as a strategy that draws on a rich concept of God in order to make good on the claim that God is incorporeal, much like one might draw on a rich concept of, say, the chemical composition of water in order to explain to a child that the clear liquid in her glass is potable. So, for example, if God is a necessary being, or is omnipotent, or eternal, or immutable, then one might have reason to think there is an important difference between God and the creation that bears upon divine incorporeality. For the created order is not a necessary being (it has a beginning in or with time); is not all-powerful, but limited and finite; is not eternal, but contingent and dependent upon divine conservation and government; and is not immutable, but changing. These may provide ancillary reasons for thinking that God is incorporeal. But they are also liable to be contested by those enamored of the view that God is a material being. For instance, God could be a material being and a necessary being if the matter/energy of the universe were eternal and God were identical to the sum of this matter/energy. Similarly, neither his power nor his eternity

4. Christian hylomorphists, such as Thomas Aquinas, deny this. For Aquinas, the soul is the form of the body and has location when conjoined with its body, throughout which it is distributed—at least, this seems to be the implication of his view in *Summa Theologiae* I, q. 76, a. 8. But I do not understand how an essentially nonphysical entity like a soul can be said to acquire extension through union with a corporeal entity as its form. On my reading of it, Aquinas's position entails that at one time my soul has extension and is distributed throughout my body, but that at somatic death, is decoupled or disentangled from the body and exists as an immaterial entity until the resurrection (*Summa Theologiae* I, q. 89, a. 1). But this means at one time I am identical to the composite of a body + soul (i.e., what appears for all intents and purposes to be a material object, being extended), and at another time I am identical to an immaterial object. This is deeply puzzling.

5. Charles Taliaferro, "Incorporeality," in *A Companion to Philosophy of Religion*, ed. Philip L. Quinn and Charles Taliaferro (Oxford: Blackwell, 1997), 271–78.

seems to *require* his being incorporeal. Many physical objects have powers; perhaps a material God could be very powerful, even omnipotent. If the world is backwardsly everlasting, as Thomas Aquinas postulated, then perhaps a material divinity could be everlasting in time, though arguing for the conclusion that God is an eternal (i.e., atemporal) material being is a more challenging prospect. It is more difficult—indeed, *very* difficult—to conceive of an immutable material deity because physical objects appear to be inherently mutable. Be that as it may, I shall not use a conceptually rich concept of God or the conjunction of two or more divine attributes as a means by which to derive divine incorporeality, though this may be another route to the same goal.

Challenges for Divine Incorporeality

So it would seem we have the testimony of Scripture and tradition in favor of the view that God is incorporeal. There may also be considerations pertaining to a rich concept of God that can be deployed in favor of the doctrine. But objections to divine incorporeality are not difficult to find.

For one thing, what bodies are thought to be, and therefore what it means for an entity to be corporeal, is a contested matter in metaphysics. This general concern has two concrete applications relevant to the claim that God is incorporeal, both of which depend on what I shall call *global monism*. The global monist claims that all that exists is composed of one sort of thing. Usually, this is understood in terms of immaterialism or materialism. Let us turn, in the first instance (and briefly), to immaterialism, which is a species of global monism that claims all that exists are minds and their ideas, with matter being a sort of fiction explicable without the need to appeal to the notion of extended unthinking substances. The eighteenth-century contemporaries Bishop George Berkeley (1685–1753) and Jonathan Edwards (1703–58) offer two historic examples of this position in the Christian tradition.[6] If immaterialism obtains, the distinction between corporeality and incorporeality is difficult to draw because there are no material objects as such, no unextended nonthinking things (for

---

6. For a recent volume that makes constructive theological use of the philosophical legacy of Berkeley and Edwards in this regard, see Joshua R. Farris, S. Mark Hamilton, and James S. Spiegel, eds., *Idealism and Christian Theology*, Idealism and Christianity 1 (London: Bloomsbury, 2016).

present purposes, I am assuming that material objects are unextended nonthinking things). In fact, it would seem that the sort of worry against which divine incorporeality is traditionally deployed does not even arise. For if there are only ideal kinds of things, then the claim that immaterial entities like God or human souls interact with, or are paired with, particular parcels of matter or particular material substances simply cannot get off the ground, for there are no material objects as such. In fact, it looks like if one is an immaterialist, then divine incorporeality is trivially true, on a par with claiming that water is wet, or that paint is colored, because all entities turn out to be immaterial. Alternatively, it is a sort of category mistake, ascribing to the Deity an attribute that has no counterpoint, perhaps no possible counterpoint, rather like ascribing to a piece of music the property of being noncolored. Music is essentially noncolored since it is aural, not physical. Similarly, in the case of God, if there is, or perhaps there can be, no such thing as an extended unthinking substance, then it is empty to predicate incorporeality of the Divine because all entities are incorporeal.

But suppose we adopt the alternative version of global monism, namely, materialism. This presents a potentially serious challenge to the doctrine of divine incorporeality. The force of this objection rests on the assertion that there is—perhaps, there can be—no such thing as an incorporeal entity. There are several ways one could construe this claim consistent with the two modalities implicit in the characterization just given. Contemporary "hard" metaphysical naturalists think that the only sorts of things that *can* exist are material or physical objects. This is clearly inconsistent with divine incorporeality. For, as I understand it, on this view the existence of incorporeal entities such as God is metaphysically impossible. This is a very strong modal claim indeed. It is equivalent to saying that there are no possible worlds in which incorporeal entities obtain. By contrast, "soft" metaphysical naturalists make the modally weaker claim that there are *in fact* no incorporeal entities. This is a modally weaker claim because it is consistent with the possibility of immaterial beings.

Strange to say, neither of these two versions of metaphysical naturalism is inconsistent with the existence of God as such, though they are often so understood in the popular imagination. What they are inconsistent with is the claim that God is incorporeal. For the weak metaphysical naturalist, it is just the case that there are no immaterial substances. But this is consistent with God's being an existing *material* substance. Suppose the metaphysical naturalist opts for the "hard" version of the doctrine instead. Even then one could, like the early modern philosopher Thomas Hobbes, argue that all substances are material substances; that God is a substance; and thus that God is a material substance. Talk of immaterial substances, or of substances without extension and without bodies, is, says the Hobbesian, meaningless. It would be a poor argument that grounded this accusation of meaninglessness in the thesis that global materialism is true—in other words, that there are as a matter of fact no immaterial substances. If I were to say, "Global materialism is true; therefore, there can be no immaterial substances," few would be persuaded. But this is not the only argument open to the Hobbesian. Hobbes himself has this to say in his *De Corpore*:

> The gross errors of certain metaphysicians take their origin from this; for from the fact that it is possible to consider thinking without considering body, they infer that there is no need for a thinking body; and from the fact that it is possible to consider quantity without considering body, they also think that quantity can exist without body and body without quantity, so that a quantitative body is made only after quantity has been added to a body. From the same fountain spring these meaningless vocal sounds, "abstract substances," "separated essence" and other similar things.[7]

Here the worry is that those who think there are immaterial thinking things predicate their reasoning on the claim that one can conceive of a thinking subject without it being conjoined to, or otherwise metaphysically coupled with, a material object. But, says Hobbes, this is just a mistake. Thinking subjects cannot be abstracted from the material substances that give rise to them or compose them, or to which they are identical (take your pick of the relations between bodies and thinking subjects open to defenders of global materialism). This is not a particularly powerful argument, but it is better than having global materialism as a premise. So even

---

7. "Hinc enim originem trahunt quorundam metaphysicorum crassi errores; nam ex eo quod considerari potest cogitatio sine consideratione corporis, inferre volunt non esse opus corporis cogitantis; et ex eo quod quantitas considerari potest, non considerari corpore; existere etiam putant quanititatem sine corpore, et corpus sine quanititate, ita ut addita ad corpus quantitate tum demum fiat quantum; ab eodem fonte nascuntur illae voces insignificantes, *substantiae abstracte, essentia separata,* aliaque similia" (Thomas Hobbes, *Elementorum philosophiae sectio prima "De corpore"* [London: Andrew Crook, 1655], 3.4, p. 22). The English translation in the body of the text is modified from A. P. Martinich's translation in Hobbes, *Computatio sive Logica* (New York: Abaris, 1981).

"hard" metaphysical naturalism is consistent with the claim that there is a God, though it is inconsistent with the claim that he is incorporeal.

Whatever we make of the strength or cogency of Hobbes's reasoning in favor of global materialism (or, indeed, any other argument for this conclusion), it should be obvious that there is no way to derive anything like a theologically orthodox account of the Deity on this basis. God cannot be a material object, at least not according to the great Abrahamic faiths. He is essentially immaterial, indeed, essentially incorporeal. So Hobbesianism is a nonstarter for anyone wanting to retain a traditional theistic conception of God.

For those beguiled by pantheism, things are rather different. For then God and the world are either numerically or qualitatively identical, and it turns out that God is a material object or has the world as a material proper part. If God and the world are numerically identical, then God = the world. That is, the indiscernibility of identicals applies to God and the world, and to talk about the world (as a mereological sum) is just to talk about God, and vice versa.

However, it may be that God and the world share almost all the same properties apart from, say, thisness or haecceity. I take it that thisness is a nonqualitative property—that is, a property an entity has independent of any other properties, relations, or qualities it might have. One way to motivate pantheism as a qualitative identity relation between God and the world would be to claim that God and the world share all and only the same properties, relations, and qualities apart from their haecceities. It might even be the case that God and the world have different persistence conditions, and yet pantheism obtains. To illustrate: the marble statue and the slab of marble are composed of the same "stuff"—namely, marble. But they are not numerically identical, and they do not have the same persistence conditions, because the marble will remain if we efface or destroy the statue. Suppose something like this way of thinking about God and the world is right. It would then be the case that God and the world are merely qualitatively identical for reasons other than the fact that they have distinct haecceities. In which case we have at least two reasons why the pantheist need not embrace numerical identity. God-plus-the-world may be a mereological sum, with the world as a proper part, if God and the world have distinct thisnesses. Or, God and the world have different persistence conditions though they are "composed" of the same "stuff."

Would this be a sufficiently close relation between God and the created order to count as pantheism? Perhaps. If not, it is a very close relative.

Clearly, the global materialist need not be a pantheist, though Hobbesianism as I have defined it is consistent with pantheism. One could also be an immaterialist and a pantheist. Jonathan Edwards has been accused of being both.[8] But there are several strong (to my mind, compelling) reasons to resist pantheism. The most obvious of these is that it requires a significant departure from orthodox, classical theism. For both views appear to undermine the claim that God is metaphysically and psychologically independent of the creation (i.e., has aseity), which bears on the relationship this view has to notions like divine sovereignty and freedom.

But perhaps the God-world relation is rather different from this. Panentheism is a step away from pantheism, toward theism. The panentheist denies God and the world are numerically identical and usually wants to claim more for the distinction between God and the world than that they have distinct haecceities. Instead, the world is somehow contained "in" God, but God is greater than the world, in or with which he is omnipresent.[9] On some versions of this doctrine, God is said to be "incarnate" in the world, which is his "body." But this seems to challenge a traditional doctrine of divine incorporeality on two fronts: it means God is not merely a spirit in abstraction, as it were, from any "body" (i.e., from the world); and it means God is essentially composite, having a part that includes or comprehends the creation, and a part that is without the creation. In which case he is composite after all and "contains" a mereological sum—the created world—that has numerous corporeal parts.

On the face of it, it may appear that the panentheist thinks God is partitioned into a part that includes the world and a part without the world. But whatever is meant by the locution "in" in the phrase "the world exists *in* God," panentheists typically do not think of this as anything like an identity claim. The world is not "in" God like the oxygen is "in" the oxyhemoglobin

---

8. By Charles Hodge in particular. See Oliver D. Crisp, "On the Orthodoxy of Jonathan Edwards," *Scottish Journal of Theology* 67, no. 3 (2014): 304–22.

9. On one standard definition, panentheism is the view according to which "the being of God includes and penetrates the whole universe, so that every part exists in Him, but His Being is more than, and not exhausted by, the universe" (F. L. Cross and E. A. Livingstone, eds., *The Oxford Dictionary of the Christian Church*, 3rd ed. [New York: Oxford University Press, 1997], 1213). There are problems fixing exactly what panentheism entails, despite this attempt at definition. But here is not the place to pursue that discussion. For present purposes, we will simply adopt the conventional denotation.

that makes up oxygenated red blood cells. Rather, the world is "in" God rather like the yoke is "in" the egg white. However, unlike the egg simile, God is said to "penetrate" or "permeate" the world. That is, he is present with every point in space-time and has immediate access to every point in space-time. This is how I understand some of the extravagant claims made for God's perichoretic relation to the world. For if God is "wholly in the world" although the world is not "wholly in God," then, whatever else this means, it cannot be that the erstwhile panentheist who endorses perichoresis means to embrace pantheism. Rather, the panentheist claims that God is incorporeal although he somehow "contains," "includes," or, perhaps better, "comprehends" the creation as well.

A distinction can be made between panentheism, on the one hand, and Neoplatonism, on the other. Often these two views are conflated in the literature and for good reason: they substantially overlap so that many Neoplatonists are also panentheists. But Neoplatonism does not necessarily include the notion that the world is contained "in" God as a proper part. Rather, for the Neoplatonist, the world is emanated from God and has a sort of attenuated or shadowy existence as the "overflow" or communication of God outside of himself, on analogy with the shadow cast by someone walking in broad daylight. Just as a shadow is radically dependent on the human being who casts it, so also the creation is radically dependent on God's continuing to emanate it from himself. But it is *emanated from* himself; it does not necessarily reside *within himself* as with panentheism. Nevertheless, this distinction between Neoplatonism and panentheism is rather thin. A paradigmatic Neoplatonist like Plotinus often says things that strongly suggest, even imply, panentheism, such as the following passage from his *Enneads*:

> In general one must think of the intelligible things as one in nature, and one nature holding them all and in a way encompassing them, not each one separate as in the things of sense . . . but all things together in one, for this is the nature of Intellect. . . . It is truly the "complete living being" composed of all living beings, or rather encompassing in itself all living beings, being one as large as all things; just as this All is one and is all that is visible, encompassing all things that are in the visible.[10]

10. Plotinus, *Ennead* VI.6–9, trans. A. H. Armstrong (Cambridge, MA: Harvard University Press, 1988), 28–31.

Is God or the ultimate principle of reality of classical panentheism or Neoplatonism incorporeal? He most certainly is. There are many species of panentheism, just as there are different versions of Neoplatonism (e.g., Plotinus's Neoplatonism, Proclus's Neoplatonism, Augustinian Neoplatonism, and so on).[11] But for Neoplatonists who are also panentheists, the divinity (or the divine principle, the One) is essentially incorporeal and cannot be tarnished with anything corporeal or material. Nevertheless, this entity has a strange relationship to the created order, which seems to be a sort of necessary product of divine creativity, "emanated" by the divine. A number of classical Neoplatonists/panentheists have also been idealists. Some, such as Jonathan Edwards, have thought that the creation is a world of minds and their ideas that are radically dependent upon the Deity for their continued existence. Those enamored of such a high-octane version of Neoplatonism have no place for materiality. Like Berkeley, Edwards thinks the world an ideal one. Unlike Berkeley, he conceives of the relation between God and his creation rather like that of the sun and its rays, or the fountain and the water it produces: God and the world are both essentially immaterial entities, though the creation is the shadowy emanation of God, the overflow of his essentially creative essence.[12]

We come to theism. I take it that theism is the claim that there is a God. *Classical* theism includes the idea that God and the world are distinct entities, though the world is created and governed by God. For the classical theist, God is an essentially incorporeal agent. God creates all things apart from himself, and the world he creates is corporeal. Although the created order is dependent upon God for its existence after the first moment of creation, the classical theist does not think that this contaminates or entangles God in the created order in a way that would compromise the essential integrity of his nature or of who he is. God is analogous to a maximally perfect soul since he is a simple substance (i.e., is not composed by more fundamental parts, unlike composite objects, like bodies) and is literally nowhere, having no location or extension. Nevertheless, he is omnipresent, for omnipresence does not imply omni-extension or

---

11. For a useful recent survey, see John W. Cooper, *Panentheism: The Other God of the Philosophers; From Plato to the Present* (Grand Rapids: Baker Academic, 2006).

12. See Jonathan Edwards, "Concerning the End for Which God Created the World," in *The Works of Jonathan Edwards*, vol. 8, *Ethical Writings*, ed. Paul Ramsey (New Haven: Yale University Press, 1989), 405–63.

location. (As Anselm of Canterbury points out, "It is our . . . practice often to predicate spatial words of things which neither are places nor are contained by spatial limits," like souls or the Supreme Nature.)[13] God is not located at every point in space. If he were, he would not be incorporeal but corporeal, or at least would possess material parts, and something like pantheism or Hobbesianism would obtain.

Incarnation and Incorporeality

Aside from these objections from different versions of global monism, pantheism, and panentheism, there are theological complications in the neighborhood that any adequate treatment of divine incorporeality will have to tackle. Chief among these in the Christian tradition is the doctrine of the incarnation. If Christ is God Incarnate, then it looks like God *can*—indeed, *does*—have a body after all. But then it appears that God is not incorporeal, or at least that he is not essentially incorporeal.

However, this is not how these matters stand in traditional, orthodox Christology, which maintains the following tenets: the Triune God is essentially incorporeal (he is a spirit); God the Son, being a divine person and member of the Godhead, is essentially incorporeal; and the human nature assumed by God the Son has a material part, that is, his human body. These are not incompatible claims, provided some model of the incarnation can be provided according to which God the Son is not numerically identical to his human body, or does not have his human body as a proper part. (This is a matter that we have already had cause to touch upon in considering Robert Jenson's position in the previous chapter.) Some traditional models of the hypostatic union have difficulty with this claim. Suppose God the Son "expands" himself at the first moment of incarnation in order to include his human nature, like a vine might be expanded by having an additional limb engrafted onto it. The limb becomes integrated into the life of the vine; it becomes a part of the vine. In a similar fashion the human nature of Christ becomes integrated into the life of God the Son; it becomes part of him. The problem this poses

---

13. Anselm of Canterbury, *Monologion* 23, in *The Complete Philosophical and Theological Treatises of Anselm of Canterbury*, trans. Jasper Hopkins and Herbert Richardson (Minneapolis: Banning, 2000), 40. Strangely enough, Anselm's metaphysics is also deeply influenced by Augustinian Neoplatonism, though it is often thought to be a paradigm of classical theism.

for incorporeality should be obvious. In becoming incarnate, God the Son acquires corporeal parts so that he is at best a compound of incorporeal and corporeal parts. But this is to compromise divine incorporeality. Even if we say that the corporeality of Christ is assumed by the divine person of the Son—so that it is not said to be brought into the divine life shared by the other two divine persons, compromising their incorporeality—this still means that God the Son has a material part. Indeed, this also means that a divine person has a material part, even if it does not mean that God *simpliciter* has a material part, strictly speaking.

However, if God is simple, at least in the sense of being a metaphysically simple substance, then perhaps his relationship to Christ's human nature, including his corporeal body, is not a mereological relation that compromises his incorporeality. This is just what the compositional model of the incarnation says, as we shall see in chapter 6. We have already noted in passing in the previous chapter that the defender of the compositional model maintains that Christ is not identical to the Word (i.e., God the Son). Suppose that is right. Then Christ is composed of three concrete parts: the Word and his human nature (comprising a human body and soul, rightly related). This much is a common feature of much classical, and especially medieval, school theology. Now, in addition to this, suppose that Christ's human nature is rather like a garment, which the Word puts on at the first moment of incarnation. Just as the garment is not identical to the person wearing it, so the Word is not identical to the human nature he assumes. The analogy, as Aquinas points out at one point, is not exact and could be misleading.[14] For my relation to the garments I wear is both contingent and temporary: I can put on another suit of clothes, and my clothes do not in any way constitute who I am in any strong, ontological sense. The same is not true of Christ, on this view. The Word is intimately related to his human nature precisely because it is *his* human nature; he has metaphysical ownership of it. But the Word is truly, although only contingently, related to a human being.[15] That is, the Word might not have become incarnate; it was not necessary, all things considered, that the Word

---

14. "Now the assumed nature [vis. Christ's human nature] is, as it were, a garment, *although this similitude does not fit at all points*" (*Summa Theologiae* III.3.7). Of course, Aquinas is not committed to the sort of compositional model I have in mind.

15. The interesting question is whether his individual human nature is only contingently united to the divine person of the Word. For a careful, nuanced account of several influential medieval accounts of the counterfactuals raised by such questions about the necessity of the

became incarnate—he voluntarily took up the work of the mediator and became incarnate in order to provide the means of human salvation from sin. But from this it is only a short, though crucial, metaphysical step to the claim, central to the compositional model, that in uniting himself with human nature the Word did not become identical with that human nature. He cannot be identical with his human nature because the Word is essentially incorporeal (so he cannot have material parts), and, according to the vast majority of classical theologians, he is metaphysically simple or noncomposite, and thus is incapable of division. In which case he cannot be identical to any of the "parts" of human nature, whether material/corporeal or immaterial/incorporeal.

It should be clear even from this briefest of outlines that the compositional model of the hypostatic union has the interesting consequence that Christ is composed of "parts," of which God the Son is the most metaphysically fundamental (being the person who sustains the human nature he assumes). But it is equally clear on this way of thinking that God the Son is not identical to his human nature. It proposes a view according to which the Second Person of the Trinity is strongly united to his human nature but not identical to it. Hence, *compositional* Christology.

The view has many virtues. For one thing, it preserves God the Son from undergoing substantive change on becoming incarnate; it also retains the distinction between the essentially incorporeal divine person and the human nature he assumes. But it also has potentially damaging drawbacks. For example, it seems to imply that the human nature of Christ is not a thing (*non aliquid*), which is equivalent to the unorthodox position known as christological nihilism (i.e., that Christ's human nature is not a concrete particular—that is, is *no-thing*). I do not think this is an implication of the view, as we shall see in chapter 6. For present purposes, it is sufficient to see that the model has the consequence that Christ and his human nature are not identical, and that it preserves important theological intuitions that have deep roots in the Western catholic tradition.

So it seems that the incarnation can be used as a sort of theological test case for divine incorporeality. How do the different metaphysical options we have surveyed fare in response to this challenge?

---

incarnation, see Alfred J. Freddoso, "Human Nature, Potency and the Incarnation," *Faith and Philosophy* 3, no. 1 (1986): 27–53.

Let us begin with the denial of divine incorporeality. If, like the Hobbesian and the pantheist who is also a global materialist, we think that God is a material object, then the incarnation does not involve the addition of one sort of substance (a material body) to another sort of substance (an incorporeal divine person). It is merely the addition of another physical part to God, who is essentially corporeal and composite. In this case, there is no problem with divine incarnation as such, because there is, or can be, no such thing as divine incorporeality. But this is a rather drastic solution to the problem the incarnation poses, and not one that will appeal to anyone committed to classical Christology or classical theism, since (as we have seen) such classical, orthodox theology stands foursquare behind the claim that God is incorporeal.

Next, we turn to the global immaterialist position. As we have already seen, immaterialism does not imply that in becoming incarnate, God the Son acquires metaphysical ownership of a material substance. Indeed, there are obvious advantages to this view for a doctrine of the incarnation, because the so-called problem of interaction (between an immaterial soul and material body) and the pairing problem (how this particular soul is paired with this particular body and no other) do not arise in the problematic way they do for substance dualists. If there are no material objects, then the incarnation cannot be a matter of acquiring a human nature that includes a physical body. This does mean that the immaterialist is in the odd position of conceding the incarnation does not involve acquisition of a physical body. But this is not obviously unorthodox. The immaterialist claim that there are, or can be, no material substances is a metaphysical thesis that seems entirely consistent with the theology of the catholic creeds, which do not require the belief that in assuming human nature God the Son acquired a concrete physical part.[16]

What about panentheism? Much depends on whether the panentheist in question is an immaterialist (like Edwards) or thinks of the world on analogy with the physical body of God, with God taking the place of a soul. Some contemporary panentheists, such as Arthur Peacocke, have argued that the incarnation is of a piece with God's gradual work of revealing himself in and through the created order in which he is immanent. God is

---

16. For a recent attempt to make the case for an immaterialist account of the incarnation, see Marc A. Hight and Joshua Bohannon, "The Son More Visible: Immaterialism and the Incarnation," *Modern Theology* 26, no. 1 (2010): 120–48.

said to "convey meaning" through the "information input" of his particular presence in the human Jesus. But this does not involve a "'descent' into the world by God conceived of as 'above' (and so outside) it . . . but as the manifestation of what, or rather of the one who, is already in the world though not recognized or known."[17] Peacocke holds to what he calls an "Emergent Monism," that is, a layered set of interlocking physical systems where certain properties or powers emerge from more basic or fundamental physical parts of the whole.[18] He also characterizes his position as a species of "theistic naturalism" whereby the physical processes of the world are also regarded as the actions of God who continuously creates them.[19]

This sort of panentheism, which is one of a family of views in the current literature on science and religion, makes the incarnation a matter of God's presence being particularly manifest or tangible in and through the life of Christ. This is often called "degree Christology" since it implies that the difference between Christ and other human beings is the degree to which God indwells him. Christ is supremely "God-conscious" or "open" to the divine. But language of Christ being God Incarnate has dropped away along with the classical metaphysics that underpinned it. Peacocke prefers to speak of events, processes, and emergence than of substances and their attributes. Divine incorporeality has an ambiguous place in such an ontology. Peacocke emphasizes the immanence of God in creation, which is somehow contained within the divine life. But he says much less about God's transcendence or the manner in which he is distinct from the creation. Moreover, if Christ is a supremely God-conscious human, then the question of how an incorporeal agent can become personally united to a human nature, including a corporeal part—his body—does not arise in quite the same way it does in traditional, classical Christology. For on Peacocke's view, God is not assuming a human nature as such, but communicating certain information in the life of Christ in whom he is specially present. But since God is omnipresent in all creation in which he is said to be "immanent," this turns out to be just a more particular manifestation

---

17. Arthur Peacocke, *All That Is: A Naturalistic Faith for the Twenty-First Century*, ed. Philip Clayton (Minneapolis: Fortress, 2007), 38–40 and 37, respectively. Peacocke wrote a lot in this vein. But this short essay, on which he was working almost until the day he died, offers a succinct and comprehensive survey of his views on God's relationship to the world, a matter that had occupied the bulk of his previous work in the science-religion debate.
18. Ibid., 12, 14, 26.
19. Ibid., 17.

of God's presence in Christ than in other humans. The benefits of this view must be weighed against the potential cost (if it is regarded as a cost) of moving away from traditional ways of thinking about Christ as being one person with two natures.

Coda

Discussion of divine incorporeality must include a range of different philosophical and theological factors. There are issues pertaining to the very definition of incorporeality as it applies to the divine nature. There are other matters having to do with the way in which God is related to the world he creates. Finally, for Christian theists and Christian theologians, there is the complication of the incarnation, which, as we have seen, may be regarded as a sort of theological litmus test used to ascertain which models of the God-world relationship are able to account for the person of Christ while retaining divine incorporeality. For those theists who do not believe the doctrine of incarnation, who may think it impossible God takes on a corporeal human nature, this last part of our treatment of incorporeality might be taken as a warning: a reason for thinking that the Christology beloved of orthodox, traditional Christian theology raises significant, perhaps insuperable problems for a concept of God's essential incorporeality. But I have argued that at least one traditional model of the hypostatic union does not have this consequence. And if one is willing to embrace immaterialism, then the incarnation does not have this consequence either, though for very different reasons. Given the fact that discussions of the relationship between God and the world are front and center in several overlapping contemporary literatures (e.g., philosophy of religion, philosophical and systematic theology, religion and science), it is unlikely that discussion of the doctrine of divine incorporeality will go away any time soon. Rather, as these themes are complicated by models of the relationship between God and the creation that move away from classical theism (e.g., panentheism), these concerns will become more pressing for theologians as they seek to understand how it is that "in him we live and move and have our being" (Acts 17:28 ESV).

4

The Christological Doctrine of the Image of God

> Despite the difference in nature that remains between humanity and the second person, the perfect hypostatic unity of the two of them in Christ makes him the perfect human image of the second person of the trinity in much the same way the perfect unity of substance between the first and second persons of the trinity makes the second the perfect image of the first. In both cases perfect unity makes for perfect imaging.
>
> —Kathryn Tanner[1]

In the previous chapters we have considered the eternal generation of the Son, the notion that God the Son exists in some sense without his flesh (*asarkos*), and the relationship between the notion of divine incorporeality and the incarnation. We might say that starting with christological "first principles" as far as the dogmatic shape of the incarnation goes, our investigation began with the Trinity and the generation of the Son, proceeded to consider his state prior to his becoming incarnate, and then tackled what it means to say that an essentially incorporeal being becomes

---

1. Kathryn Tanner, *Christ the Key* (Cambridge: Cambridge University Press, 2009), 13.

incarnate. Now that we have considered these matters, we are in a position to ask a further question. We can put it like this: human beings are said to be made in the divine image, a doctrine that has been put to much use in theological anthropology as well as recent accounts of the doctrine of creation. However, exactly what is meant by the doctrine of the image of God has been hotly contested. Yet, if Christ is the eternally generated Son Incarnate, might it be that this throws light on the meaning of the image of God in human beings? Might it be that the reason why the incorporeal God takes on human flesh is in order that human beings may be made in his image in some important respect? That is the question we shall consider in this chapter.

Introduction

To begin with, we must of course ask, what *is* the "image of God"? What is it for human beings to be created "in God's image"? There are a number of different answers to these questions in the Christian tradition. The account this chapter sets out and recommends we shall call *the christological doctrine*. On this view the image of God is borne by one individual, Christ. Other human beings are made in the image of God to the extent that they are conformed to the likeness of Christ. We might say that they are ectypes of the archetype of the divine image in Christ. Rather like the prototype of an automobile and the production model that is based upon the blueprints of the prototype, Christ is the "prototypical" human. We are made in *his* image, as it were, so that we reflect God in some measure as we image Christ, the God-man.

In the biblical tradition, human beings are said to have been created in the image (*tselem*) and likeness (*demut*) of God (Gen. 1:26–27). There has been much theological debate about whether the terms "image" and "likeness" in the Primeval Prologue to Genesis are synonyms or should be distinguished as two different states or stages of human moral development.[2] However, it appears that these two terms refer to the same thing, namely, the human person taken as a whole, acting as the divine representative on

---

2. The distinction can be traced to a number of the fathers. See Nonna Verna Harrison, "The Human Person as Image and Likeness of God," in *The Cambridge Companion to Orthodox Christian Theology*, ed. Mary B. Cunningham and Elizabeth Theokritoff (Cambridge: Cambridge University Press, 2008), 78–92.

earth (*tselem*).³ By contrast, in the New Testament, Christ is said to be the image (*eikōn*) of the invisible God, the firstborn over all creation, by whom all things are made (Col. 1:15–16), the exact representation of the being of the Father (Heb. 1:3), and the image of God (2 Cor. 4:4). St. Paul tells us in Romans 8:29 that "those whom he foreknew he also predestined to *be conformed to the image of his Son*, in order that he might be the firstborn among many brothers" (ESV). On the basis of such biblical claims, St. Irenaeus writes:

> For in times long past, it was said that man was created after the image of God, but it was not [actually] shown; for the Word was as yet invisible, after whose image man was created, wherefore also he did easily lose the similitude. When, however, the Word of God became flesh, He confirmed both these: for He both showed forth the image truly, since He became Himself what was His image; and He re-established the similitude after a sure manner, by assimilating man to the invisible Father through means of the visible Word.⁴

Similarly, Athanasius writes that after the fall, God was faced with the prospect of a defaced image in human beings:

> What, then, was God to do? What else could He possibly do, being God, but renew His Image in mankind, so that through it men might come once more to know Him? And how could this be done save by the coming of the very Image Himself, our Savior Jesus Christ? Men could not have done it, for they are only made after the Image; nor could angels have done it, for they are not the Images of God. The Word of God came in His own Person, because it was He alone, the Image of the Father, who could recreate man after the Image.⁵

---

3. This is an instance of Hebrew parallelism. For discussion, see Richard J. Plantinga, Thomas R. Thompson, and Matthew D. Lundberg, *An Introduction to Christian Theology* (Cambridge: Cambridge University Press, 2010), 182–85. Also relevant are R. W. L. Moberly, *The Theology of the Book of Genesis*, Old Testament Theology (Cambridge: Cambridge University Press, 2009), ch. 2; Gerhard von Rad, *Genesis* (Philadelphia: Westminster, 1961), 56; William Dyrness, "The *Imago Dei* and Christian Aesthetics," *Journal of the Evangelical Theological Society* 15, no. 3 (1972): 161–72, esp. 162.

4. Irenaeus, *Against Heresies*, in *Ante-Nicene Fathers*, vol. 1, *The Apostolic Fathers, Justin Martyr, Irenaeus*, ed. and trans. Alexander Roberts and James Donaldson (Peabody, MA: Hendrickson, 1994), 5.16.2, p. 544.

5. Athanasius, *On the Incarnation*, trans. A Religious of C.S.M.V. (Crestwood, NY: St. Vladimir's Seminary Press, 2003), §13.

The argument that follows takes as its point of departure these patristic accounts of the image of God as they reflect the biblical traditions. It has three parts. In the first, two traditional approaches to the doctrine of the image of God are set out and assessed. Then in a second section the christological doctrine is offered as an alternative to the two traditional approaches to the divine image. In a third section some objections to this model are considered.

Two Approaches to the Divine Image

Often in historic discussion of the image of God, it has been identified with some capacity or power, or something about the nature of human beings that sets them apart from other creatures. Thus John Calvin writes that

> although the soul is not the man, there is no absurdity in holding that he is called the image of God in respect of the soul; though I retain the principle which I lately laid down, that the image of God extends to everything in which the nature of man surpasses that of all other species of animals. Accordingly, by this term is denoted the integrity with which Adam was endued when his intellect was clear, his affections subordinated to reason, all his senses duly regulated, and when he truly ascribed all his excellence to the admirable gifts of his Maker. And though the primary seat of the divine image was in the mind and the heart, or in the soul and its powers, there was no part even of the body in which some rays of glory did not shine.[6]

This is not just a Protestant approach to the divine image. Similar ideas can be found in the *Catechism of the Catholic Church*, which states, "By virtue of his soul and his spiritual powers of intellect and will, man is endowed with freedom, an 'outstanding manifestation of the divine image.'"[7]

---

6. John Calvin, *Institutes of the Christian Religion*, ed. John T. McNeill, trans. Ford Lewis Battles (Philadelphia: Westminster, 1960), 1.15.3.

7. See *The Catechism of the Catholic Church* III.I.1, art. 1, 1705, located online at http://www.vatican.va/archive/ccc_css/archive/catechism/p3s1c1a1.htm. Some of the Protestant Confessions are more ambiguous—e.g., the Westminster Confession, which says, "After God had made all other creatures, He created man, male and female, with reasonable and immortal souls, endued with knowledge, righteousness, and true holiness, after His own image" (4.2). Wolfhart Pannenberg makes it clear that "the classical understanding of the divine likeness in Christian theology relates it to the soul" (Pannenberg, *Systematic Theology, Vol. 2*, trans. Geoffrey Bromiley [Grand Rapids: Eerdmans; Edinburgh: T&T Clark, 1995], 206). This is broadly correct. For a recent and accessible account of the image of God that equates it with possession

This sort of view is often referred to as *the substantive account of the image of God*, since it equates the image with something substantive about human beings, such as possession of an immaterial substance, or soul, or certain powers associated with the soul or the human person, such as rationality.[8] (These are not mutually exclusive, of course. For instance, one might identify the divine image with rationality *as exemplified by* the human soul.) Calvin represents a substantive account of the divine image in human beings, in keeping with the Augustinian tradition in which he stands. For Calvin, the divine image shines in all parts of unfallen humanity but is especially present in the soul with its various powers, especially the powers of the intellect and affections, rightly governed by reason. It is this pristine state from which human beings fell in Adam, so that fallen human beings bear at most a defaced remnant of this divine image that requires the secret work of the Holy Spirit in order to be renovated and restored.[9]

The problems with this doctrine are well known. Here are some of the most obvious. First, if the image of God is a capacity or power (construed broadly to include things like the capacity to think, and therefore, rationality, as in the *Catechism of the Catholic Church*), it is difficult to demarcate human beings from other sorts of created entities. Do certain sorts of simians have such rationality? Do dolphins? Surely angels do. Yet the image of God is usually thought to be a property of human beings alone among God's creatures. If that is right, then the divine image cannot be identified with rationality, for it is not at all clear that it is a characteristic unique to human beings.

This approach also raises worries about the measure of the given power or capacity necessary to exemplify the image. Take rationality once more, since it has been a popular candidate in historic discussion of the topic.[10]

---

of a soul, see J. P. Moreland, *The Recalcitrant* Imago Dei: *Human Persons and the Failure of Naturalism* (London: SCM, 2009).

8. Sometimes this substantive view is called the structural view (thus, Hoekema). However, the benefit of the former appellation is that it makes clear the fact that according to this way of thinking, the image of God is something about human beings that is essential or substantive, e.g., a property, power, or nature that belongs to a certain sort of entity.

9. Calvin is a somewhat frustrating interlocutor on this matter because he appears to say different things in different places in his corpus about whether the divine image has been effaced post-fall or merely severely damaged. In keeping with most Calvin interpreters, I am reading him as a proponent of the latter, less extreme view, which does seem to represent the preponderance of his writings on this matter.

10. See Aquinas, *Summa Theologiae* I.93.6. The patristic discussion of the divine image has informed all subsequent debate in Christian theology. For an interesting recent treatment

What are we to make of human beings that fail to exemplify this capacity, such as those in utero, or infants, or those who are severely mentally impaired, or in permanent vegetative states, or that are born encephalic? For most Christians, moral intuitions will press in the direction of including most if not all such entities within the bounds of human personhood. Yet none of these sorts of individuals actually possess rationality (though some may have the dispositional property of rationality, such as infants). But then it looks like there are some humans (perhaps, human persons) that lack a necessary condition for being made in the divine image, which is an outcome few Christian theologians will want to embrace given that the divine image is not usually thought to be something accidental, but essential to human persons. (Humans are, after all, said to be *made in* the divine image in Gen. 1:26–27; cf. 9:6.)

As we have seen, Calvin is more expansive in what he thinks falls under the image of God. He includes the body as a part of human beings in which the rays of the image shine. Following his lead, other Reformed theologians have also argued that the whole human person must be included within the notion of the divine image, not merely human rationality, or even a human soul. But it is difficult to see how the defender of a substantive doctrine can make good on this claim since God is essentially disembodied. How can a corporeal body be said to be made in the image of an essentially immaterial agent, such as God? This seems to be a straightforward category mistake.[11]

Suppose the claim is that God's image in human beings is essential and has to do inextricably with rationality. Presumably, human beings image God in this respect in virtue of having the capacity for a certain sort of complex mental life. Even if one thinks that human beings are material objects, as with physicalism, this does not necessarily mean that human bodies are in the image of God. All it requires is that humans exemplify

---

of this material, see Frances Young, *God's Presence: A Contemporary Recapitulation of Early Christianity* (Cambridge: Cambridge University Press, 2013), ch. 4.

11. Herman Bavinck is one Reformed theologian who thinks that human bodies must be included within the ambit of the divine image in humans. Gresham Machen resists this for the reasons given here. A useful discussion of these matters can be found in Anthony A. Hoekema, *Created in God's Image* (Grand Rapids: Eerdmans, 1994), 67–68. Hoekema sides with Bavinck. He says, "If it is true that the whole person is the image of God, we must also include the body as part of the image" (ibid., 68). We shall see that Hoekema's intuition, which reflects the Primeval Prologue in Genesis, can be included within the christological doctrine. This is one reason for preferring it to what we might call the *merely* substantive doctrine.

certain properties requisite for certain mental states, such as rationality. Since properties are not physical objects, it makes no sense to say that the instantiation of those properties in human beings has to do with the corporeality of human beings, as if being embodied were somehow a constituent of the divine image in human beings.

Having said that, although this approach appears to be mired in difficulties, which is why many contemporary theologians have begun to look elsewhere for ways of conceiving the image of God, I do not claim that the defender of such a position is without resources or potential responses. Nevertheless, there are significant obstacles in the way of an attempt to rehabilitate this approach to the image of God without recourse to supplemental theses and additional arguments—as we shall see in due course, when considering the christological doctrine.

More recently, theologians have thought that a better way of characterizing the image as it is set forth in Genesis 3 is what is often called *the relational account of the image of God*. On this view, human beings bear the divine "image" as they relate to one another and to God and act as divine regents over the created order. Thus, David Fergusson writes:

> In its Hebraic context, the divine image refers not to the possession of an immortal soul (as in the Greek tradition) but more to the role exercised by human beings in the cosmic order. As those who can hear and obey the divine word, human beings are charged with acting on God's behalf in relation to one another and to the rest of creation. This more functional or relational account of the divine image makes better sense of the succeeding verses that speak of the roles of human beings in the world already made.[12]

Although variations on the relational doctrine are in the ascendency in biblical studies and modern theology, there is reason to doubt that this really captures all that is meant by the divine image in human beings. For one thing, it does not really do justice to the claim in Genesis 1:26–27 that human beings are made *in* or *after* God's image, unless one connects

---

12. David Fergusson, "Creation," in *The Oxford Handbook of Systematic Theology*, ed. John Webster, Kathryn Tanner, and Iain Torrance (Oxford: Oxford University Press, 2009), 74. Other influential modern theologians that espouse a relational view of the image of God include Karl Barth, Jürgen Moltmann, and Wolfhart Pannenberg. It is a view one can find among Christian philosophers too. One example is Kevin Corcoran's *Rethinking Human Nature: A Christian Materialist Alternative to the Soul* (Grand Rapids: Baker Academic, 2006), 81.

this image to those versions of social trinitarianism, according to which there are three centers of consciousness in the divine life relating to one another in eternal perichoresis. Then human beings image God as they (somehow) reflect this irreducible relationality within the Godhead. However, for those that find such social views of the Trinity unappealing (such as the present author), or who find the supposed connection between the divine life, human relationality, and the image of God tenuous or even implausible, this provides no motivation for a relational doctrine of the image of God.

One might hold to a relational view of the divine image without appeal to social trinitarianism, however. For instance, it might be that the divine image has to do with oversight and care for the creation, with human beings acting as divine vice-regents, relating to one another, to the other creatures over whom they have a certain derived authority and responsibility, and to God their Creator. This seems to be what Fergusson has in mind in the passage just cited.

However, as with the substantive doctrine, it is not clear how this adequately distinguishes human beings from other entities. That is, it is not apparent from such a characterization of the divine image why *only* human beings bear it. Other creatures relate to one another, to the rest of the creation, and (possibly) to their Creator. Certainly, angels do this. Yet they are not traditionally thought to be image-bearers in the way that human beings are. It might be thought that there is something about the divinely bestowed role of overseeing the creation that makes human beings unique. In virtue of this role they relate to the creation (and to God) in a way that no other creature does, not even angels. There is textual and exegetical support for this view. However, this also presents challenges for contemporary constructive theologians. For instance, some are uncomfortable with notions of human "dominion" over other creatures, which seem to them to be quaint or imperialistic, even speciesist. However, supposing some mileage can be gotten from the notion that human beings have a unique role in overseeing the created order, how does this in and of itself provide a reason for thinking that this exhausts what is meant by the divine image? How does it account for the way in which the New Testament identifies the image with Christ and the redeemed? At the very least this reading of the biblical material leaves a number of important theological questions unanswered.

In recent theology there have been other attempts to find a relational basis for the image of God that does not fall foul of this worry about human uniqueness. One example can be found in the systematic theology of the Lutheran Robert Jenson, whom we have already encountered in the second chapter. He has argued that "our specificity in comparison with the other animals is that we are the ones addressed by God's moral word and so enabled to respond—that we are called to *pray*." Jenson goes on to say that "the final specification of 'the image of God' is *love*."[13] Is he right about this? Can the divine image be identified with certain relations humans normally possess, and specifically with loving and praying? Although these might be thought to be improvements upon the medieval notion that the image was to be identified—or (at least) intimately bound up—with rationality, these alternatives do not appear able to overcome the worry about human uniqueness. Are we to say of those incapable of prayer (e.g., patients in a permanent vegetative state, and so forth), or those who do not pray, that they have nothing of the divine image or, alternatively, only some reduced amount of it? As for those who are impaired in their capacity to love (e.g., sociopaths or the severely mentally handicapped), do they possess less of the divine image because they are incapable of appropriately giving and receiving love?

This does not seem at all theologically satisfactory. For one thing, it suggests that certain human individuals suffering from particular personality disorders, such as sociopaths, or from particular mental incapacities do not instantiate the divine image in the same manner as do other human beings. But, as with the objection from human uniqueness applied to substantive views, so too here: an argument for the image of God that excludes *ex hypothesi* a certain group of human persons from consideration, or calls their inclusion in the divine image into serious question, is hardly theologically satisfying if the image is thought to be an essential human characteristic.

In addition to these worries, it could be objected that relational views of the divine image rely upon implied ontological claims that render them, at bottom, substantive after all. J. P. Moreland writes, "Even if we functionalize the image or treat it in largely relational terms . . . it is still true

---

13. Robert W. Jenson, *Systematic Theology*, vol. 2, *The Works of God* (New York: Oxford University Press, 1999), 58–59 and 72, respectively.

that a thing's functional abilities or relational aptitudes are determined by its kindedness"—in other words, by the natural kind to which it belongs. "Thus, even the functional, relational aspects of the image of God have ontological implications."[14] Thus, if humans do represent God in their dominion over creation, they do so because they have the requisite properties and powers by means of which they exercise such dominion. Alternatively, if humans image God in their interpersonal relations (which, some suppose, are analogues to divine relationality), then this obtains just in case the humans in question have certain powers and properties and are the sort of thing that can exemplify relationality (like God). So it looks like the relational account of the divine image depends upon ontological claims of the sort we find in the substantive account. If that is right, then relational accounts of the divine image are not really distinct from substantive views but supplement or extend them.

Yet these are not the only alternatives on the doctrine of the image of God.[15] Suppose human beings image God as they are conformed to the image of Christ, who, being the Son of God incarnate, is the image of the invisible God (i.e., the image of the Father) in human flesh. Such a notion provides the basis for a christological gloss on Genesis 1 that makes sense of the New Testament claims about the relation between Christ as the principle image-bearer and fallen human beings as those that are being conformed to the divine image by being united to Christ. It is this doctrine, which is very ancient indeed and can be traced back to patristic theologians like Irenaeus and Athanasius, that we will explore in the remainder of the chapter.

I will argue that it is an improvement on various iterations of the substantive and relational doctrines of the image of God because it is able to include within the scope of the divine image the whole human being, not just certain powers or capacities that supposedly distinguish humans from all other creatures. What is more, it provides a reason for thinking that there is an important relational dimension to the image of God because those made in his image are conformed to the likeness of Christ. Finally,

---

14. Moreland, *Recalcitrant* Imago Dei, 4. Hoekema makes similar claims in *Created in God's Image*.

15. Joshua Farris distinguishes between a functional and relational view of the image of God. However, it is not clear to me from the examples he provides that there is a real difference between these two views, so I have conflated them. See Farris, "An Immaterial Substance View: Imago Dei in Creation and Redemption," forthcoming in *Heythrop Journal* (2016).

by making Christology the theological frame for discussion of the divine image, it provides a reason for thinking that human beings possess the divine image in a way that it is not present in other creatures. This is an important consideration, given the amount of ink that has been spilled trying to discover some reason for thinking that the image of God is unique to human beings.

The Christological Argument

Traditional substantive accounts of the image of God often make reference to the importance of Christ as an archetype of the divine image. Thus, the *Catechism of the Catholic Church* states, "It is in Christ, 'the image of the invisible God,' that man has been created 'in the image and likeness' of the Creator. It is in Christ, Redeemer and Savior, that the divine image, disfigured in man by the first sin, has been restored to its original beauty and ennobled by the grace of God."[16] The idea seems to be this: Adam and Eve were endowed with the image of God, understood as possession of a human soul and the intellectual powers of rationality and will. As a consequence of the fall, these gifts were impaired. Christ is the Second Adam (per Rom. 5:12–19). He possesses in an untarnished state the divine image because he is without sin (Heb. 4:15). Fallen human beings can have the divine image repaired in them by the secret working of the Holy Spirit in regeneration and sanctification, conforming fallen human beings to the image of God in Christ.

Yet this is not the only way to understand the excerpt from the *Catechism of the Catholic Church*. In keeping with fathers such as Irenaeus and Athanasius, it could be read in a rather different manner, one that makes the divine image not merely something that Christ repairs but rather something that he instantiates as the archetype and divine *eikōn*. On this way of thinking, human beings are made in the image of God *by being made in the image of Christ*. An illustration will help make this clearer. Imagine Michelangelo's statue of David. There is an original statue carved from a single slab of marble and housed in the Accademia

---

16. *Catechism of the Catholic Church*, 1701. Cf. Pannenberg: "In him alone do we see that our destiny of fellowship with God is the point of the divine likeness which Genesis 9:6 adduces as a basis for the inviolability of the human person and therefore for human dignity" (*Systematic Theology*, 176n2).

di Belle Arti in Florence, Italy. There are also multiple copies of this artistic marvel, including several in the environs of Florence itself. What relationship do the copies bear to the original? We might say that they reproduce the physical properties of the original—often in a different medium, such as bronze. Suppose we take a cast of the original marble statue and from this generate ten impressions in bronze. Then we have ten copies of the original. Although the copies are in bronze and not marble, they look almost identical to the original from which they have been cast (allowing for minor differences and defects that are incorporated in the replication process). Yet the ten bronzes are clearly copies or facsimiles of the original. This would be true even if they were composed of the same material.

Now, suppose Christ is like the original statue. Just as the marble slab that felt the impress of the hands of Michelangelo is the original from which the facsimiles in bronze were derived, so Christ is the "original," the archetypal human being who bears the image of God. Although (according to classical Christian theology) human beings are descended from an original human pair, they are not made in the image of Adam and Eve, strictly speaking. Rather, on this way of thinking, Eve, Adam, and every other human being are made in the image of Christ, who is the image of the invisible God. Hence, the divine image you and I bear is, as it were, a facsimile of that image borne by Christ; it is ectypal. Although he lived long after any first putative human community, he is the one who bears the archetypal divine image, after whose divine image the rest of humanity is fashioned.

In a recent essay on this topic, Mark McLeod Harrison says, "When a 'regular' human is made, she is made from scratch as a copy of God. But Jesus preexists his human incarnation and thus, in a sense, *he copies humans* when he is made the incarnate God. Whereas we all resemble one another because we copy God, Jesus resembles us because he copies us."[17] It seems to me that McLeod Harrison is right about this, from a certain point of view. In a sense the human nature of God the Son is a copy of the sort of nature all other human beings possess, yet without sin. In his respect he "copies humans" when he becomes incarnate. However, without further explanation this could be misleading from the standpoint of the

---

17. Mark McLeod Harrison, "On Being the Literal Image of God," *Journal of Analytic Theology* 2 (2014): 158.

christological doctrine of the divine image with which we are concerned here. For on this view it is not merely that Christ possesses a copy of human nature in virtue of his assumption of human nature. That is true, of course, but it is not terribly theologically interesting. Much more important for the present argument is the claim that God has ordained from before the foundation of the world that Christ would be the archetype of true humanity, and that his human nature (in hypostatic union with God the Son) would be the blueprint for all other human natures. He is the image of God, as the New Testament declares. And his being the image of God has to do with the fact that God makes human nature capable of bearing union with the divine and capable of bearing the divine imprint or image in order to do so.

Another illustration. Suppose I wanted to go to a masquerade. In order to do so, I need to purchase a disguise. It needs to "fit" my face. So I have a mask made that conforms to the contours of my visage. It would not fit your face in the same way because it is bespoke; it is made to fit me, not you. In a similar manner, the human nature of Christ is fashioned in order that it might conform to, and be in personal union with, God the Son. What I am suggesting is that in order to do this, God ordained that human nature have certain properties and powers that would mean that the particular human nature God the Son assumes at the first moment of his incarnation conforms to, and is capable of being in personal union with, a divine person. Human nature is created in order that it might reflect the divine image and be united to God. In the case of Christ, that union is unique and personal; he has metaphysical ownership, as it were, of the human nature he assumes (just as I have ownership of my human nature). But all human beings have a nature that is capable of such hypostatic union, in principle. And all human beings are given a nature that has the requisite image of God so that God the Son may unite himself with human nature. Indeed, Christ is the archetype whose human nature is the blueprint for all other human natures.

This goes a considerable way toward explaining why the image of God we bear includes the whole of human nature (whatever that turns out to be). It is not just that I bear the divine image in my soul (if I have a soul), or in virtue of having rationality, or the capacity to love, or pray, or whatever. Rather, I bear the divine image in virtue of the fact that human nature is in principle created with the capacities and powers necessary and sufficient to be in hypostatic union with a divine person.[18] This includes both my mind (and soul, if I have a soul) and body, rightly configured. To abstract from human nature one aspect that is in the likeness of God is to divide what is united in Christ. He assumes a complete human nature, not merely human rationality or a human soul (if humans have souls). It is his whole human nature that images God by being made with the capacity for hypostatic union with a divine person.

What is more, this picture of the divine image makes sense of Calvin's worries about the vitiation of that image because of human sin. Suppose with much traditional, classical Christian theology that there is a primeval fall from grace that entails the moral defacing of the divine image in human beings thereafter. We bear a defaced image, whereas Christ, who is without sin, bears the perfect image. Our image must be restored through the secret working of the Holy Spirit in regeneration. Christ's human nature does not require such repair because it is miraculously generated without sin (Heb. 4:15). For this reason, he is able to act in such a way as to provide the restoration of that image in fallen human beings through an act of atonement (whatever the mechanism is by means of which he brings about that state of affairs). That is, because he does not bear a defaced divine image, he is able to act on behalf of those who do bear a defaced divine image, providing the means by which that image may be restored in redemption.

Additionally, this view dovetails with the New Testament emphasis upon Christ as the *eikōn* of God, along with the Old Testament view of the Primeval Prologue to Genesis, according to which the image of God has to do with representing the divine on earth. Peter Enns expresses this consensus view among biblical scholars when he writes that the image of God in Genesis "refers to humanity's role of ruling God's creation as God's representatives." He goes on:

> We see this played out in the ancient Near Eastern world, where kings were divine image-bearers, appointed representatives of God on earth. This concept is further reflected in kings' placing statues of themselves (images) in

---

18. Compare a suit of armor, which in principle provides necessary and sufficient protection from sword thrusts. However, it only actually provides me this protection if I am wearing the suit when attacked by another knight. Just so, human nature in principle has the necessary and sufficient conditions for hypostatic union with God, but will only actually be in such union if assumed by a divine person.

distant parts of their kingdom so they could remind their subjects of their "presence." Further, idols were images of gods placed in ancient temples as a way of having a distant god present with the worshipers.[19]

According to Enns, the image of God in Genesis is not "that spark in us that makes us human rather than animal," such as reason, the soul, and other candidates put forward by defenders of the substantive view of the divine image. Instead, it has to do with representing God in the world.[20]

But this makes complete sense if we understand the divine image according to the christological view. If Christ is the archetype of humanity, then the representational role the image of God plays in Genesis is consistent with the christological focus of the New Testament. For then Christ is the archetypal human being, who represents God to humanity and humanity to God in his incarnation. He is also the prototypical human being, after whose image all other human beings are fashioned. Humans are able to represent God in the world in virtue of being made in the image of the God-man, the archetypal image-bearer.

This means that there is a very good biblical and theological case to be made for the christological view. It is able to incorporate the central issues of both the substantive and relational views of the divine image and to reconcile the apparent tensions between Old and New Testament material concerning the nature of that image. It also provides a way of thinking about humanity that is shaped by specifically christological concerns rather than more general theological or philosophical ones. For these reasons it seems to me that the christological view has much to commend it.

Objections

However, there are objections to this christological alternative to the merely substantive and merely relational views (understood as discrete, independent positions). The first and most important is this: Can Christ be the archetypal image and we the ectypes when the New Testament connects

---

19. Peter Enns, *The Evolution of Adam: What the Bible Does and Doesn't Say about Human Origins* (Grand Rapids: Brazos, 2012), xv. Cf. J. Richard Middleton, *The Liberating Image: The Imago Dei in Genesis 1* (Grand Rapids: Brazos, 2005), 121, where Middleton also opts for this sort of reading of the divine image in Genesis.
20. Enns, *Evolution of Adam*, xv.

bearing the image that Christ renews with redemption? That is, it looks like those who bear Christ's image are the redeemed, not all of humanity (cf. Col. 3:10; Eph. 2:10; 4:24). As Wolfhart Pannenberg puts it, "Christian theology must read the OT saying about our divine likeness in the light of the Pauline statements that call Jesus Christ the image of God . . . and that speak of the transforming of believers into this image." When the Pauline doctrine is examined, it is clear that "participation in the likeness attributed to Christ is promised only to believers."[21]

However, this reading of the biblical material is not the only one possible. Here is an alternative that is consistent with the christological doctrine. God eternally ordains that Christ be the archetype of human beings. The creation of human beings is in the "image" of Christ, as embodied rational animals capable in principle of being hypostatically united to a divine person. The first humans possess the nature of embodied rational animals modeled on Christ. The first human community falls from grace, thereby vitiating the embodied rational nature they each possess and disrupting the relations in which they stand to one another and to God, whose vice-regents they are. The restoration of this image obtains through the redemptive work of Christ, applied to believers through the secret work of the Holy Spirit in regeneration. Those united to Christ by this work of salvation are in a process of sanctification that includes the renewal of the divine image, which will be completed in the afterlife, whereupon they will be elevated to a moral state that enables them to enjoy the eschatological vision of God (*visio dei*).

This way of understanding the Pauline material does justice both to the Old Testament texts about the embodied divine image and to the role human beings play as divine representatives on earth. It also makes sense of the way in which the New Testament material identifies the divine image with Christ, as well as of the way in which its renewal is correlated to redemption in Christ.

A second, related objection is this: How can an entity that begins to exist later than the first in a series be the archetype or prototype for the series? Normally one would expect a prototype to begin to exist chronologically prior to the production model, for obvious reasons: the prototype is tested and examined in order to make sure that the production-line models are

---

21. Pannenberg, *Systematic Theology*, 208. Cf. Friedrich Schleiermacher, *The Christian Faith*, trans. H. R. MacIntosh and J. S. Stewart (Edinburgh: T&T Clark, 1999), §89, which makes a similar point in a rather more indirect manner.

up to specification and work properly. However, according to the christological doctrine, Christ begins to exist a long time after human beings appear on the scene. This seems deeply counterintuitive; some explanation is surely required.

However, this objection only goes through if Christ is *merely* human. That is, it would obtain if Christ is merely a human person. For then his being the prototypical human being, the archetype of all subsequent humans, would make no sense because he begins to exist at a moment chronologically subsequent to the first moment at which human beings began to exist. However, there is very good theological reason for resisting this position. The christological doctrine depends on two classical christological claims. The first is that Christ is the God-man, a divine person to whom is joined a human nature. The second is that he is eternally generated according to his divine nature, so that his divine nature preexists his human nature, although his human nature begins to exist at a particular moment in time. God has ordained that the human nature God the Son assumes be the prototype of all other human natures. Although in one sense the concrete particular that is his human nature begins to exist subsequent to the moment at which the human race begins to exist, it is possible for his human nature to be the archetype of all other human natures because its generation is eternally in view, as it were, in the mind of God, logically prior to his ordination of all subsequent human beings. What is more, it is eternally ordained that this be the human nature God the Son assumes. For this reason Christ is able to say in the Fourth Gospel, "Before Abraham was, I am" (John 8:58 ESV).

This state of affairs is rather like one in which an author plans a work of science fiction. Suppose she begins the process with the protagonist, the heroic leader of a race of aliens. This leader is introduced some way into the narrative, situated in a make-believe history that includes a complex backstory about the race of which he is a member. Nevertheless, the characteristics of the race were conceived prior to the writing of the narrative in which the leader is situated. They were based upon the characteristics of the leader, who was the first element in the fiction thought of by the author. She inserts the protagonist some way into the narrative, though in point of fact he was envisaged by the author prior to any other character in the book. *Mutatis mutandis*, Christ is ordained (not conceived!) as the prototypical human being, the archetype of the whole race, logically, though not chronologically, prior to the existence of any other human being in the mind of God.[22]

A third objection is this: Does the christological doctrine require a first human pair? More generally, is such a doctrine consistent with an evolutionary account of the generation of human beings? Let me address these two related concerns in order. First, I do not think that the doctrine *requires* a first human pair, understood to mean a first specially created human pair from whom all other humans are descended by normal generation. One could assume a story according to which human beings gradually emerge from earlier ancestors over time, including the complex history of evolutionary development that such stories entail in the current scientific literature on human origins. This does no violence to the christological doctrine; it is consistent with it. For on this view, God ordains Christ as the human archetype and then sets in motion (and superintends) the created order, in which the emergence of human life over vast eons of time is an intended outcome. This might be true even if the particular biological steps toward this goal are not "fixed" by divine decree, just as the outcome of a battle with an invincible pugilist is known in advance even if the particular stages of the fight are not. Suppose for the sake of argument that this is right. Then God ordains that human beings will emerge at a certain stage in evolutionary development even if he does not ordain the stages of development that precede it. Moreover, he ordains that the humans that emerge conform to the image of Christ.

Exactly how the emergent human community falls from a state of moral innocence, vitiating human nature, is more difficult to discern given this framework. Perhaps hominids reach a particular stage of social, moral, and physical development at a particular moment in prehistory, the time at which *homo sapiens* begin to exist as a stable hominid community. Very soon after this, there is some moral disruption that corrupts these early humans. After that, the rest of the creation-fall-redemption arc of the biblical metanarrative follows without much perturbation. The christological doctrine is consistent with this story. It, or something very like it, is not beyond the bounds of the broad contours of contemporary evolutionary theory, as far as I can discern. In which case the christological doctrine is consistent with at least one such story, though it is also consistent with the traditional theological account of the fall of an aboriginal human pair.

---

22. I have dealt with the election of Christ in more detail in *God Incarnate*, ch. 1.

A fourth and final objection has to do with the limit cases that entangled the merely substantive and merely relational accounts of the divine image. Recall that in each case, worries were raised about certain sorts of human beings that did not appear to be a good "fit" with the notion of the divine image in view. Does the christological view fare any better on this score? Can it account for those, such as the severely mentally impaired, or infants, or those born encephalic, that are what we might call (in a nonpejorative sense of the word) *liminal* cases of human beings? I think it can, although I can only indicate here how to respond to some of these cases. Earlier I indicated that Christians normally have views about physical or mental impairment (including the lack of certain important physical constituents, such as a brain in the case of the encephalic) that do not necessarily exclude such entities from counting as human beings, even human persons. On that assumption, let us apply benefit of the doubt reasoning to our three cases. Of these, human infants are rather different because they are not physically or mentally impaired, only immature in some respects (e.g., with respect to the exercise of rationality). Nevertheless, is it the case that humans that are physically and/or psychologically immature or impaired in some significant respect fail to bear the divine image? I don't see why. Human beings gain and lose parts all the time. So it cannot be that, just in virtue of losing a physical part, the humanity of our liminal cases is in question. Nor can it be the case that the humanity of infants is in question in virtue of their being physically and psychologically immature. Although the divine image may be underdeveloped or impaired in some respects in each of the three liminal cases (vis. the substantive and relational aspects of the image), all three are the sorts of entities that are capable of bearing hypostatic union with God. And all three sorts of entities belong to the natural kind of which Christ's human nature is also a member. Hence, I conclude that in each of the three cases the entity in question is arguably both human and an image-bearer, although the instantiation of that image may be immature (in the case of infants) or impaired (in the case of the severely mentally handicapped and the encephalic).

Conclusion

I have argued that a christological version of the doctrine of the image of God is able to give a more satisfying and comprehensive account of the divine image than those versions of the doctrine that privilege either the substantive or the relational aspects of the image. It also makes good sense of the biblical traditions—indeed, better sense than merely substantive or merely relational accounts. It is also able to meet several important objections. Given its ecumenical importance and its deep roots in patristic theology, a version of this doctrine has much to commend it. It may also provide resources for other theological loci, such as the doctrines of original sin and of atonement. For these reasons it seems to me that the christological doctrine has much to commend it. There are other concerns the doctrine raises that have not been dealt with here. For example, the nature of the divine image has not been elucidated in detail,[23] nor has the question of how the christological doctrine helps make sense of the vitiation of the image in Adam and its repair in regeneration been addressed. (And I am sure there are other concerns besides these.) However, I trust that enough has been provided to give the reader an indication of how these two issues might be addressed in a more expansive account of the doctrine.

---

23. This is where Mark McLeod Harrison's essay is useful. He is sympathetic to the patristic doctrine of Christ as the *eikōn* of God, even if he may not agree with the particular way in which I have construed that doctrine here.

5

Desiderata for Models of the Hypostatic Union

> Thus the official record of both substances represent him as both man and God: on the one hand born, on the other not born: on the one hand fleshly, on the other spiritual: on the one hand weak, on the other exceedingly strong: on the one hand dying, on the other living. That these two sets of attributes, the divine and the human, are each kept distinct from the other, is of course accounted for by the equal verity of each nature.
>
> —Tertullian[1]

Thus far we have analyzed several interrelated issues in Christology. Each of these has to do with protology, or the doctrine of first things. We have considered how God the Son is eternally generated; whether we can speak of Christ in abstraction, as it were, from his human nature; how an essentially incorporeal deity can acquire human flesh; and we set forth a christological account of the vexed issue of the image of God. The upshot of these studies is that Christology has a fundamental role to play in matters pertaining to "first things."

---

1. Tertullian, *Treatise on the Incarnation*, trans. Ernest Evans (London: SPCK, 1956), §5, pp. 18–19.

Alongside these considerations are methodological ones having to do with the intellectual desiderata for accounts of the incarnation. We may ask, on what basis should we construct our Christologies? Indeed, what method should we adopt? What authorities should we appeal to when pondering these deep matters of the faith? Although these may seem like questions that admit of obvious answers, in the history of modern theology, they have been given anything but traditional responses. Some want to develop Christologies on the basis of what can be shown via historical investigation, independent of any appeal to traditional theological authority, such as the catholic creeds or the Bible understood as Christian Scripture. Usually, this involves an appeal to a certain cluster of practices and methodological assumptions that are loosely collected together under the name Historical Biblical Criticism (or HBC). Some, though by no means all, practitioners of HBC seem to think that this is the only viable means by which to get at what can be known about the historical Jesus.[2] This often goes hand-in-hand with a rather condescending attitude toward theological accounts of Christ that take, say, the Bible as Scripture or the catholic creeds as data for the generation of theological claims about Christ. A celebrated example of this can be found in the work of Rudolf Bultmann, who writes:

> Also finished by knowledge of the forces and laws of nature is faith in spirits and demons. For us the stars are physical bodies whose motion is regulated by cosmic law; they are not demonic beings who can enslave men and women to serve them. . . . Likewise, illnesses and their cures have natural causes and do not depend on the work of demons and on exorcising them. Thus, the wonders of the New Testament are also finished as wonders; anyone who seeks to salvage their historicity by recourse to nervous disorders, hypnotic influences, suggestion, and the like only confirms this. . . . We cannot use electric lights and radios and, in the event of illness, avail ourselves of modern medical and clinical means and at the same time believe in the spirit and wonder world of the New Testament.[3]

---

2. There has been some discussion of the methods of HBC among Christian philosophers, especially Alvin Plantinga, Peter van Inwagen, and Eleonore Stump. For a recent (and critical) response to Plantinga and Stump from a practitioner of HBC, see C. L. Brinks, "On Nails, Scissors, and Toothbrushes: Responding to the Philosophers' Critiques of Historical Biblical Criticism," *Religious Studies* 48, no. 1 (2013): 1–20.

3. Rudolf Bultmann, "New Testament and Mythology," reprinted in *New Testament and Mythology and Other Basic Writings*, ed. and trans. Schubert M. Ogden (Minneapolis: Fortress, 1984), 4.

It is such issues of christological desiderata that are the focus of attention in this chapter. To begin with, we shall consider some preliminary issues that frame discussion of the hypostatic union. Then, after a note on the consensus view bequeathed to Christian theology via the canons of the Council of Chalcedon of AD 451, we focus upon what the desiderata for discussion of the hypostatic union consist in. This leads to discussion of the notions of persons, natures, and wills "in" Christ. A concluding section pulls the argument together, summarizing the implications this has for work in Christology. This provides the groundwork for a particular model of the hypostatic union, which is set forth in the next chapter.

Preliminary Matters

Accounts of the person of Christ that begin with history and progress to theological claims about Christology are usually termed "Christologies from below." Those that begin with certain theological givens—data that are thought to be divine revelation, or approved and authoritative theological statements that depend upon divine revelation, such as the creeds—are usually called "Christologies from above." Neither term is very helpful as a description of what the particular theological trajectories involve. Christologies from below often make tacit assumptions about who Christ is at the outset, just as Christologies from above make judgments about how to treat differing reports about christological texts in the canonical Gospels. And, for the most part, sophisticated Christology involves both textual work (including the sort of work familiar to practitioners of HBC) as well as appeals to what we might call ecclesiastical tradition, broadly construed. Nor is it true that approaches to Christology that privilege a method "from below" will inevitably yield "lower" Christologies than those that adopt an approach "from above." (Here "lower" and "higher" refer to where one pegs Christ metaphysically. If a particular Christology assumes that he is more than merely human, it is a "higher" Christology than one in which he is assumed to be merely human.) This may often be the case, but it need not be. There is certainly nothing like an entailment between, say, Christology "from below" and low Christology, or, for that matter, between Christology "from above" and high Christology. We can point to historic examples that buck this trend, the supreme instance of which is the disciples of Jesus who became the apostles of the early church. Their knowledge of Christ was largely (though not exclusively) "from below," so to speak, but they came to think of Christ in the most exalted terms, as the Son of God. As Richard Bauckham puts it, the "earliest Christology was already the highest Christology." He goes on to say that this "was not a mere stage on the way to the patristic development of ontological Christology in the context of a Trinitarian theology. It is already a fully divine Christology, maintaining that Jesus Christ is intrinsic to the unique and eternal identity of God. The Fathers did not develop it so much as transpose it into a conceptual framework more concerned with the Greek philosophical categories of essence and nature."[4]

There are also historical examples of those whose Christology emphasizes an approach "from above," but whose conclusions are not as high as classical Chalcedonian Christology. Arianism might be thought of as a candidate here, where certain metaphysical assumptions about the unique and undivided nature of God and of how to fit Christ into the divine identity led to a doctrine of the person of Christ according to which Christ is only of *like* substance to the Father (i.e., *homoiousios*).

Rather than wade into this debate—something I have attempted elsewhere[5]—I shall simply stipulate that responsible Christology ought to pay attention to the biblical and postbiblical traditions in formulating arguments for substantive conclusions about the person and work of Christ. This is not to deny that discrimination and judgment will have to be exercised in appeals to different sorts of theological authority. Allowing that Christology should attend to biblical and extrabiblical sources, including canonical and confessional documents, is one thing. The weighting of these different sources in forming christological judgments is another, and I will not go into that in detail here.[6] Instead, I will assume with the great majority of Christian theologians down through the ages that Scripture is the norming norm in theology this side of the grave. Other theological norms, such as the canons of ecumenical councils or the confessions of particular ecclesial communities, or even the arguments of theologians, are to be understood in light of Scripture and as ancillary to Scripture. To

---

4. Richard Bauckham, *Jesus and the God of Israel: God Crucified and Other Studies on the New Testament's Christology of Divine Identity* (Grand Rapids: Eerdmans, 2008), x.

5. Crisp, *God Incarnate*, ch. 1. See also Crisp, *Divinity and Humanity*.

6. I do go into this in *God Incarnate*, ch. 1.

my mind there is also considerable merit in approaching the theological task in general, and the christological one in particular, with what Thomas Oden has recently called "consensual Christianity" in mind[7]—that is, paying attention to the consensus about a wide range of theological matters, especially matters pertaining to what is central and defining within the Christian tradition. Marginal voices often do help us to see things in a different light and can lead to reevaluations of the canonical consensus. But in formulating Christian doctrine, especially *christological* doctrine, more weight should be given to the consensus than to those at the margins. Part of the reason for this is that the consensus view on christological matters was reached via a complex process of debate, discussion, and reflection in the first five centuries of the life of the church, during which the very language of Christology was forged. Pains were taken to ensure that the church had certain christological parameters and dogmatic markers in place that indicated the bounds of orthodoxy in this matter.

This is not true of every theological topic. For instance, there is no real consensus view on the atonement, though this is hardly a marginal topic in Christian theology. On the face of it, this seems rather odd. However, the early church debates about Christology were generated because the church was trying to get clear *who* and *what* Christ is. Surely he is more than a mere human. But how is he different from other mere humans? Is he a sort of superman, an angelic being, or a divine entity who merely appears to be human? Or is he both divine and human—not a hybrid of these two things but God and man both together in one person? And if he is both God and man, is he fully God and fully man? How can these things be predicated of one individual when it appears that such a view yields contradictions of the sort that imply one person is both omnipotent and impotent, both omniscient and yet limited in knowledge, both omnipresent and yet circumscribed by a human nature, and so on?

The fact is the same attention was not paid to the doctrine of atonement as was paid to the incarnation, which is why the church today continues to wrangle over how we should understand the nature and scope of this aspect of the work of Christ. But two things must be borne in mind here. The first is that the early Christians all believed that Christ was the Savior

---

7. Thomas Oden, *Classic Christianity: A Systematic Theology* (San Francisco: HarperOne, 2009), xvi–xxi. He echoes Vincent of Lérins's claim that the catholic faith is "that which is believed everywhere, always, and by all" in this respect.

of the world and that salvation was obtained through his work. This much was not in dispute. The second thing is that many of the theologians of the early church did not think of the atonement as a separable constituent of the work of Christ that could be abstracted from and analyzed independently of other aspects of his work, or, more importantly, from his person. They believed that the incarnation and atonement were two aspects of one organic whole. Both were parts or phases of the one seamless work of Christ.[8] The idea was not merely that the incarnation is a necessary prerequisite to the atonement (though this is true). It was that the incarnation is part of the work of Christ that culminates in the atonement and resurrection. This makes a considerable difference not only to how we view the person and work of Christ but also to how we think of their relative places in Christian dogmatics. We might put it like this: the mechanism of atonement and its scope (i.e., the extent of Christ's salvific work in its accomplishment and application) were not matters that were so controverted that they required dogmatic definition. The question of who and what Christ is—that is, what it means to say he is the Savior of the world, and how it is that he can be such a Savior—was a matter that was a pressing problem for the church as she sought to establish what the faithful should believe about Jesus of Nazareth.

It is often said that the christological settlement at which the church arrived after much vituperation was as much a political as a theological resolution—some might say a *merely* political resolution. It is undeniable that the christological controversies were hard and often bitterly fought, that some theologians were misunderstood or even misrepresented, and that politics played a significant role in the outcome. However, this fact alone says nothing one way or another about the truth value of the outcome. A decision can be reached for complex religious and political reasons and still be the right result. I suggest that God would not permit the church to come to a substantially mistaken account of the person of Christ and to encode this in a canonical decision in an ecumenical council, for what we think about the person of Christ touches the heart of Christian doctrine and therefore the heart of the gospel. It is an impoverished doctrine of providence that claims otherwise.

---

8. A particularly clear example of this can be found in Athanasius, *On the Incarnation*. Kathryn Tanner has reaffirmed this patristic view in her recent work *Christ the Key*, which also owes much to the Christology of Thomas Torrance.

Before turning to consider the Christology bequeathed to Christian theology by Chalcedon and the dogmatic desiderata its canons provided, one other preliminary matter requires comment. In some recent theology there is a concern to approach the theological task "without metaphysics" or in a "postmetaphysical" manner. In the hands of some theologians, this claim has to do with addressing a particular philosophical project, usually the project associated with the Continental tradition, especially Martin Heidegger and his interlocutors.[9] Other theologians seem to think that one can (even ought to) approach the theological task absent metaphysics per se. But without further explanation this claim is liable to misunderstanding. For it is not that such theologians eschew the project of presenting theological arguments that are ontological in nature. What they reject is the idea that one can make ontological claims on the basis of the most general metaphysical categories and notions. Instead, it is said, the theologian should begin with the specific and concrete and work from this to general ontological claims. Bruce McCormack articulates a specifically christological version of this "postmetaphysical" method. He says,

> The word "metaphysical" has often been taken as synonymous with "ontological." It is not so used here. . . . "Metaphysics" is a way of speaking about transcendent (supramundane) realities, which begins with general concepts rather than concrete particulars. A move is made from a general concept (often a totality that has been abstracted from the individuals of which it is composed) such as "world" or "humanity." The problem is that a totality is only an idea; it is not given to us directly to know. We do not encounter it anywhere. It is simply postulated in order to introduce and explain the unity of a group of items. As such, it lacks reality.[10]

McCormack goes on to relate this specifically to Christology, saying, "It is also possible to construct an ontology . . . on the basis of an individual as a possibility made necessary by the belief that Jesus Christ is God incarnate. In him, that which 'deity' is and that which 'humanity' is are 'universals' made concretely real in an individual."[11] This christological

---

9. See Kevin Hector, *Theology without Metaphysics: God, Language, and the Spirit of Recognition* (Cambridge: Cambridge University Press, 2011).

10. Bruce L. McCormack, "The Person of Christ," in *Mapping Modern Theology: A Thematic and Historical Introduction*, ed. Kelly M. Kapic and Bruce L. McCormack (Grand Rapids: Baker Academic, 2012), 168n54.

11. Ibid.

method is not "metaphysical," he says, "since it does not draw inferences from general concepts." But because it does result in an account of what a divine and human being is, it counts as "ontological." It is a *post*metaphysical method because it was only recognized "after the failings of both classical and modern metaphysics had become clear."[12]

There is certainly something to be said for the claim that Christian theology should be shaped in fundamental respects by the doctrine of the incarnation, or by christological concerns more broadly construed. But that is not the same as a method that proceeds on the assumption that ontological claims must begin with the concrete moving from there to the abstract. What is more, we have just seen that on McCormack's reckoning, abstract metaphysical notions are ideas that lack reality independent of the concrete things from which they are abstracted. Yet they are also universals made concretely real in an individual. Whatever one makes of these claims about universals, concrete particulars, and kind terms like "humanity" or "deity," they are nothing if not metaphysical in nature. We might think of McCormack's comments as the recommendation of a particular sort of metaphysical method. On this reading of his remarks, he begins with the presumption that concrete particulars are the most fundamental ontological things and that any conceptual apparatus that may be devised on the basis of these concrete things is a kind of purely mental construction that does not carve nature at the joints. But this is not novel, and it is not postmetaphysical in the sense of being nonmetaphysical or beyond metaphysics or even ametaphysical in nature. It is representative of the sort of approach to metaphysics advocated by those who are nominalists about predicates and concepts. Rather than exchanging metaphysics for ontology, McCormack appears to be rejecting one way of conceiving metaphysics (a way often associated in traditional theology with realism about universals and abstract objects) for another, apparently nominalist-sounding, approach.

But I can see no reason why a Christian theologian might not adopt McCormack's general proviso that theology ought to be framed by means of christological concerns (e.g., that Christology be the "lens" through which we view a particular theological locus, such as the church or Scripture) without commitment to the sort of nominalism he seems to think

12. Ibid.

necessary for the successful execution of such a project. To put it another way, McCormack's approval of a christologically focused theology is appealing (at least to this reader). But for those who are nonplussed about his claim that classical and modern metaphysics have failed, there are other options available. In fact, systematic metaphysics is back in vogue among Anglo-American philosophers, including neo-Aristotelian metaphysics that countenances much that would be recognizable to our medieval and patristic forebears. Far from "failing" or heading toward extinction, such "classical" metaphysics is alive and well and, if anything, flourishing once more.

A Note on the Chalcedonian "Consensus"

With these methodological considerations in mind, we can turn to the question of desiderata. Since I am approaching this question from the perspective of consensus Christianity, and since there is a classical consensus of sorts encapsulated in the Christology of the ecumenical Council of Chalcedon of AD 451, it is its so-called definition of the person of Christ that is our point of departure. I do not deny that there are other ways of thinking about the person of Christ, some of which have been historically important. It is just that we will be concerned to think about Christology within this dogmatic frame of reference, the frame of reference that has been accepted by the vast majority of Christians in history as a trustworthy summary statement about the person of Christ and that encapsulates important theological notions found in Scripture.

The Chalcedonian definition is not without its problems, however. For one thing, it does not give us anything like a complete account of the person of Christ or of the natures he possesses. As several recent treatments of the matter have reminded us, it is ambiguous with respect to certain claims that can be made about the hypostatic union. Thus, Richard Sturch observes, "It has long been recognized that the main purpose of most of the early Councils was not so much to lay down an orthodox line as to rule out lines which were *not* orthodox. Provided that these were unambiguously repudiated, language could be, and was, used which allowed other ambiguity, or at least a certain latitude of interpretation."[13]

13. Richard Sturch, *The Word and the Christ: An Essay in Analytic Christology* (Oxford: Oxford University Press, 1991), 214. He goes on to say that Chalcedonian Christology is sufficiently

So, for instance, we are told that Christ is one person subsisting in two distinct, unconfused natures (human and divine). But we are not told what a nature is, or what a person is in this instance. Nor are we told how one person can be said to have two natures, nor even how someone who is fully human can be consubstantial with the Godhead.[14] What we have in the Chalcedonian definition is, I suggest, a group of theological statements that constitute a sort of *dogmatic minimalism*, which we see elsewhere in the historic affirmations of the Christian faith. It is minimalistic because the definition says as little as doctrinally possible about the hypostatic union while making clear that certain ways of thinking about the person of Christ are off-limits or unorthodox. We might say that the Chalcedonian definition draws a veil over the hypostatic union, so that what we know about substantive questions regarding the union of Christ's human to his divine nature is severely limited. Nevertheless, it does make clear that certain views about the person of Christ are to be avoided, and this in turn gives us certain (minimal) dogmatic claims with which we can construct theological desiderata for the purposes of contemporary systematic theology.

Suppose this claim about dogmatic minimalism is granted. There is a further question in the neighborhood that has to do with the relationship between dogmatic minimalism and the metaphysics of the incarnation. We could frame it thus: Does assent to Chalcedon commit the theologian not only to a particular theological framework for understanding the incarnation but also to a particular metaphysics?

This is an important question, and much turns on it. I have already laid down that Scripture is the norming norm for all theological judgments, and that creeds, including the Chalcedonian definition, are subordinate norms that depend upon Scripture as the norming norm. But we might think of Scripture as a sort of data source from which are drawn certain doctrinal

open-textured as to permit the believer to conceive of Christ in "scriptural, patristic, medieval or modern terms."

14. Sarah Coakley makes the same point when she says, "The relatively undefined character of the key terms 'nature' (*physis*) and 'person' (*hypostasis*) in the so-called Definition . . . draws attention to the open-endedness of the document, its unclarity about the precise meaning of key terms. If anything is 'defined' in the 'Definition' it is not these crucial concepts. To be sure, these terms had a prehistory, but it was an ambiguous one and the 'Definition' does not clear up the ambiguity" (Coakley, "What Does Chalcedon Solve and What Does It Not? Some Reflections on the Status and Meaning of the Chalcedonian 'Definition,'" in *The Incarnation*, ed. Stephen T. Davis, Daniel Kendall, and Gerald O'Collins [Oxford: Oxford University Press, 2002], 148).

theories, such as the creeds. These in turn form the basis for particular theological models, which provide conceptual structures by means of which the theologian postulates certain ways of understanding the content of the creeds that is metaphysical in nature.[15] The advantage of thinking of matters in this way is that it does not require the contemporary theologian to ensure that her metaphysics are the same as those of the church fathers of the fifth century. But it does take seriously the need to engage with the theological tradition in formulating metaphysical models of the incarnation. Both the Chalcedonian fathers and the modern theologians wishing to stand in the Chalcedonian tradition speak of "one person subsisting in two natures." Both mean by this that Christ is a divine person with a human nature. But their theological accounts of "person" or "nature," respectively, may depend upon somewhat different metaphysical views of "persons" or "natures."

I have belabored the point about the dogmatic minimalism of Chalcedon (as I see it) because I think theologians are sometimes too quick to say what the hypostatic union does or does not entail, or what it is that they find confusing, befuddling, or downright incoherent about the Chalcedonian account (often as a prelude to some departure from it). As Sarah Coakley has pointed out, the definition is not merely a means by which to regulate our language about the incarnation (though it does include this). Nor is its language purely metaphorical, offering us a picture of how we might think about Christ. And it certainly does not give us a set of necessary and sufficient conditions by means of which we can analyze the incarnation.[16] However, if we bear in mind that the dogmatic hardcore of classical Christology is rather thin, and deliberately so, it should help us to see that there may be many different Christologies that are consistent with the canons of Chalcedon. It may not be too strong to say that the Chalcedonian definition is commensurate with a number of distinct models of the hypostatic union. Hence, a certain intellectual humility is called for in our reflections upon this topic.

What, then, are the dogmatic desiderata for models of the hypostatic union consistent with Chalcedon?

---

15. A similar account of the relationship between Scripture (as data), creeds (as theories), and metaphysical models of the incarnation (as a second tier of theory) derived from the work of Peter van Inwagen is discussed by Robin Le Poidevin in "Incarnation: Metaphysical Issues," *Philosophy Compass* 4, no. 4 (2009): 703–14, esp. 706.

16. See Coakley, "What Does Chalcedon Solve and What Does It Not?"

Desiderata Outlined

According to Chalcedon, Christ is one person with two natures, one human and the other divine. He is fully divine. He is fully human. His two natures subsist in a personal (hypostatic) union without being mixed together into some sort of hybrid thing and without either nature losing its essential integrity. Yet there are not two persons subsisting in Christ. Rather, he is fundamentally a divine person who may be said (in some manner) to acquire a human nature in addition to the divine nature he already possessed prior to the first moment of incarnation.

So, minimally, any Chalcedonian Christology will include the following tenets:

1. Christ is one person.
2. Christ has two natures, one divine and one human.
3. The two natures of Christ retain their integrity and are distinct; they are not mixed together or confused, nor are they amalgamated into a hybrid of divine and human attributes (like a demigod).
4. The natures of Christ are really united in the person of Christ—that is, they are two natures possessed by one person.

Taken together, these four claims comprise what is usually called the two-natures doctrine. But matters are complicated by the decisions reached by two further ecumenical councils, Constantinople II in AD 553 and Constantinople III in AD 681. For our purposes, the relevant decisions reached by Constantinople II were (a) the reaffirmation that the person of Christ and the Second Person of the Trinity are one and the same, and (b) the notion that the human nature assumed by God the Son at the incarnation was not "personal"—that is, that it was not a person or the human nature of a person independent of or prior to its assumption by the Son. This latter claim is often summed up in a distinction that has since gained wide currency, although the fathers of the council did not utilize it. The first part of this distinction is that the human nature assumed by the Son is *anhypostatic*—that is, it is not a person independent of the Son. The second part is the claim that the human nature of Christ is *enhypostatic*—that is, is made personal, or is personalized, in the very act of incarnation by means of which the human nature in question becomes (as it were) the human nature of the Son. Let us call the conjunction of these claims the an-enhypostatic distinction.[17]

As is probably apparent from the characterization just given, this an-enhypostatic distinction is puzzling at least in part because it is not clear from what was just said exactly what a nature is, or what it would mean for a nature to be "personalized." We shall return to this matter presently, when considering the concepts of persons and natures in the context of clarifying the desiderata.

Constantinople III is particularly remembered in the christological literature for its canonization of dyothelitism, the claim that Christ has two wills. Under the influence of St. Maximus the Confessor in particular, it was argued that if Christ is truly and fully human as well as truly and fully divine (as Chalcedon had claimed) then he must have a human will as well as a divine will. To deny this is to deny his full humanity, or so the argument went. The concern was to rebut the monothelites, who claimed that one person = one will. If Christ is one divine person who acquires a human nature in the incarnation, then he must have one will. For, they reasoned, how can one person have two wills without being fundamentally dysfunctional or fractured? Once again, much depends on what is meant by a person and a nature in this debate, as well as what is meant by a human will and a divine will.

I have already noted that in modern theology there is disagreement about whether Chalcedonian Christology is coherent, or whether it should be the point of departure for contemporary reconstructions of the doctrine. But there is also disagreement about the additions to Chalcedonian Christology made by the fathers of Constantinople II and III. In explicating what he calls the "impasse" of the two-natures Christology of Chalcedon, Jürgen Moltmann writes this about the an-enhypostatic distinction that encapsulates an important theme of Constantinople II:

---

17. I have dealt with the an-enhypostatic distinction in more detail in *Divinity and Humanity*, ch. 3. For a useful discussion of the distinction and its importance in the development of Chalcedonian Christology in the context of the seven ecumenical councils, see Fred Sanders, "Introduction to Christology: Chalcedonian Categories for the Gospel Narrative," in *Jesus in Trinitarian Perspective: An Introductory Christology*, ed. Fred Sanders and Klaus Issler (Nashville: B&H Academic, 2007), 1–41. For a summary of the anathemas of Constantinople II, see John H. Leith, *Creeds of the Churches: A Reader in Christian Doctrine from the Bible to the Present*, 3rd ed. (Louisville: John Knox, 1982), 45–50.

If the eternal Logos assumed a non-personal human nature, he cannot then be viewed as a historical person, and we cannot talk about "Jesus of Nazareth." The human nature that was assumed would then seem to be like the human garment of the eternal Son—something which he put on when he walked on earth. It becomes difficult to find an identity here between this human nature and our own. Or has the eternal Son of God taken on "human nature without personhood" in the modern sense, so that he has assumed the human being who is really a "non-person"? . . . Or is the "true" human nature itself anhypostatically enhypostasized in the divine person . . . ? But then "real," actual human personhood would in itself already have to be termed the sin of egocentrism.[18]

And in a well-known passage in *The Christian Faith*, Friedrich Schleiermacher writes this of dyothelitism, which was canonized at Constantinople III:

> The utter fruitlessness of this way of presenting the matter becomes particularly clear in the treatment of the question whether Christ as one person formed out of two natures had also two wills according to the number of the natures, or only one according to the number of the person. For if Christ had only one will, then the divine nature is incomplete if this is a human will; and the human nature, if it is a divine will. But if Christ has two wills, then the unity of the person is no more than apparent, even if we try to conserve it by saying that the two wills always will the same thing. For what this results in is only agreement, not unity; and in fact the answer to the problem thus is the return to the division of Christ. And one or the other will is always simply a superfluous accompaniment of the other, whether it be the divine will that accompanies the human or *vice versa*.[19]

Much in these debates turns upon two matters. On the one hand, there is the formal question of whether Chalcedonian Christology is still serviceable and, if it is, whether it is incumbent upon modern theologians to take into consideration the judgments of Constantinople II and III in addition to the canons of Chalcedon as dogmatic pronouncements that

---

18. Jürgen Moltmann, *The Way of Jesus Christ: Christology in Messianic Dimension*, trans. Margaret Kohl (London: SCM, 1990), 51.

19. Friedrich Schleiermacher, *Christian Faith*, §96, 394. This same worry is echoed in more recent theology. See, e.g., Gordon D. Kaufman, *Systematic Theology: A Historicist Perspective* (New York: Scribner's Sons, 1968), 188, who harks back to Schleiermacher's discussion, and John Macquarrie, *Jesus Christ in Modern Thought* (London: SCM, 1990), who speaks of dyothelitism as "a pathological condition" that should not be affirmed of Christ (167).

offer the appropriate way to construe what Chalcedon leaves ambiguous (regarding the an-enhypostatic distinction and dyothelitism, respectively). On the other hand, there is the more material consideration of whether the terms of reference that Chalcedon bequeathed to the Christian tradition are helpful, and if they are, how we should construe them. Let us consider these two matters in reverse order, beginning with the key theological terminology of Chalcedon.

One Person, Two Natures

How are we to understand the claim that Christ is one person with two natures? To begin with, let us invoke an axiom implied by the four tenets of Chalcedonian Christology, outlined above. Call it the *Chalcedonian Axiom* (CA). It is this:

> (CA) Christ has one of whatever goes with the person and two of whatever goes with natures.[20]

This much is implied by the dogmatic minimalism of Chalcedon. But a moment's reflection on what this means quickly takes us beyond the letter of Chalcedon, as it took the fathers of the church in the post-Chalcedonian christological controversies that culminated in the canonical decisions of Constantinople II and III. Hence, there is one person in Christ. So there is one subject of predication, one fundamental entity to which we refer when we speak of Christ. But this person has two complete, unconfused natures. So (presumably) there must be two wills, one belonging to his human nature, one to his divine nature; two centers or ranges of consciousness, one belonging to his human nature, one to his divine nature; two sets of predicates that apply to the respective natures; and so on. But given that at least some of these alleged implications of Chalcedon are disputed, we need to say something about persons and natures before going any further.

Much ink has been spilled in trying to make sense of these two terms. It may not be too much to say that the christological controversy from the

---

20. I owe this to Garrett J. DeWeese's essay "One Person, Two Natures: Two Metaphysical Models of the Incarnation," in *Jesus in Trinitarian Perspective: An Introductory Christology*, ed. Fred Sanders and Klaus Issler (Nashville: B&H Academic, 2007), 115.

fifth and sixth centuries onwards depends on what we take these terms to mean. Let us begin with the term "person."

It is often said in discussions of the hypostatic union, or of the Trinity, that the term "person" as understood in the patristic christological debates should not be conflated with modern psychologically influenced notions of persons. Brian Daley makes the point well. He is adamant that "when Greek theologians in the early church speak of the 'hypostasis' of Christ, or of the three 'hypostases' of the Trinity, it is clear that they are not referring to what we moderns might call a 'person': an independent subject, constituted by a unique and unrepeatable focus of self-consciousness, practical autonomy, and some measure of psychological freedom."[21] Instead, he observes that the church fathers "developed their notion of hypostasis [i.e., person] to meet the needs of clarifying the apostolic faith, with the aid of contemporary philosophy but not necessarily determined by its conclusions."[22] Note, in this connection, his affirmation of the ancillary role philosophical notions played in the theological task. The dogma was fundamental; the philosophy a means to clarifying what was believed.

What was the concept of "person," or hypostasis, in play, then? He maintains that a hypostasis "was essentially a particular individual within a universal species, identifiable as such or such a thing by the qualities it (or he or she) shared with similar individuals, yet marked off as unique by a set of characteristics all its own. It was the kind of thing so unique and unrepeatable you could call it by name—not just 'horse,' but 'Silver'; not just 'man,' but Peter or Paul or John, or even Jesus."[23] But beyond this, the fathers did not stray. Their account stopped once the job of clarifying the apostolic faith had been achieved. In this sense, their position was dogmatically minimalist. Suppose Daley is right about this. Then a person is a particular sort of entity, one that may belong to a species but is unique, distinguished from others of its kind by the characteristics that make it the concrete particular to which we give the name "Peter" or "Paul" or "John."

21. Brian Daley, "Nature and the 'Mode of Union': Late Patristic Models for the Personal Unity of Christ," in *The Incarnation*, ed. Stephen T. Davis, Daniel Kendall, and Gerald O'Collins (Oxford: Oxford University Press, 2002), 193–94. Daley analyzes the Christologies of Leontius of Byzantium, Maximus the Confessor, and John of Damascus—three key figures in the consolidation of the Chalcedonian doctrine.
22. Ibid.
23. Ibid.

As is well known, Boethius's definition of a person as an individual substance of a rational nature was widely discussed in the West, and it is the definition Aquinas appeals to in *Summa Theologiae* Ia, q. 29.[24] It was important for much medieval work on the metaphysics of the hypostatic union and seems, on the face of it, to be consistent with Daley's conclusions about representative Greek Christologies. Borrowing from Aristotelian metaphysics, the medieval school theologians thought of fundamental substances or supposits as the subjects of predication. Such entities have natures, such as human nature. These are called secondary substances, or (perhaps more helpfully) substance-kinds. A particular fundamental substance has a particular substance-kind that it instantiates. So, we might say that the particular person Fred instantiates the particular substance kind *human*. Fred is made human, so to speak, by instantiating the substance-kind *humanity*. It should be clear from this that the substance-kind a particular person instantiates is essential to that person; the person cannot obtain without it. Thus, it is essential to Fred that he be human, not horse. The connection between the fundamental substance and the substance-kind it instantiates is necessary *de re*. Such fundamental substances also have accidents or properties that are predicated of them, such as shape, color, size, mass, and so on. So, we might say, Fred is a human. That is essential to his being Fred. But he can change his shape as he grows, have a different size, augment or reduce his mass, and so on. Accidents are not essential to Fred in the same way as is his substance-kind. For Fred can change his size and shape (to some extent), but he cannot cease to be a member of the kind human. Thus, on this way of thinking, we have the following understanding of persons in relation to their natures: persons are fundamental substances of a rational nature. They are concrete things. Natures are substance-kinds that are predicable of certain sorts of things, like humanity is predicable of Fred. Accidents are predicates or attributes of a particular entity that are nonessential, that refer to the fundamental substance as the bearer of properties.[25]

---

24. Boethius defines a person in his *Liber de persona et duabus naturis*, caput III. He writes, "Persona est naturae rationalis individuis substantia. Sed nos hac definitione eam quam Graeci ὑπόστασιν dicunt terminavimus" ("A Person is an individual substance of a rational nature. But our definition of this is what the Greeks termed a hypostasis").

25. For two very clear presentations of the Aristotelian metaphysics underlying much medieval school discussion of the incarnation, see C. J. F. Williams, "A Programme for Christology," *Religious Studies* 3, no. 2 (1968): 513–24, and Marilyn McCord Adams, *Christ and Horrors*

However, without some finessing, this way of construing the metaphysics of the incarnation poses a problem for the Boethian definition. It proves too much. For if a person is an independent substance of a rational nature, then the human Christ looks like a candidate for being a person. But we do not want to affirm that, on pain of Nestorianism. One way of avoiding this consequence is to add to the Boethian definition the proviso that in addition to being an independent substance of a rational nature a person cannot be composed with another substance.[26] On the Aristotle-inspired metaphysics just outlined, this would mean that the human nature of Christ fails to be a person, though an individual with a complete human nature would normally form a fundamental substance that does not compose part of another fundamental substance, thereby forming a person.

In contemporary discussion of the topic, some philosophical theologians have opted for something like this Aristotle-inspired medieval account. Others have developed different ways of construing the metaphysics of the incarnation while affirming the same Chalcedonian two-natures doctrine.[27] The debate seems to turn on whether one thinks that the human nature of Christ is fundamentally a concrete particular—that is, a substance or substance-like thing—or whether one thinks of it as fundamentally an abstract object, such as a property or trope. But several things are nonnegotiable, dogmatically speaking, whichever way one construes the metaphysics. The first of these is that whatever we say of the person of Christ, we must be able to affirm that he is the Second Person of the Trinity. In other words, our doctrine of the incarnation must fit with our doctrine of the Trinity. It would be a grave theological mistake to affirm that Christ is a person of one sort whereas the divine persons of the Trinity were persons of a different sort. Second, the person of Christ is the subject or fundamental

---

(Cambridge: Cambridge University Press, 2006), ch. 5. Also of use in this regard is Swinburne, *Christian God*, ch. 9. The previous paragraph is indebted to these accounts.

26. A point made by Richard Cross in *The Metaphysics of the Incarnation: Thomas Aquinas to Duns Scotus* (Oxford: Oxford University Press, 2002), 240. But this goes back at least to Peter Lombard. In *The Sentences*, bk. III, dist. V, ch. 3 (16), he tackles the objection that a person was united to a person in the incarnation, citing Boethius's definition as the source of this problem (for if a person is a "rational substance of an individual nature," then it looks like Christ's human nature is a person independent of its union with the divine Word). He replies, "But this does not follow, because the soul is not a person when it is united personally to another thing, but when it exists by itself" (Lombard, *The Sentences Book 3: On the Incarnation of the Word*, trans. Giulio Silano [Toronto: Pontifical Institute of Medieval Studies, 2008], 23).

27. I discuss this in detail in *Divinity and Humanity*, ch. 2.

substance to whom a human nature is joined. Third, the natures exist "in" Christ; they are possessed or instantiated by him. His divine nature is essential to him because he is a divine person. But his human nature is contingently related to him, as the nature he voluntarily assumes.

Beyond these minimal dogmatic affirmations, Chalcedonian Christologists are divided, depending on what is meant by "nature" in relation to the person of Christ. It is not my task here to adjudicate which way of construing the metaphysics of persons and natures best represents Chalcedonian Christology. I am only interested in outlining the desiderata for such Christology, consistent with the dogmatic minimalism of the Chalcedonian definition.

Personalizing the Natures, Distinguishing the Wills

We come to the question of rightly interpreting the Chalcedonian legacy in the canons of Constantinople II and III.

Recall that Constantinople II defends the Chalcedonian settlement, including the claim that Christ is a divine person with a human nature (and therefore a member of the Trinity) and the claim that his human nature is "personalized" in the life of the Second Person of the Trinity, so to speak. It has no existence independent of the Second Person. This latter claim is encapsulated in the an-enhypostatic distinction. Now, depending on what one makes of the terms "person" and "nature," one will have a slightly different account of the an-enhypostatic distinction and the personhood of Christ. This brings us to Moltmann's objection, cited earlier. In truth, there are several aspects to Moltmann's objection. First, he worries that the an-enhypostatic distinction implies that Christ's humanity is somehow unreal, that it would be "like the human garment of the eternal Son," something he puts on and can take off again. Second, he thinks this tells against Christ being a truly historical person. For what sort of concrete, real person has a nonpersonal human nature? Finally, he worries that this an-enhypostatic distinction means that "the eternal Son of God" has "taken on 'human nature without personhood'" and that this has implications for how we should think of human personhood, since Christ does not need to be a human person to be fully human.

Let us examine this more carefully. Does the an-enhypostatic distinction imply Christ's humanity is unreal, that it is merely a garment worn by the Son, or even that it is not really connected to him? Nothing could be further from the truth. The anathemas of Constantinople II make it clear that God the Son unites himself to a complete human nature. However, it is true that (in one respect) this is only contingently related to God the Son. For the Chalcedonian doctrine reiterated by Constantinople II is that in the incarnation we are dealing with a divine person. So he is a person who has the divine nature essentially. He does not have the same relation to his human nature precisely because he voluntarily assumes that human nature as part of his work as the mediator of salvation. He takes it up and (in theory at least) he could lay it down, though in point of fact he will not do so. For, to press the logic of this view, he is eternally God Incarnate. He eternally deigns to take on this role and therefore to unite himself to human nature, something that he will not revoke. This brings us to Moltmann's worry about Christ's humanity being nonhistorical if it is nonpersonal. Once again, this misses the point of the Chalcedonian Christology elaborated upon by Constantinople II. The whole point of the two-natures doctrine is to preserve the claim that there is only one hypostasis, or one person "in" Christ, as it were. This is God the Son, the divine person who takes on a human nature. The human nature he assumes cannot be a person independent of the Son, on pain of Nestorianism. But this does not mean his humanity is "nonpersonal"—at least not in any theologically damaging way. Nor does it mean there is something lacking in Christ's humanity that is present in our humanity. That is to conflate being human—that is, belonging to the kind humanity—with the particular human to which we are referring, namely, Christ the God-man. If humanity is a substance-kind as many school theologians taught, then Moltmann's concern is wide of the mark. If human nature is a property of God the Son from the incarnation onwards, then it is odd to think that this means there is something lacking in Christ, for he possesses the property in common with all other humans. For, on this way of understanding the matter, humanity just is a kind-essence or property had by God the Son and by every other human being. The difference between Christ and the rest of humanity lies not in the property of human nature he acquires but in the relation he has to his human nature. So, whether we understand the humanity of Christ as fundamentally an abstract-nature (that is, a property or property-like thing) or as a concrete-nature (that is, as a substance, or a substance-like thing), Moltmann's concerns are avoided.

Let us turn to Schleiermacher's rejection of dyothelitism, the doctrine canonized at Constantinople III. His objection is subtler than Moltmann's and therefore rather more difficult to rebut. Recall our Chalcedonian Axiom stated earlier, that *Christ has one of whatever goes with the person and two of whatever goes with natures*. Schleiermacher embraces this consequence of Constantinople III and reasons that this means one of two things. Either there are not enough wills in Christ for him to be fully human and fully divine (because either he is a divine person with a human nature, and so lacks a human will, or is a human person with a divine nature, and so lacks a divine will), or he has two wills, one human and one divine. But then, he says, "the unity of the person is no more than apparent," for what results is "agreement, not unity,"[28] which is to divide Christ rather than unite him. If, in other words, the wills go with the person, there can only be one, and we end up with monothelitism. One person, one will—that is the logic of the claim being made here. Alternatively, if the wills go with the natures, there must be two of them, but then we end up dividing Christ. No dyothelite wants that. Notice the care with which he puts this latter objection. He does not say that if the two wills go with the two natures then Nestorianism results. That does not necessarily follow because dyothelitism does not imply two persons. One would have to show that possession of two wills in two distinct natures requires there to be two persons "in" Christ. But no dyothelite will concede that. Instead, Schleiermacher says that the problem is that this way of carving up the wills would divide Christ. In other words, it tells against the unity of the person. For if one person has two distinct wills that belong to two distinct natures, "then the unity of the person is not more than apparent."[29] Christ might be like someone with multiple personality disorder. Or, as some Christologists have speculated, he might be like the subject of a neurological commissurotomy, where the corpus callosum connecting the two hemispheres of the brain is severed in order to reduce the electrical activity between them that is so damaging to patients suffering from grand mal epilepsy. Such patients suffer significant disruption in their mental lives, rather as Schleiermacher seems to imagine obtains with the dyothelite Christ.

It seems to me that Constantinople III makes it plain that the wills of Christ go with the natures. He has two wills, or two theaters of operation,

28. Schleiermacher, *Christian Faith*, §96, p. 394.
29. Ibid.

in which he acts as a human being and as a divine person, respectively. If Christ's human nature is a property or property-like thing (i.e., an abstract nature), then in acquiring human nature the Son acquires the properties necessary and sufficient to will as a human. His human way of willing is just the Son willing certain things as a human, and he is able to do this because he is a human in virtue of acquiring the property *humanity*. By contrast, if Christ's human nature is concrete—that is, a substance or substance-like thing—matters are a little more complicated. Normally, human substances are fundamental substances—that is, persons—capable of willing as humans. Christ is not fundamentally a human substance, though he has a human substance, on this view. But if it is possible for God the Son to assume a human substance such that it does not form an entity independent of the Son, and therefore does not become a fundamental substance independent of the Son, then maybe he can will as a human by means of that substance. This concrete-nature view, or something very like it, is how at least some of the school theologians understood the metaphysics of the incarnation, in line with Chalcedon and Constantinople III. It may be somewhat awkward and unwieldy, but it is not clear (to me, at least) that it dissolves the personal union of the Son with his humanity. Indeed, if the Son is a divine person and therefore a metaphysically simple entity, there may be good reason for opting for some version of a concrete-nature view since then Christ is a composite in which God the Son is a metaphysically simple component.[30]

Recently, several evangelical philosophical theologians have argued in favor of monothelite accounts of the hypostatic union. Garrett DeWeese maintains that evangelicals need not balk at this because monothelite Christology follows the Cyrillian tenor of Chalcedonian Christology in virtue of its emphasis on the unity of the person of Christ. He also argues that evangelicals are not bound by conciliar decisions if they turn out to be problematic.[31] He gives two examples of such potentially mistaken creedal statements: the decision of the seventh (and last) ecumenical council, Nicaea II, to endorse iconography in churches, and the Nicene-Constantinopolitan creedal statement that "we believe in one baptism for the remission of sins." Neither of these claims forms a part of what evangelicals take to be biblical religion, so evangelicals should not feel

---

30. This, in a nutshell, is the model of the hypostatic union to be developed in the next chapter.
31. DeWeese, "One Person, Two Natures," 148.

bound by them. In a similar way, perhaps the decision of Constantinople III to endorse dyothelitism is a step away from biblical religion.

The principle that Protestants should not be bound by the ecumenical creeds if they can be shown to conflict with Scripture is a venerable one. It is enshrined in confessions like the Thirty-Nine Articles.[32] But the Thirty-Nine Articles also say, "The Three Creeds, Nicene Creed, Athanasius's Creed, and that which is commonly called the Apostles' Creed, ought thoroughly to be received and believed: for they may be proved by most certain warrants of Holy Scripture." Even if ecumenical councils may err and have erred, few Protestants would want to withhold confession of the Nicene Creed. Nicaea II is a different matter. Where confessional Protestants are concerned to uphold the Nicene-Constantinopolitan symbol, few are worried about the iconoclastic controversy. Indeed, many will be unsympathetic to iconography. But I think that is regrettable. To my mind, Protestants should take the decisions of *all* seven ecumenical councils very seriously indeed, Nicaea II included. It is not at all clear to me that the decision of Nicaea II regarding the right use of icons is contrary to Scripture.[33] What is more (and returning to the matter in hand), dyothelitism was understood by the fathers of Constantinople III and by the vast majority of Christians ever since as the right way to understand the two-natures doctrine of Chalcedon. They reasoned that if Christ has a complete human nature, he must have a human will. Whether one thinks of the natures as abstract or concrete, as a property or property-like thing, or as a substance or substance-like thing, sense can be made of this claim. But (obviously) how one construes it will be different, depending on the metaphysics one adopts. Dyothelitism is part of the catholic faith. It is a deliverance of an ecumenical council. It is not contrary to Scripture, and it has been held by the vast majority of Christians down through the ages who affirm Constantinople III as the legitimate extrapolation of Chalcedonian

---

32. Article XXI states, "General Councils may not be gathered together without the commandment and will of Princes. And when they be gathered together, (forasmuch as they be an assembly of men, whereof all be not governed with the Spirit and Word of God) they may err, and sometimes have erred, even in things pertaining unto God. Wherefore things ordained by them as necessary to salvation have neither strength nor authority, unless it may be declared that they be taken out of holy Scripture." Cf. the Westminster Confession, 31.4, which says, "All synods or councils since the apostles' times, whether general or particular, may err, and many have erred; therefore they are not to be made the rule of faith or practice, but to be used as a help in both."

33. See, for example, St. John of Damascus's *Three Treatises on the Divine Images*, trans. Andrew Louth (Crestwood, NY: St. Vladimir's Seminary Press, 2003).

Christology, over against monophysitism and monothelitism. I think this is good reason to retain the doctrine as one of the desiderata for contemporary models of the hypostatic union.

Summary

Let us take stock. Chalcedon provides us with the following dogmatically minimal claims requisite to orthodox Christology:

1. Christ is one person.
2. Christ has two natures, one divine and one human.
3. The two natures of Christ retain their integrity and are distinct; they are not mixed together or confused, nor are they amalgamated into a hybrid of divine and human attributes (like a demigod).
4. The natures of Christ are really united in the person of Christ—that is, they are two natures possessed by one person.

This yields the following Chalcedonian Axiom:

(CA) Christ has one of whatever goes with the person and two of whatever goes with natures.

Following Boethius, I have reasoned that a person is a fundamental substance of a rational nature. If one adopts the view of at least some of the medieval school theologians, the natures of Christ are to be understood as fundamentally concrete substance-like things, not as fundamentally rich properties, though natures may include properties or predicates. This is the view I favor. However, I do not think that this particular account of the metaphysics of the divine person of Christ or his two natures is the only permissible way of understanding these matters. Other ways of construing both the "person" and the "natures" in the two-natures doctrine are consistent with orthodoxy and have found advocates in the church. The main alternative family of views depends on the claim that Christ's human nature is fundamentally an abstract thing, like a property or trope. This difference over the metaphysics of the incarnation is permissible given the dogmatic minimalism of Chalcedon, which does not prescribe the ontology that underpins its theological affirmations.

I have also argued that there is a significant dissimilarity between the two natures in Christ, and failure to attend to these differences can lead to theological mistakes. The nature of God the Son is divine, and the divine nature is something that we have much less grip on than human natures, since the divine essence or nature is in a number of important respects mysterious. Nevertheless, I have affirmed that there is good theological reason for holding to the christological additions or appendices to Chalcedonian Christology provided by Constantinople II and III. We should affirm that Christ's human nature is an-enhypostatic; and we should affirm that Christ has two wills, though this is not without difficulties. I submit that these are the desiderata for Christology, as understood by consensus Christianity. Far from eliminating the need for further theological discussion and debate, it seems to me that a right understanding of the dogmatic parameters for Christology provides a basis upon which fruitful work can be done on this central and defining doctrine of the Christian faith. Such fruitful work is the focus of the next chapter, when we consider one contemporary model of the hypostatic union, namely, the compositional account.

6

Compositional Christology

> On the other hand, God's passion for material creation expresses itself in a Divine desire to unite with it, not only to enter into personal intimacy, but to "go all the way" and share its nature in hypostatic union.
>
> —Marilyn McCord Adams[1]

Having set out the desiderata for models of the hypostatic union in the previous chapter, we are now in a position to consider one such model, which we shall call the compositional account. This is the focus of the present chapter.

According to compositional Christologists, in the incarnation the Second Person of the Trinity assumes a human nature, understood to be a concrete particular. The concrete human nature and divine nature of God the Son together compose Christ. That is, God Incarnate is a whole composed of the proper parts of God the Son and (the parts of) his human nature. According to many compositional Christologists, this human nature comprises a human body and a human soul.[2] In which case Jesus

---

1. Adams, *Christ and Horrors*, 39.
2. References to "human nature" in what follows are to concrete particulars of a sort—that is, to human body-soul composites, or what I have elsewhere labeled "the concrete nature view" (see *Divinity and Humanity*, ch. 2).

Christ consists of God the Son, a human soul and a human body, which together compose Christ. Put another way, Christ is a composite of various parts. Elsewhere I have called this sort of view a three-part concrete nature account of the incarnation.[3]

However, this is not the only live metaphysical option for those committed to a compositional account of the incarnation. One could hold to a two-part Christology while maintaining that Christ's human nature is a concrete particular. One obvious way to make sense of this is to say that Christ is composed of God the Son and a human body capable of sustaining human mental life, where Christ's human body just is his human nature. Such an option might be attractive to those who maintain that human beings are essentially material beings but think that human natures are fundamentally concrete particulars of a certain sort. This need not entail Apollinarianism, provided some account can be given of Christ's human mental life consistent with the creedal claim that Christ possessed a human body and a "reasonable" soul.[4] There may well be other ways of carving up the number of parts in the incarnation alongside a commitment to Christ's human nature being a concrete particular, consistent with theological orthodoxy.[5] But in what follows, I shall concern myself only with three-part concrete nature versions of compositional Christology. Following in the steps of important patristic and medieval theologians, including Thomas Aquinas and Duns Scotus, a number of recent philosophical theologians have articulated this view.[6] But we will

3. See ibid.
4. I have argued for this elsewhere in "Materialist Christology," in *God Incarnate*. Apollinarianism is the heresy according to which Christ has a human body but fails to have a human "reasonable soul." One could construe "reasonable soul" as equivalent to "human mind." This appears to be consistent with at least some materialist accounts of human beings.
5. For instance, perhaps a mind-body dualist of the Cartesian persuasion could claim that Christ's human nature was an immaterial entity—his human soul—that acquired a certain bundle of properties that, when collocated, constitute a human body. The Cartesian might claim human natures just are human souls and that human souls may or may not have an accidental relationship to a property-bundle that constitutes a human body. In which case what is nonnegotiable in the incarnation is the assumption by God the Son of a human soul (i.e., a human nature). Possession of a human body (i.e., beginning to exemplify a certain property-bundle that constitutes a particular human body) is not a necessary condition for being human. However, this does have the rather odd consequence that God the Son could have been fully human without being incarnate.
6. For discussion of the medieval school theologians, see Marilyn McCord Adams, *What Sort of Human Nature? Medieval Philosophy and the Systematics of Christology*, The Aquinas Lecture of 1999 (Milwaukee: Marquette University Press, 1999); Adams, *Christ and Horrors*,

have to narrow the focus of our argument still further in order to make the analysis that follows manageable. Hence, this chapter is concerned with one particular understanding of three-part compositional Christology. I shall call this *the three-part compositional model of the hypostatic union*, or just *three-part compositional model* for short.

I shall outline this version of compositional Christology and then set out five problems with it that have been raised in the recent literature, including the objection that the three-part model implies Nestorianism, the heresy that Christ is composed of two persons. I shall then defend this three-part model against these objections. I argue that the model is able to withstand these five objections, although in the case of one of the objections some residual difficulties remain. I do not claim that the three-part composition model is the sober metaphysical truth about the hypostatic union. But, if the argument given here is sound, the model offers an account of the metaphysics of the hypostatic union that is more robust than some recent authors suggest.

A Three-Part Compositional Model of the Hypostatic Union

According to the three-part compositional model of the hypostatic union, God the Son is not identical to Christ, though God the Son and Christ's human nature together compose Christ. Christ's human nature bears an accidental or contingent relation to God the Son. We might say that the human nature of Christ is the instrument of God the Son, in which he is "embedded" post-incarnation. An analogy often used to illustrate the three-part composition model is that of a garment. The Second Person of the Trinity puts on human nature like a garment. He is said to be "clothed" by his human nature, but he is not identical to it. The analogy is, of course, limited but may serve to illustrate something of the model we are concerned with.[7] In the recent literature it has been updated by Brian

---

ch. 6; and Cross, *Metaphysics of the Incarnation*. Recent defenders of compositional Christology include Thomas Flint, Alfred J. Freddoso, Brian Leftow, Eleonore Stump, and Peter van Inwagen.

7. Cf. Aquinas: "Now the assumed nature is, as it were, a garment, *although this similitude does not fit at all points*, as has been said above (2, 6, ad 1)" (*Summa Theologiae* III.3.7, emphasis added). See also Marilyn McCord Adams, *What Sort of Human Nature?*; Cross, *Metaphysics of the Incarnation*, ch. 1; Heiko Oberman, *The Harvest of Medieval Theology: Gabriel Biel and Late Medieval Nominalism* (Cambridge, MA: Harvard University Press, 1963), ch. 8; and J. L. A. West, "Aquinas on Peter Lombard and the Metaphysical Status of Christ's

Leftow, who speaks of Christ's human nature as being like a diver's dry suit. The suit is intimately connected to the body of the diver, enabling its wearer to maneuver and act in an alien environment without getting wet.[8]

This cameo of the model can be adapted by those who think God is in time, such as temporalists, as well as by atemporalists or eternalists, who think that God is without time. For the temporalist, it is true to say that at some particular time God the Son assumes human nature. For the temporalist who adopts the three-part composition model, this means at the moment of incarnation God the Son is embedded in a particular human nature ("his" human nature), to which he is intimately related at all times thereafter, unless he chooses to decouple himself from that human nature.[9] The human nature thus assumed is rather like an environment suit for God the Son that enables him to act in the world among human beings. But advocates of the atemporal account of the divine nature can also appropriate the three-part compositional model. Then God the Son eternally has the relevant accidental relation to his human nature, into which he is "embedded." His human nature, like the diver's dry suit, insulates him from the alien environment his human nature occupies while allowing him to live and act in that environment. (The suit gets wet, of course, but the diver does not. Similarly, the human nature of Christ is in time, but his divine nature is not.)

Leftow is one contemporary author who has recently articulated what is effectively an atemporalist version of the three-part compositional model. Although he does not explicitly align his view with the model, his work draws on medieval accounts of the metaphysics of the incarnation, embracing the central tenets of the three-part model as I have set them out. Thus Leftow:

> Perhaps the most formal, abstract thing one can say about the incarnation is this (following such as Aquinas): for the Son to become incarnate

---

Human Nature," *Gregorianum* 88 (2007): 557–86. One potential problem for the three-part composition model is that if the human nature of Christ is really garment-like, it looks like it is no thing (*non aliquid*), and this entails christological nihilism, the view according to which Christ's human nature is not a concrete entity as such. But as we shall see, this need not follow if the three-part composition model is expounded carefully enough.

8. Leftow, "Timeless God Incarnate," 292–93.

9. Orthodox Christology presumes God the Son never decouples himself from his human nature. At the very least he is incarnate from the first moment of incarnation onward, forevermore. Or, if God is atemporal, God the Son is eternally God Incarnate. In what follows, I shall simply assume this deliverance of orthodoxy without further comment.

is at least for there to come to be a whole consisting of certain parts. Let "the Son" name the Trinity's second person and "Jesus Christ" name the whole consisting of the Son + B [the particular human body assumed by the Son] + S [the particular human soul/mind assumed by the Son]. Then, for the incarnation to take place is for Jesus Christ to come to be, by the joining of the Son, S and B.[10]

A little later he adds, "The Son is not identical with Jesus Christ. The Son is instead just part of Jesus Christ, the part which determines who Christ is."[11] So it seems the three-part composition model has at least one defender in the recent spate of literature on compositional Christology.

Perhaps this is not so surprising. After all, there is much to commend three-part compositional versions of the hypostatic union. For one thing, if God the Son is not identical to Christ and bears only an accidental relation to his human nature, then it would appear that he is insulated from certain potentially metaphysically undesirable consequences of becoming incarnate. For example, he need not undergo substantive change that might be theologically damaging, such as being composed in part by, or becoming identical to, some parcel of matter.[12] What is more, for those who maintain God is eternal and essentially metaphysically simple, having no distinct parts whatsoever (i.e., those who endorse the doctrine of divine simplicity), the three-part compositional model offers a way of making sense of the incarnation without identifying Christ's human nature with one of the Persons of the Trinity. For an entity that is only accidentally related to a particular human nature may be shielded from any essential, intrinsic changes, such as "growing" or "expanding" to include a human nature as a proper part. At the very least, an entity that has this sort of relation to a human nature is not wholly or partially composed of the parts of that human nature. In which case the three-part composition model has the considerable advantage of preserving the metaphysical integrity of the divine and human natures of Christ in the hypostatic union.

10. Leftow, "Timeless God Incarnate," 287.
11. Ibid., 290.
12. This is theologically damaging if, like traditional Christian theists, one thinks that God is an essentially immaterial—indeed, incorporeal—agent and that God has all his attributes essentially. On this way of thinking, an essentially immaterial entity cannot be said to begin to have material parts, as we saw when considering the relationship between incorporeality and incarnation in ch. 3.

Problems with the Three-Part Composition Model

But there are potentially significant drawbacks to the three-part composition model too. Here are five of the most serious: one theological problem in two parts (or perhaps two closely related theological problems that share certain commonalities), and four metaphysical concerns.

We begin with the theological objection. The very fact that, on the three-part composition model, God the Son is not identical to his human nature raises the question of whether this is an unorthodox account of the incarnation. There are two related concerns here. The first comes from those who maintain that the catholic creeds imply that God the Son is identical to Christ. For instance, the Chalcedonian "definition" of the Person of Christ says, "So, following the saintly fathers, we all with one voice teach the confession of *one and the same* Son, our Lord Jesus Christ . . . *one and the same* Christ, Son, Lord, only-begotten . . . *one and the same only-begotten* Son, *God, Word*, Lord Jesus Christ."[13] If the phrase "one and the same" is construed as an identity statement, such that God the Son = Christ, then it looks like the three-part composition model of the hypostatic union is in theological hot water, for it entails that God the Son is not identical to Christ. This we shall dub *the orthodoxy problem*.

The second theological concern is that the three-part composition model implies Nestorianism. If God the Son is not identical to Christ, and Christ's human nature is composed of a human body-soul composite, or a body and soul rightly related, what prevents this view from being Nestorian?[14] Human persons are composed of body-soul composites, or of a body and soul rightly related. One might be forgiven for thinking that when a human body and soul are present and rightly related, a human person is present. By insisting on a metaphysical cleavage between God the Son and the human nature of Christ (i.e., denying God the Son is identical to Christ or identical to his human nature), the three-part composition

---

13. Norman P. Tanner, ed., *Decrees of the Ecumenical Councils*, vol. 1, *Nicaea I–Lateran V* (London: Sheed & Ward; Washington, DC: Georgetown University Press, 1990), 86 (emphasis added).

14. Recently, Richard Cross has made a similar claim with respect to Leftow's repristination of the three-part composition model. Behind "Leftow's impressive strategy" lies "the danger of a Nestorian denial that the Son of God (as opposed to the whole of which it is a part) is human, or has human attributes, at all." From Cross, "The Incarnation," in *The Oxford Handbook to Philosophical Theology*, ed. Thomas P. Flint and Michael C. Rea (Oxford: Oxford University Press, 2009), 462.

model implies there are two entities present in the incarnation—one divine, the other human. Yet this appears to be straightforwardly Nestorian.[15] Christ's human nature seems to have all the concrete parts necessary for a human person—a human body and human soul, rightly related. But then what is it exactly that prevents the human nature of Christ from being a human person distinct from the Second Person of the Trinity? Call this *the Nestorianism problem*.

But there are also metaphysical difficulties for the advocate of the three-part composition model in addition to the theological ones, the first of which is closely related to the foregoing objections. It looks like the three-part composition model means God the Son is not human, because God the Son is not identical to a human nature. Traditional, orthodox Christology implies that at the incarnation, God the Son *becomes* human in addition to being divine. If the three-part composition model denies this or entails the denial of this, then it is an unorthodox model of the incarnation. Let us designate this *the identity problem*.

A further metaphysical difficulty concerns what we shall refer to as *the insulation problem*.[16] It looks like the three-part composition model insulates God the Son from having the properties of his human nature and performing the actions performed by his human nature. In some cases this may not be a big drawback from the point of view of a defender of the three-part composition model who is also a traditional Christian theist. God cannot suffer, so God the Son cannot suffer. Yet clearly, Christ suffers. So (the traditional Christian theist says) this must be parsed to mean, "Christ suffers in his human nature." But even if we are willing to swallow this—via the deployment of reduplicative language, say[17]—do we want to concede that God the Son does *no action* that Christ is reported

---

15. For present purposes, Nestorianism is the heresy according to which God Incarnate is composed of two distinct persons—one human, the other divine.

16. I owe this objection to Thomas P. Flint's unpublished paper, "A Puzzle concerning the Mereological Model of the Incarnation."

17. Reduplicative language as used in traditional Christology is of the form S *qua* N is P. The idea is that by relegating particular attributes Christ has to one or other of his natures, one is able to avoid the inference from "S is N *qua* P" to "S is N." There are several ways in which this sort of language has been used in Christology. Cross has a brief recapitulation of the issues in "The Incarnation." For two recent treatments of reduplication in Christology, see Timothy Pawl, "A Solution to the Fundamental Philosophical Problem for Christology," *Journal of Analytic Theology* 2 (2014): 61–85, and Michael Gorman, "Christological Consistency and the Reduplicative Qua," *Journal of Analytic Theology* 2 (2014): 86–100.

as doing in the canonical Gospels? Do we want to concede that he has *none* of the properties that Christ has? That seems like rather too much for an orthodox Christologist to swallow.

Another concern with the three-part composition model that follows upon the heels of the insulation problem is what I shall call *the no-person objection*.[18] We can frame it thus: *Who* weeps over Lazarus in John 11:35? Not God the Son, as has already been established. He is insulated from all that his human nature undergoes. He is incapable of suffering. But neither can Christ be said to be the subject weeping at Lazarus's grave, because Christ is not a person. Christ is just the mereological sum of God the Son and his human nature. And it certainly cannot be that Christ's human nature is a person, on pain of Nestorianism. So Christ's human nature is also discounted from being the subject of the weeping reported in John 11:35. But then it appears that no person is the subject of the weeping. And this is surely theologically intolerable.

A final obstacle for the three-part compositional model is actually common to other orthodox accounts of the incarnation, and it is a particular concern for those versions of orthodox Christology that presume Christ's human nature is a concrete particular. This is what we might call *the too-many-thinkers objection*. Trenton Merricks points out that the majority of substance dualists hold to the thesis, central to textbook Cartesianism, that human persons are identical with souls and only contingently related to a certain physical body, which is not a part of that human person. So, says Merricks, if one objects to this central claim of textbook Cartesianism, one is objecting to a central claim of the majority of substance dualists. Some substance dualists deny that human persons are identical with souls. Instead, they posit that human persons are soul-body composites. But, says Merricks, this raises a serious problem for this minority "composite" version of dualism. For "the dualist who denies that a person is identical with a soul must say that there are two objects with mental properties (a person and her soul) where normally we think there is one."[19] This sort of problem has application to the three-part

---

18. This is also found in Flint's helpful paper, "A Puzzle concerning the Mereological Model of the Incarnation."
19. See Trenton Merricks, "The Word Made Flesh: Dualism, Physicalism, and the Incarnation," in *Persons: Human and Divine*, ed. Peter van Inwagen and Dean Zimmerman (Oxford: Oxford University Press, 2007), 282n2.

composition model and to other versions of compositional Christology too. It looks like Christ's human soul is a thinking entity. In fact, if some version of substance dualism is true with respect to human beings, then in order to be fully human it is necessary that Christ possess a human soul. In which case Christ has a human soul that is a thinking substance. But God the Son is a thinking substance. In fact, he is the person who assumes human nature, including as one constituent of the human nature an additional thinking substance, the human soul of Christ. At this point it begins to look suspiciously like the compositional Christologist has introduced too many thinkers into one person.[20] And this raises the question of Nestorianism once again.[21]

In Defense of the Three-Part Composition Model

These are serious theological and metaphysical problems. What can be said in defense of the three-part composition model? More than one might think at first glance. Let us consider responses to the objections in the order given above.

First, the theological worries. It does not seem at all obvious that the catholic creeds require that God the Son is *identical* to Christ. When the excerpts from the Chalcedonian "definition" are read in their context, this becomes clearer. I give the whole "definition" below, highlighting the relevant phrases cited earlier:

> So, following the saintly fathers, we all with one voice teach the confession of *one and the same Son*, our Lord Jesus Christ: the same perfect in divinity and perfect in humanity, the same truly God and truly man, of a rational soul and a body; consubstantial with the Father as regards his divinity, and the same consubstantial with us as regards his humanity; like

---

20. I presume that a human brain is, for the Cartesian, a sort of thinking mechanism, though it is not the subject of human thought—the soul is. If Merricks is right, then hylomorphists have an additional thinker to contend with in the incarnation over and above these two immaterial ones. But this is controversial. Eleonore Stump, for one, appears not to take Thomist hylomorphism to have this consequence. She thinks of the human soul as similar to an Aristotelian form, or configurational state, that "informs" or organizes the matter of the body such that, once configured, the two "substances" (body and soul) form one distinct entity, a human. We shall return to this matter later.

21. Another version of the too-many-thinkers objection is raised by Joseph Jedwab in his unpublished paper "Against Mereological Christological Concretism."

us in all respects, except for sin; begotten before the ages from the Father as regards his divinity, and in the last days the same for us and for our salvation from Mary, the Virgin God-bearer, as regards his humanity; *one and the same Christ, Son, Lord, only-begotten,* acknowledged in two natures which undergo no confusion, no change, no division, no separation; at no point was the difference between the natures taken away through the union, but rather the property of both natures is preserved and comes together into a single person and a single subsistent being; he is not parted or divided into two persons, but *is one and the same only-begotten Son, God, Word, Lord Jesus Christ*, just as the prophets taught from the beginning about him, and as the Lord Jesus Christ himself instructed us, and as the creed of the fathers has handed it down to us.[22]

The defender of the three-part composition model can argue with some plausibility that, although the model is inconsistent with *Jesus Christ = God the Son*, it is commensurate with *the person who is Jesus Christ = God the Son*.

As Leftow points out, the copula "is" in the second of these italicized statements is not the "is" of identity.[23] And, on the face of it, this appears to be commensurate with the statement given by the fathers of Chalcedon.[24] Phrases that speak of "one and the same Son, our Lord Jesus Christ," who is said to be "but one and the same only-begotten, Son, God, Word, Jesus Christ," are not necessarily inconsistent with the second of our italicized statements above. "One and the same Son, our Lord Jesus Christ" seems commensurate with "There is exactly one person in Christ, namely, God the Son." "One and the same only-begotten Son, God, Word, Jesus Christ" may be similarly parsed as "There is exactly one subject in the incarnation who is referred to in various ways; this subject is God the Son." This need not imply that Christ and God the Son are identical—which is not to deny that the Chalcedonian "definition" is consistent with our first italicized statement. In fact, it looks like the Chalcedonian "definition" is consistent with both italicized statements. That is, this particular part of the symbol appears to be metaphysically underdetermined.

22. Tanner, *Decrees of the Ecumenical Councils*, 1:86–87.
23. Leftow, "Timeless God Incarnate," 294.
24. This is moot, of course. But even Cross, who interprets the relevant statements of the Chalcedonian "definition" in terms of identity between God the Son and Christ, will only go so far as to say that Chalcedon seems to be affirming this. See "Incarnation," 452, 461. Later he acknowledges that his reading of Chalcedon "is not universal amongst scholars" (ibid., 472n1).

However, the Chalcedonian definition is not the only catholic symbol relevant to this objection. The Second Council of Constantinople in AD 553 issued a series of solemn anathemas in defense of the Chalcedonian settlement and against the Nestorianism of, among others, Theodore of Mopsuestia—by then deceased. Several of these anathemas are of relevance to the question of the nature of the hypostatic union. For example, Anathema III says, "If anyone declares . . . that the God the Word was . . . in him [Christ] in the way that one might be in another, but that our lord Jesus Christ was not one and the same, the Word of God incarnate and made human . . . let him be anathema."[25] At first glance, this does seem to fit better with the first, rather than the second, of our italicized statements. But the advocate of the three-part composition model can agree that the only person "in" Christ is identical with God the Son. In this sense the person "in" Christ is "one and the same" with God the Son, which is the important claim being made here. Similarly, the three-part composition model is consistent with the notion that this person is "the Word of God incarnate and made human." Strictly speaking, God the Son is not Jesus Christ, of course. One could take the phrase "one and the same, our Lord Jesus Christ" as equivalent to "God the Son = Jesus Christ." But it would be perverse to claim this was the only construal of this passage that made theological sense.

In fact, when one puts what is said in the third anathema alongside some of the later comments of the Second Council of Constantinople, the picture that emerges is one that is consistent with the three-part composition model. (It may even offer some support to the model.) Take, for instance, Anathema VII. It speaks of the hypostatic union as a union "in which neither the nature of the Word has changed into the nature of human flesh, nor the nature of human flesh changed into that of the Word (each remained what it was by nature, even after the union, as this had been made in respect of subsistence)."[26] This is echoed in Anathema VIII: "In saying that it was in respect of subsistence that the only-begotten God the Word was united, we are not alleging that there was a confusion made of each, of the natures into one another, but rather that each of the two remained what it was, and in this way we understand that the Word

---

25. Tanner, *Decrees of the Ecumenical Councils*, 1:114.
26. Ibid., 1:117.

was united to human flesh."[27] In both of these passages a similar claim is made about the hypostatic union. This is that the two natures united in Christ are not changed through being united in Christ. Each nature "remained what it is by nature," even when the personal union had taken place. This, I suggest, is a significant dogmatic statement. Suppose we construe "change" here to mean "fundamental, or essential change." Some changes occur in the hypostatic union, such as the human nature of Christ beginning to exist, or acquiring the property "being a human nature in personal union with a divine person." But perhaps fundamental change, that is, change that would alter the nature of a thing, does not—perhaps cannot—occur at the incarnation. (It certainly cannot occur in the divine nature if God is essentially immutable.) Then, given what Anathemas VII and VIII state, whatever else happens in the hypostatic union, the divine nature of Christ cannot be fundamentally, or essentially, changed by it or as a consequence of it.

As mentioned in chapter 1 on the eternal generation of the Son, I take it that the divine nature is essentially a metaphysical simple. By that I mean the divine nature is not composed of more fundamental parts. It is, in this limited respect, metaphysically primitive. Recall that this claim is distinct from the traditional doctrine of divine simplicity, according to which the divine nature is not just a metaphysical simple but is an entity that has no parts *whatsoever*. The paradigm of the sort of immaterial metaphysical simple I have in mind is the soul. It is an immaterial entity that is not composed of more fundamental parts.[28] It cannot be divided or partitioned as my body can because it is essentially a simple, though (I presume) it has distinct properties. In these respects, souls are different from bodies (which are composed of more fundamental parts), can be partitioned or divided in virtue of having proper parts, and are not metaphysically primitive. Now, plausibly, the divine nature is analogous to a soul in being essentially a metaphysical simple. God the Son has the divine nature (he is a divine person). So God the Son is a metaphysical simple.[29] Now, recall the words

27. Ibid., 1:118.
28. Cf. Roderick Chisholm, "On the Simplicity of the Soul," in *Philosophical Perspectives*, vol. 5, *Philosophy of Religion*, ed. James Tomberlin (Aterscadero, CA: Ridgeview, 1991), 157–81.
29. This is ambiguous between the claim that (a) each divine person in the Godhead is a metaphysical simple, and a second claim that (b) the divine essence is a metaphysical simple. I am sympathetic to the latter, although I will not offer an argument for this here.

of Anathemas VII and VIII cited above. The hypostatic union of Christ's human and divine natures cannot fundamentally change the natures thus united through, or as a consequence of, the act of union. So Christ's divine nature, being essentially a simple, cannot begin to be composite at the first moment of incarnation by, say, "expanding" to include a concrete human nature as a proper part or parts—for this would constitute a fundamental change to the divine nature of God the Son. This is consistent with the three-part composition model, according to which God the Son does not fundamentally change at the first moment of incarnation. The relation he has to his human nature is an accidental one, the human nature he assumes being like an instrument in which he is embedded.[30]

The claim that God the Son is a metaphysical simple is a theologically respectable one, though many in the tradition would want to go beyond it to claim God has no parts whatsoever. The three-part composition model is able to accommodate this notion that God is a metaphysical simple along the lines required by Anathemas VII and VIII. When the earlier are set beside the later anathemas, the overall picture of the hypostatic union that emerges is, I suggest, consistent with the three-part composition model. But it seems to be consistent with other accounts of the incarnation too. That is, it appears that the anathemas of the Second Council of Constantinople, like the relevant dogmatic claims of the Chalcedonian "definition," are metaphysically underdetermined, since both symbols appear to be consistent with the three-part composition model as well as the stronger metaphysical claims made by those Christologists who think God the Son is identical to his human nature. But that is all to the good. It means that there is no reason to think the three-part composition model falls foul of catholic orthodoxy—as expressed in the Chalcedonian "definition" and the anathemas of the Second Council of Constantinople. And it also offers some indication as to why the orthodoxy of the three-part composition model has been mistakenly called into question: the two

---

30. Granted, this may not be the only way one could construe the metaphysics of the hypostatic union in keeping with the Anathemas of the Second Council of Constantinople. But I am not concerned with other ways of construing the metaphysics of the incarnation here. Nevertheless, here is an example of one sort of alternative view consistent with the Anathemas of the Second Council of Constantinople: if one allows that human nature is fundamentally a property rather than a concrete particular, exemplifying this property need not entail a fundamental change in the person who begins to exemplify it if, say, it is an accidental property of the one who possesses it.

catholic symbols we have considered appear to be consistent with more than one metaphysical account of the incarnation.

But what of the second theological objection, which was that the three-part composition model yields Nestorianism? The Chalcedonian two-natures doctrine implies that Christ is *a divine person with a human nature*. By contrast, the three-part composition model appears to mean Christ is a divine person and a human person, somehow united. What will the defender of the three-part composition model say to that? The obvious response involves attempting to block the inference from human nature to human personhood. One could claim that the logic of the three-part composition model is that there are not two persons in Christ, because his human nature is subsumed into a larger whole. Or, his human nature fails to be a person distinct from God the Son in virtue of being part of a larger composite that includes God the Son.[31] Another way to block the nature-person inference is to argue that no proper part of a person constitutes a person, on analogy with the claim that no proper part of a member of a natural kind constitutes a member of the same natural kind. This is the line Leftow takes, utilizing the famous 1,001 cats example of Peter Geach.[32]

The analogy goes like this. Consider Tibbles, a domestic cat. His being a cat makes him a member of the biological family *felidae*. We might say that the domestic cat Tibbles is an instance of the natural kind *felidae*.[33] But Tibbles has numerous proper parts, including the part that is composed of all of Tibbles's parts, minus one hair. Call this Tibbles-Minus. Question: does Tibbles-Minus compose another cat, numerically distinct from Tibbles? It certainly looks like it. But if that is the case, then apparently the removal of two of Tibbles's hairs will generate a third cat, and so on, until it seems we have at least 1,001 cats—presuming Tibbles has at least 1,001 hairs. But it seems bizarre to think that there are at least 1,001 cats sitting on the mat, composed of proper parts of Tibbles. How do we resist this conclusion? By claiming that no proper part of a member of a given

---

31. This is Eleonore Stump's suggestion in "Aquinas' Metaphysics of the Incarnation," in *The Incarnation*, ed. Stephen T. Davis, Daniel Kendall, and Gerald O'Collins (New York: Oxford University Press, 2002), 208–9.

32. See Peter Geach, *Reference and Generality*, 3rd ed. (Ithaca, NY: Cornell University Press, 1980), 215, cited in Leftow, "Timeless God Incarnate," 281n22.

33. All that is important here is that "cat" maps onto a particular natural kind. I am not making the broader claim that all biological families have a one-to-one correspondence with natural kinds.

natural kind constitutes another member of the same natural kind. That is, no proper part of Tibbles, such as Tibbles-Minus, constitutes a member of the kind *felidae*. There is only one felid on the mat, and that is Tibbles.

Leftow enjoins us to apply this reasoning to the incarnation in the following way:

> Given a set of parts composing at time t a member of a natural kind (e.g., cat), no subset of that set composes at t a member of the same natural kind. Well, then: persons are a natural kind. So if at t S [the human soul], B [the human body] and the Son compose a person, no subset of {S, B, and the Son} does so.[34]

This looks plausible. And it offers the friend of the three-part composition model a way of resisting the accusation of Nestorianism. God the Son is the only person present in Christ. His human nature never composes a human person distinct from God the Son because (a) no person can have a person as a proper part (from Leftow's adaptation of the 1,001 cats maneuver above), and (b) at no time does the human nature of Christ exist apart from God the Son, the divine person who assumes it at the first moment of its existence. So the human nature is never in a position to form a fundamental substance or supposit distinct from God the Son, which, on the medieval way of thinking, is a necessary condition for the instantiation of personhood—presuming the Boethian definition of person as an "individual substance [i.e., fundamental substance] of a rational nature," which we encountered when setting out the desiderata for models of the hypostatic union in the previous chapter.[35]

This does have the puzzling implication that Jesus of Nazareth is not identical to God the Son, strictly speaking. But that is just a feature of the model: if Christ is a composite whole of which God the Son is a part, then clearly God the Son cannot be identical to Christ. But, for good theological reasons—reasons having to do with preserving the metaphysical simplicity of the divine person involved—the model must affirm this, on pain of introducing composition into the divine nature!

This brings us to the identity problem. To recap: the identity problem is that, according to the three-part composition model, God the Son is

---

34. Leftow, "Timeless God Incarnate," 282.
35. See Aquinas, *Summa Theologiae* I.29.1.

not human because he is not identical to a human nature. Traditional, orthodox Christology implies that at the incarnation, God the Son *becomes* human in addition to being divine. If the three-part composition model denies this, or entails the denial of this, then (so the objection goes) it is unorthodox. But in order to make good on this claim, one would have to concede that there is sound theological reason to think that God the Son becoming human entails God the Son becoming identical to a particular human nature. But why concede this? All that orthodoxy requires is that in the incarnation, the Second Person of the Trinity assumes human nature. Orthodox Christologists are agreed that the relation God the Son bears to his human nature is a contingent one: he is not required to assume human nature; there is no necessity for him to assume human nature; in becoming human he freely assumes a human nature. In one sense, the assumption of human nature means God the Son does "become human": he "becomes" the divine person who is Jesus Christ. But for the atemporalist this boils down to the claim that God the Son is eternally the divine person who is Jesus Christ. No temporal "becoming" occurs here. (Matters are more complicated for the temporalist. But I shall ignore this complication since, like Leftow, I am interested in the atemporal view of the matter.) Clearly this does not imply that God the Son is identical to his human nature, as we have already seen. There is no creedal pressure to assume "becoming" here implies some identity between God the Son and his human nature. So I conclude that the three-part composition model is not required to embrace the idea that God the Son is identical to a particular human nature.

We come to the insulation problem. The most difficult version of this problem arises for atemporalists who are advocates of the three-part composition model, such as Leftow. As already mentioned, divine immutability and impassibility are constituents of traditional, classical Christian theism and of the views of those theologians who have deployed this sort of thinking about theology proper in their accounts of the incarnation. So this is not a new problem. The claim that the divine nature of Christ must be shielded from human emotion as well as other sorts of change, such as property changes, is the sort of problem common to any account of the incarnation that is committed to the atemporalist picture, according to which God does not change in any substantial way. It is not a problem peculiar to the three-part composition model of the incarnation. This much we can say ad hominem, but of course this does nothing to alleviate the difficulty posed. The real issue here is whether God the Son is so insulated from the actions and mental states of his human nature that although Christ suffers, weeps, performs physical acts, and so on, God the Son does not. His human nature does these things; he does not.

But consider a rather different way of thinking about this matter, according to which God the Son acts in the incarnation through his human nature rather like one might use a tool to perform a particular task. In a similar way, Professor Stephen Hawking talks, but he uses an electronic box to do it.[36] When we speak to Professor Hawking, we are really speaking to a human-box composite, a joint system that produces the words we hear. If we ask who speaks when we hear these words, the answer is in one sense the box, but in a more fundamental sense Professor Hawking. The sounds issue from the electronic box. But it is the Professor who speaks through the medium of the box. He is the one who programs it to make the sounds he intends to convey as speech. Something similar obtains with respect to the incarnation, according to the three-part composition model. God the Son is present in the world through his human nature. He uses his human nature rather like Professor Hawking's electronic box, as an instrument that enables him to perform certain sorts of tasks. If we ask the question, who weeps at Lazarus's grave in John 11 or eats broiled fish on the beach after the resurrection in John 21?, the answer is also similar to the Professor Hawking example. In one sense the human nature of Christ does these things. It is what we might call the proximate cause of the weeping and so forth. But the ultimate cause is surely God the Son. He acts through his human nature in order to bring about Christ's weeping at Lazarus's grave and eating broiled fish. When we deal with Christ weeping or eating or performing some other human action, we are faced with a human-divine composite, a "joint system" that produces the human acts we see.

This looks like it implies causal overdetermination—Christ's human nature and his divine nature both cause a given action, such as weeping at Lazarus's grave. But this need not follow if, say, the divine person *moves* the human nature to bring about the action in question. Richard Cross worries that this means that the Trinity moves Christ's human nature to bring about the actions of the human Christ because of the so-called trinitarian law: *opera trinitatis ad extra indivisa sunt* (the external acts of

---

36. I owe this example to Brian Leftow.

the Trinity are indivisible).[37] If all the external acts of God are trinitarian acts, then if God the Son moves his human nature to eat broiled fish, the Trinity moves Christ's human nature to eat broiled fish. But I do not see why this is a special problem for the version of the three-part composition model with which I am concerned. The trinitarian law applies to all the external acts of God. The Trinity upholds and sustains Christ's human nature at every moment it persists through time. The Trinity concurs with every mundane act the human Christ brings about, just as the Trinity concurs with every mundane act I bring about—given a doctrine of God's general concurrence with the mundane actions of creatures. As it is usually understood, the trinitarian law still provides metaphysical room, so to speak, for external acts of the Trinity that terminate on particular divine persons, such as the incarnation. We say that God the Son assumes human nature. But really, this is a trinitarian act that terminates on one divine person in particular, God the Son. Similarly, God the Son moves his human nature to eat broiled fish. This is a trinitarian act in one sense, but it terminates upon the person of God the Son in particular, since it is *his* human nature (i.e., the human nature he assumes; it is not assumed into the divine essence) that is in view.

Is this sufficient? It does mean God the Son *simpliciter* does not weep or eat broiled fish. But then what is so strange about that? We have already established in chapter 3 that God the Son is an essentially immaterial being. He is incapable of weeping or eating. But his human nature is capable of these tasks. In the same way, as a consequence of his physical condition, Professor Hawking is incapable of making the sounds of audible human speech. But his electronic box is capable of performing this task. Of course, there are limits to the analogy with Professor Hawking. I take it that the personal union brought about by the incarnation is much more intimate than that between Hawking and his electronic speech apparatus. For one thing, God the Son seems able to bring about basic actions in his human nature, such as Christ's weeping at Lazarus's grave, whereas Hawking is not able to do this with his electronic apparatus, which has

---

37. Cross, *Metaphysics of the Incarnation*, ch. 10. Cross, following Scotus, thinks that a better way to make sense of the action of God the Son "in" or "through" his human nature is to say that the human nature causes the human acts of Christ (weeping, eating, etc.) but that these acts are predicated of God the Son via the *communicatio idiomatum* (communication of attributes), which, as we have already noted, involves predicating the attributes (actions, etc.) of the individual natures of Christ to the person "in" Christ, namely, God the Son.

to be programmed manually. This is not necessarily inconsistent with the point being made here about God the Son's insulation from the properties and acts of his human nature. For, to change the analogy for a moment, the Cartesian can say, "My soul brought about the raising of my arm." But no one would think this implies that the soul of the Cartesian has an arm. I conclude that although God the Son is insulated from the changes his human nature undergoes, this does not necessarily constitute a problem for the three-part composition model.

We turn now to the no-person objection. Granted that God the Son is insulated from physical or emotional changes that his human nature experiences, we can ask the further question: If Christ weeps over Lazarus, *who* is the subject of this action? Not God the Son, as has already been established. He is insulated from all that his human nature undergoes. He is incapable of suffering. Not Christ, because Christ is not a person on the three-part composition model. Christ is just the mereological sum of God the Son and his human nature. Nor can it be that Christ's human nature is a person, on pain of Nestorianism. So Christ's human nature is also discounted from being the subject of the weeping reported in John 11:35. But then it appears that no person is the subject of the weeping.

What are we to say to this? Perhaps the doctrine of the communication of attributes may be of some use at this juncture. Elsewhere I have defined this as follows:

> *Communicatio idiomatum:* The attribution of the properties of each of the natures of Christ to the person of Christ, such that the theanthropic [i.e., God-mannish] person of Christ is treated as having divine and human attributes at one and the same time, yet without predicating attributes of one nature that properly belong to the other nature in the hypostatic union, without transference of properties between the natures and without confusing or commingling the two natures of Christ or the generation of a *tertium quid* [third sort of thing].[38]

This version of the communication of attributes blocks the inference from "S is N according to his F nature" to "S is N." The human nature of Christ weeps. God the Son does not—indeed, cannot—if he is essentially impassible. Yet God the Son is said to be the person who weeps, according to

38. Crisp, *Divinity and Humanity*, 7–8.

his human nature. The property "being the entity that weeps at Lazarus's grave" belongs to the human nature of Christ. But the property "being the person who weeps at the grave of Lazarus" belongs to God the Son. In virtue of the hypostatic union, the property in question is attributed to God the Son via the communication of attributes.

But can we run this in the opposite direction? That is, can we say S is the person who does N, when strictly speaking it is the nature F possessed by S that has or does N? Let us return to our earlier example of Christ's weeping in John 11. According to orthodoxy, Christ is one divine person who assumes a human nature, in addition to his divine nature. The two natures must not be confused or (fundamentally) changed through, or as a consequence of, the event of hypostatic union. So if we ask who it is that is weeping at Lazarus's grave, the answer according to orthodoxy must be the person "in" Christ. There can be only one person in Christ (again, according to orthodoxy). So it is God the Son who weeps. But God the Son cannot weep, on account of being an essentially immaterial being that is immutable and impassible. Well then, we are left with saying this: the human nature of Christ weeps. The divine person who possesses this human nature is the one that moves his human nature to weep. He does not weep "in" his divine nature, but only "in" his human nature. Granted, on this way of thinking, one cannot say, "The divine person weeps," if this means "The divine person *simpliciter* weeps." But if we mean by this "The divine person moves his human nature to weep," or even just "The divine person weeps in his human nature," then we can affirm it.[39] This, I think, is one of the least satisfactory parts of the three-part composition model. And it is here that the defender of the three-part composition model has to take considerable care so as not to fall into the trap of conflating that which is ascribed to the person with that which applies only to one of the natures of Christ.

Finally, we come to the too-many-thinkers objection. Assuming Christ has a human body and human soul (or human body-soul composite),

---

39. There are ways of finessing this application of the communication of attributes—for instance, with the concept of synecdoche (that is, ascribing to the person "in" Christ the property that is had by only a part of Christ, his human, or his divine, nature) or, as Marilyn McCord Adams has recently suggested, by emphasizing the fact that Christ's human nature is not essential to God the Son. Then, applied to the three-part composition model, God the Son has the attributes of deity *simpliciter* but has human attributes only in a qualified way. See Adams, *Christ and Horrors*, 135–36.

Christ's human brain is a thinking substance. Christ's human soul is a thinking substance. God the Son is a thinking substance. But this adds up to too many thinking substances for only one subject of the incarnation.

But consider again textbook Cartesianism, mentioned earlier. According to the Cartesian, humans are identical with their souls, which are "plugged into" or "interface with" a human brain at the pineal gland. It looks like both the human soul and the human brain on the Cartesian account are thinking entities. So textbook Cartesianism appears to have an analogous too-many-thinkers problem. But perhaps not: the Cartesian could reason that the human soul is a thinking substance that uses the human brain with which it is "attached" to act in the corporeal world. The brain, then, is something like an instrument of the soul. (Recall the Professor Hawking example used earlier.) Expand this to include the incarnation. Then God the Son assumes a human nature, including a human soul "attached" to a human body. According to this textbook Cartesian story, normally when a human body and human soul are rightly configured, the human person present (i.e., the human soul) uses its brain to think and perform actions through its body in the physical world. But in the case of the three-part composition model, this does not occur because, although the natural endowment of a human person is present (a human soul, which, in this case is united to a human body), this fails to form a fundamental substance, a supposit. The Second Person of the Trinity is the fundamental substance in the incarnation. He is the person who assumes his human nature. And he uses both the human body (including the human brain) and the human soul of Christ as his instruments. Now there is no need to think that there are too many thinkers. Although there are three thinking substances present in the incarnation, there is only one subject, God the Son, who acts upon, or through, his human nature—the human nature in which, so the three-part composition model states, God the Son is embedded post-incarnation.

Of course, this is only a model. It may be that some other version of substance dualism better approximates to the truth of the matter. (Perhaps one where the relationship between body and soul is much more intimate and more carefully drawn, such as that offered by Richard Swinburne in his modified Cartesian account in *The Evolution of the Soul*.)[40] Be that as it

---

40. Richard Swinburne, *The Evolution of the Soul* (Oxford: Oxford University Press, 1986). Swinburne's most recent treatment of these matters is in *Mind, Brain, and Free Will* (Oxford: Oxford University Press, 2013).

may, it seems to me that the too-many-thinkers objection need not obtain if the advocate of the three-part composition model makes clear that the incarnation involves God the Son using his human nature as his instrument, much as the human soul of a human person normally uses its brain in a manner similar to an instrument. Adding an additional "thinker" in the person of God the Son need not make matters more difficult, if something like the medieval metaphysical story of the assumption of human nature by the Son is co-opted by the defender of the three-part composition model—including the commitment to two ranges of consciousness in the incarnation, one essential to the divine person and another accidentally related to him via his assumption of human nature.

Conclusion

I have argued that the three-part composition model of the incarnation is consistent with the dogmas of Chalcedon and the Second Council of Constantinople. It does not entail Nestorianism. And it has the resources with which to withstand the versions of the identity objection, the insulation problem, and the too-many-thinkers objection proffered here. It is possible to use the communication of attributes to help make some sense of the no-person objection. But this, I concede, is a tricky area in the metaphysics of the hypostatic union, in which more work needs to be done. The objective throughout this chapter has been merely to defend central tenets of the three-part composition model rather than to endorse the model. I have not suggested that the three-part composition model is the *right* way to conceive of the metaphysics of the hypostatic union. (After all, a model is a simplified description of much more complex data that only approximates to the truth of the matter.) But if the argument offered here is successful, a number of intellectual impediments to the model will have been removed or (in the case of the no-person objection) significantly reduced.

7

The Union Account of Atonement

> What is real in the union between Christ and his people, is the foundation of what is legal; that is, it is something really in them, and between them, uniting them, that is the ground of the suitableness of their being accounted as one by the Judge: and if there is any act, or qualification in believers, that is of that uniting nature, that it is meet on that account that the Judge should look upon 'em, and accept 'em as one, no wonder that upon the account of the same act or qualification, he should accept the satisfaction and merits of the one, for the other, as if it were their satisfaction and merits: it necessarily follows, or rather is implied.
>
> —Jonathan Edwards[1]

We have traversed a lot of theological territory in the previous chapters. Beginning with matters of protology, we discussed the eternal generation of the Son, the existence of Christ in abstraction, as it were, from his human nature, the relationship between God's incorporeality and the incarnation, and the christological doctrine of the image of God. Then there were two chapters on the hypostatic union, looking at desiderata for models of the hypostatic union and then presenting one such model, the three-part composition account. With this chapter we return to where

1. Jonathan Edwards, "Justification by Faith," in *Sermons and Discourses, 1734–1738*, 158.

we left off in discussing the image of God. If God has created us all in the image of Christ, who is the image of God, to what end has he created us? Here I want to unpack a particular account of the atonement that speaks to a strong doctrine of union with Christ, which we will focus upon in more detail in the final two chapters. Here, we want to consider the nature of atonement and how it is that Christ's work deals with human sin. I propose a model of atonement that speaks to these matters—one that gives us a "joined up" account of both human dereliction from God and the divine act of reconciliation in Christ.

The atonement is one of the central and defining doctrines of Christian theology. Yet the nature of the atonement—that is, *how* it is that Christ's life and death on the cross actually atone for human sin—remains a theological conundrum. Over the centuries, a number of different models of the atonement have been proposed that attempt to make sense of the biblical data and offer an account of the nature of the atonement. But none have won universal support. This chapter offers a new argument for the atonement, which I shall call the *union account of the atonement* since it is predicated on a particular understanding of the union of human beings with Christ in his atoning work.

We shall proceed as follows. First I shall set out the theological context for the argument. This involves giving some account of alternative models of the atonement in the tradition and why the union account might be thought a particularly appealing way of thinking about the atonement. Then I shall set forth an argument for the union account that involves the application of an idea found in some Augustinian accounts of the transmission of sin from Adam to his progeny. At the end of this exposition, I offer some brief comments on the metaphysics undergirding the theology of this argument. In a final section, several theological and philosophical objections to this reasoning are discussed.

Some Models of Atonement

Systematic theologies usually include a discussion of a number of different accounts of the atonement found in the Christian tradition. Although different taxonomies could be offered, I shall discuss the following: the ransom account, the satisfaction account, the moral exemplar account, and penal substitution. These are not all the doctrines of atonement one can find in the Christian tradition, but they are arguably the most influential.[2]

Some version of the ransom model is often thought to be the majority view in the patristic period of the church. It is certainly not the view of all the fathers, but it is often thought to reflect the work of a number of patristic authors.[3] A standard version of the story informing the ransom view runs like this: by sinning against God, human beings have sold themselves into slavery to the Devil. God, not wishing to see humanity remain in this benighted situation, deigns to bring about the means by which human beings can be emancipated from their vitiated moral condition and indentured state. This involves the incarnation and work of Christ, who tricks the Devil into bringing about his death on the cross. Instead of destroying Christ, this act actually enables Christ to pay the ransom price required to liberate human beings. Thus, the work of Christ achieves two interconnected goals: to break the hold evil (in the person of Satan) has over human beings, and to enable human beings to be reconciled with God.

The ransom account (expressed in the sort of story just given) was dusted down in the mid-twentieth century by the Scandinavian theologian Gustav Aulén, whose book *Christus Victor* claimed that the ransom model was the "classic" view of the atonement, which had been overlaid

---

[2]. The best and most reliable single-volume account of the history and development of the many different doctrines of the atonement is still R. S. Franks, *The Work of Christ* (Edinburgh: Thomas Nelson and Sons, 1962). Recently it has become popular to eschew talk of atonement "models" or "theories" in favor of "metaphors" and "motifs" as well as models that offer a kaleidoscopic approach that borrow key ideas from different historic accounts. However, it seems to me that the historic models of atonement each provide distinct *mechanisms* for human reconciliation. So they are not merely "metaphors" or "motifs." What is more, kaleidoscopic approaches to atonement look suspiciously like yet another model rather than a collection of metaphors or motifs. For these reasons, I have resisted this recent trend to downgrade traditional atonement models or relegate them to one among a cluster of different metaphors of the work of Christ. Two influential accounts that take this more popular recent approach are Colin E. Gunton, *The Actuality of Atonement: A Study of Metaphor, Rationality, and the Christian Tradition* (London: T&T Clark, 1988), and Mark D. Baker and Joel B. Green, *Recovering the Scandal of the Cross: Atonement in New Testament and Contemporary Contexts*, 2nd ed. (Downers Grove, IL: IVP Academic, 2011).

[3]. St. Gregory of Nyssa's *Great Catechism* is often thought to epitomize the ransom view among the patristic authors, whereas parts of Athanasius's *On the Incarnation*, especially chapters 2 and 4, seem much more like a primitive satisfaction account of the atonement. I have discussed this doctrine in more detail in "Is Ransom Enough?," *Journal of Analytic Theology* 3 (2015): 1–11. Benjamin Myers argues (to my mind, convincingly) that ransom is not the view of the fathers in "The Patristic Atonement Model," in *Locating Atonement: Explorations in Constructive Dogmatics*, ed. Oliver D. Crisp and Fred Sanders (Grand Rapids: Zondervan, 2015), ch. 3.

by centuries of theological accretions.[4] He maintains that this classic view is superior to later accounts of the work of Christ and should be preferred to other ways of thinking about the atonement. Aulén's work has been widely discussed, particularly among systematic theologians, but it is not without problems.

One concern with Aulén's work is that it is not obvious that the ransom view is *the* "classic" account of the atonement, or the best or most comprehensive way of thinking about the nature of atonement. That would have to be argued. Even if the ransom view is the majority position among the fathers (which it is not), this does not automatically give it a privileged status above other models of the atonement. The venerable pedigree of a given model is not, after all, a cast-iron guarantee of its being the best explanation of the data. A second problem is that the ransom account, as expressed by the story just given, involves a rather naïve understanding of the relationship between the fall, human sin, and enslavement to the Devil, with unpleasant overtones of God being implicated in an act of deception. That said, the conceptual hardcore of the doctrine is that Christ's work is remedial, being the price required to purchase or buy back some number of fallen humanity enslaved to evil. It is perfectly feasible to set out such a doctrine without the paraphernalia of the story about deceiving the Devil. Then Christ's work would bring about the reconciliation of some number of fallen humanity, including their release from the power of evil—the language about the personification of evil having been removed.[5] This would have the advantage of divesting the account of the unwelcome consequence of God's involvement in deception. However, if the core of the account can be stated without the need for personified evil, to whom is the ransom price of Christ's work paid? It might be possible to amend the theory in the direction of a satisfaction account of the atonement at this point. In which case God, whose moral governance has been impugned by human sin (let us say), requires the ransom as the price for human wickedness. Taken in this way, Christ's work is not so much a question of paying the ransom demand of the Devil as paying the price demanded by the divine

---

4. Gustav Aulén, *Christus Victor* (London: SPCK, 1931).
5. Some recent accounts of atonement take up elements of the *Christus Victor* view and press them in a rather different direction, namely, "nonviolent" accounts of atonement. See, e.g., J. Denny Weaver, *The Nonviolent Atonement*, 2nd ed. (Grand Rapids: Eerdmans, 2011). I discuss this development in "Is Ransom Enough?"

moral law for human sin. This moral demand might be thought a ransom in a loose, nonphilosophical sense since it involves payment of a price set in order to bring about the reconciliation of some number of fallen human beings. But it is not a ransom in the sense of a payment made to a diabolical entity that has enslaved humanity.

There are other problems with the *Christus Victor* view apart from these, including the fact that it doesn't appear to provide a complete model of atonement at all. Be that as it may (and there is not space to argue for that claim here),[6] it may be simpler to put to one side those aspects of this account that are objectionable and search for an atonement model able to account for what is helpful in this understanding of the work of Christ. I suggest there are good theological reasons for pursuing such an alternative. For one thing, New Testament references to the payment of a ransom (e.g., the Greek word *lytron* used in Matt. 20:28 and the parallel in Mark 10:45) do not require a ransom account of atonement to be rendered plausible or consistent with other things in Scripture. In the context of these passages, the idea of ransom has to do with saving fallen humans ("the many") from a condition of oppression through an act of self-sacrifice. In fact, there is little biblical evidence for thinking God enters into some unholy pact with the Devil over the enslavement and ransom of humanity (although, Heb. 2:14–16 is suggestive in this regard). Moreover, satisfaction or penal substitution models of atonement can make sense of this biblical idea of ransom, along the lines of Christ's work being able to "buy back" some number of fallen humanity from the moral consequences of sin, without the unhelpful elements of the ransom view.[7]

This brings us to the satisfaction account, elements of which we have already segued into the ransom account. Satisfaction is a doctrine of atonement that is given its first systematic exposition in Anselm of Canterbury's magisterial *Cur Deus Homo* (Why the God-Man). Famously, Anselm's version of satisfaction theory is set up *remoto christo*—that is, setting aside the incarnation and reasoning simply on the basis of more general theological claims to the necessity of the incarnation of a God-man for atonement to be made. Anselm thinks that the nature of God is such that

---

6. I have dealt with this objection in "Is Ransom Enough?"
7. Other atonement doctrines may also offer a way of making sense of the biblical material on ransom, e.g., the governmental account of the atonement. I am not suggesting satisfaction or penal substitution models are the only plausible alternatives.

he *requires* satisfaction for sin committed against him. God cannot set aside satisfaction without in some way compromising his own perfect character, which is impossible. Because human sin is committed against a being of infinite worth and honor (i.e., God), it generates a correspondingly infinite demerit that no finite human being can annul, even if he or she were without sin.[8] Any putative redeemer would have to be without sin because only then would such a person be in a position to perform an act of supererogation—that is, an act that is nonobligatory and generates a merit sufficient to atone for human sin (i.e., a merit of infinite worth). Any sinful human would be incapable of producing such an act since he or she is already infinitely indebted to God on account of his or her sinful condition. A sinless human would still be incapable of producing a supererogatory act of sufficient merit to balance off the sin of all humanity, since no mere human moral action generates an infinite merit that can be applied to all humanity. Although he does not make this explicit, the logic of Anselm's position means that some other creature—for example, a sinless angel—cannot act on behalf of human beings in this regard. Nor could an angel generate an act of sufficient merit to balance off human sin, because angels cannot perform acts that have an infinite merit, on account of being finite creatures.[9] In fact, reasons Anselm, only God is capable of producing a supererogatory act that would be of sufficient merit to offer satisfaction for human sin. But since one of the stipulations for satisfaction, according to Anselm, is that a human being acts on behalf of other human beings in atonement,[10] only a being that is at one and the same time both fully divine and fully human can provide satisfaction for human sin. Hence, Anselm arrives at the conclusion that only the God-man can perform an act of supererogation that has the worth requisite to provide satisfaction; God must become human in order to atone for human sin.

---

8. This does have the apparently counterintuitive consequence that all sin entails an infinite demerit, which appears to make all sin equal for the purposes of culpability. There are possible responses to this problem, but it would take us too far from the main argument to discuss them. See, for example, Oliver D. Crisp, "Divine Retribution: A Defense," *Sophia* 42 (2003): 35–52, and the literature cited there.

9. Like Augustine of Hippo, Anselm does think that one motivation for the redemption of fallen human beings is that their number make up the number of angels that fell with the Devil. See *Cur Deus Homo* I.16–18 in *Anselm of Canterbury: The Major Works*.

10. "But the obligation rests with man, and no one else, to make the payment referred to. Otherwise mankind is not making recompense" (*Cur Deus Homo* II.6). Cf. II.7 in *The Major Works*, 320–21.

On the Anselmian account, the mechanism for atonement has to do with the God-man performing some infinitely meritorious act that may be used as a merit (at least) sufficient to balance out the demerit of human sin. Christ performs such an act in his atonement, offering the merit to God on behalf of fallen human beings. His meritorious act is performed in order to satisfy the moral law to which fallen humans are, as it were, indebted. But it is no part of this theory that the God-man take upon himself the penal consequences of human sin, standing in the place of fallen humans as a penal substitute, as with the penal substitutionary theory of atonement.[11] The sobriquet "the commercial theory of atonement," by which the Anselmian view is known in some older textbooks of theology, underlines the transactional character of the Anselmian satisfaction theory.

In the modern literature, Richard Swinburne has defended a modified version of satisfaction theory, without Anselm's commitment to the notion that God *requires* satisfaction for sin, the moral claim that sin is infinitely heinous, or the idea that Christ's atonement must be strictly equivalent in value to the sin committed against God.[12] He speaks of his doctrine in terms of the biblical idea of sacrifice, which he regards as the most helpful way of conceiving of the work of Christ found in Scripture—namely, Christ offering himself up as a sacrifice for human sin. But in Swinburne's hands this notion of sacrifice is construed in a way that is consistent with a version of satisfaction. Christ offers up some supererogatory act of sacrifice to God, and fallen human beings are able to somehow access that work in order to bring about their own redemption. In some respects, this echoes the more moderate version of satisfaction theory advocated by Thomas Aquinas, according to which Christ's satisfaction for sin is a most fitting means of atonement but not necessarily the only one possible, all things considered. That said, Aquinas does suggest that the atonement is consequentially necessary in some sense—that is, necessary as a consequence of God ordaining to bring about the sort of world he did, with human

---

11. However, if Anselm says that Christ satisfies the demands of the moral law, then there may be a punitive element to the model after all—provided the demands of the moral law are inflexible and must be met by their author. For an argument that presses in this direction, which he calls "reparative substitution," see S. Mark Hamilton, "Jonathan Edwards, Anselmic Satisfaction and Moral Government," *International Journal of Systematic Theology* 17, no. 1 (2015): 46–67.

12. Richard Swinburne, *Responsibility and Atonement* (Oxford: Oxford University Press, 1989).

beings who would sin and require salvation.[13] Swinburne distances himself from this language about the consequential necessity of atonement and several other aspects of the Thomist understanding of Christ's work in his own account of Christ's work.

The concept of atonement that Swinburne uses to do much of the work in his doctrine includes four distinct components: repentance, apology, reparation, and penance. Humans are able to repent and apologize to God for their sin. But they are not able to offer adequate reparation or penance; God must arrange this. Swinburne thinks that "the way in which we humans can use Christ's life and death as a means of removing sin is by offering it as our reparation and penance. To do so, we must join to it our feeble repentance and halting words of apology."[14] He concedes that God may set aside satisfaction and simply forgive sin. But God has good reason not to do this. Human beings need to understand the moral seriousness of their sins, just as children need to be corrected when they have gone astray. And it is permissible for God to bring about some supererogatory act of satisfaction through the work of Christ, though there is no necessity for God to do so, all things considered. If we think of Swinburne's doctrine as a moderate version of satisfaction, as I am suggesting, then it looks like the hardcore of satisfaction theories has to do with the issue of God's honor and/or moral law being satisfied by some act of supererogation that is performed by the God-man and to which we join our own act of penitence. Whether Christ's act is a requirement for satisfaction, what moral value it must have (if it must have a particular moral value at all) and in what sense it is necessary, all things considered (if it is necessary at all), appear to be matters that not all satisfaction advocates agree upon.

We come to the moral exemplar account, the first clear statement of which is often thought to be traceable to elements of Peter Abelard's doctrine of atonement, written at least in part in response to Anselm's work. However, caution needs to be exercised in evaluating this claim, often repeated in textbooks of Christian theology. Recently, Philip Quinn has challenged the idea that Abelard's account of the atonement is reducible to something like the idea that Christ is *merely* a moral example whose work we should emulate and whose act of love in the atonement

---

13. Aquinas, *Summa Theologiae* III.46.1–4.
14. Swinburne, *Responsibility and Atonement*, 161.

ought to stimulate in us a reciprocal response of love to God.[15] Whether or not Abelard's medieval theory has elements that sound at times like an embryonic version of a moral exemplar doctrine, it is certainly true that the moral exemplar view enjoyed a vogue in early modern theology with the advent of Socinianism, which, in the work of Faustus Socinus, sought to overthrow the arguments of advocates of penal substitution and satisfaction theories of atonement.[16] Interest in this view continued in nineteenth-century liberal theology. A modern version of this sort of doctrine can be found in the work of the British philosopher of religion John Hick.[17] As part of his bid to provide a religiously pluralist account of Christology, he argues that Christ's work must be seen primarily in terms of a moral example of self-sacrificial love and what, following Friedrich Schleiermacher, we might call "God-consciousness." There is no satisfaction brought about by the work of Christ, on this view, since no such satisfaction is necessary. Indeed, one persistent objection to this sort of account of the work of Christ is that it is not really a doctrine of atonement at all, since the logic of this view is that no reconciliation between God and humanity needs to take place. On Hick's version of the doctrine, human sin is really a matter that, though not trivial, may be forgiven without any reparation being exacted as satisfaction. But even if this view does not necessarily trivialize sin, it does raise a rather serious problem about the moral price involved in the incarnation and death of Christ. One is left wondering why God could not have provided the requisite moral example for human beings to emulate without such terrible cost to himself.

15. Phillip L. Quinn, "Abelard on Atonement: 'Nothing Unintelligible, Arbitrary, Illogical, or Immoral about It,'" in *Reasoned Faith*, ed. Eleonore Stump (Ithaca, NY: Cornell University Press, 1993), 281–300. See also Caroline Walker Bynum, "The Power in the Blood: Sacrifice, Satisfaction, and Substitution in Late Medieval Soteriology," in *The Redemption*, ed. Stephen T. Davis, Daniel Kendall, and Gerald O'Collins (Oxford: Oxford University Press, 2004), 177–86.

16. Franks says that for Faustus Socinus, "the death of Christ operates to redeem us in so far as it is an example of obedience, leads us to trust God, and gives us hope of deliverance from punishment" (*Work of Christ*, 366). The major work on the atonement by Socinus is *De Jesu Christo Servatore* (1594). A historical-theological reassessment of Socinus's importance can be found in Alan W. Gomes, "*De Jesu Christo Servatore*: Faustus Socinus on the Satisfaction of Christ," *Westminster Theological Journal* 55 (1993): 209–31.

17. John Hick, *The Metaphor of God Incarnate: Christology in a Pluralist Age* (London: SCM, 1993), 112–33. Another influential modern theological statement of the moral exemplar view sans commitment to religious pluralism can be found in Hastings Rashdall, *The Idea of Atonement in Christian Theology* (London: Macmillan, 1919).

This is not to deny that Christ's atonement is a moral example and act of love. The question is whether the work of Christ is *reducible* to these elements. In my view, it is not. As I have just indicated, something more needs to be said about the nature of Christ's work in order for it to be a work of atonement, although Christ's work certainly includes the components of the moral exemplar doctrine. Here much depends on the theory of punishment one adopts. Defenders of the moral exemplar view reject the idea that retribution—where there must be a moral fit between crime and punishment—is part of the theory of punishment that informs the work of Christ. God is not "wroth with sin"; he is not bound to punish. In fact, in some versions of this theory he is bound not to punish but to forgive sin. All of this stands in stark contrast to the other accounts of atonement canvassed here, which in various ways include retributive punishment as a constituent of divine distributive justice.[18]

The final doctrine of atonement we shall consider is penal substitution. This is the family of views of the atonement according to which Christ's atoning work on the cross consists in his acting as a penal substitute, being punished for that sin in place of the sinner. As I have already intimated, this atonement theory is able to incorporate the core ideas of the other models we have discussed while offering a different understanding of the nature of the atonement.[19] Hence, the advocate of penal substitution can agree that Christ's work is remedial, as per the ransom account. It also includes the concept of satisfaction (of divine moral law). And, in common with the moral exemplar, satisfaction, and ransom doctrines, defenders of penal substitution may speak of Christ's work as providing a moral example in life and death of obedience to the will of God that Christians ought to emulate.

In the theological literature, the relation between Christ's penal substitution for the sinner and the sinner's sin and/or guilt is usually (though

---

18. Swinburne's doctrine means God could set aside divine retribution, though he does not. But saying God may not exact some reparation or satisfaction from humanity for human sin is not the same as saying God cannot exact some reparation or satisfaction from humanity because the very idea that God would act in this way is somehow immoral or beneath the divine dignity. Those moral exemplarists that make this latter claim seem to be committed to a very different understanding of divine justice, according to which Christ's work is about reconciliation but not atonement. See, e.g., Weaver, *Nonviolent Atonement*.

19. This is not a novel idea. In the modern literature, it is discussed in J. I. Packer, "What Did the Cross Achieve? The Logic of Penal Substitution," in *The J. I. Packer Collection*, ed. Alister McGrath (Downers Grove, IL: InterVarsity, 1999), 94–136.

not always) interpreted according to what I shall call a *forensic fiction*.[20] God treats Christ as if he is guilty of the sin of fallen human beings and "punishes" him accordingly, bringing about his death on the cross, which is a suitable act of atonement. God also treats the sinner as if she were sinless in view of Christ's work on the cross, provided the sinner appropriates that work for herself. How that is done is beyond the scope of this chapter. However, the important thing to see here is that on this forensic fiction account of penal substitution, the innocent Christ really is treated as if he were the guilty sinner, though he is not. And God really does punish the innocent in the place of the guilty. Christ is said to "represent" the sinner in his act of atonement.

There are, as the philosopher David Lewis points out, definite analogues to penal substitution in human systems of justice, and in many ways we humans are of two minds about penal substitution, irrespective of whether or not we believe in its theological application.[21] We allow it under certain conditions for certain sorts of crime, where the penal consequences of the crime committed are pecuniary in nature. But we do not allow it when the crime is, say, first-degree murder. In that case, the penal consequences of the crime committed have to be met by the one guilty of the crime, and we would consider it unjust if a substitute were to serve the punishment in place of the perpetrator. Cases of crimes where the penal consequences involved are pecuniary, or monetary, need not be trivial. They can be very serious crimes, such as large-scale fraud, which carry with them crippling financial consequences for the person convicted of that crime. In such circumstances, what is important is that the fine is paid, not that the perpetrator pays it. Someone generous enough might pay the full penalty on behalf of the fraudster if they had the financial wherewithal. The law would be satisfied, even though the perpetrator of the crime has not actually paid the penal consequence set out by the law; a substitute has done so instead. But importantly, we find no examples of legislation allowing substitution when the crime is a serious felony, such as murder. In such cases, the one guilty must meet the penal consequences

---

20. John Murray, *The Imputation of Adam's Sin* (Grand Rapids: Eerdmans, 1959), offers a classic treatment of this. The nineteenth-century Presbyterian theologian Charles Hodge has an idiosyncratic version of the forensic fictional view that is noteworthy. See Charles Hodge, *Systematic Theology*, vol. 2 (Grand Rapids: Eerdmans, 1940).

21. See David Lewis, "Do We Believe in Penal Substitution?," *Philosophical Papers* 26 (1997): 203–9.

of that crime, and we would consider it a terrible miscarriage of justice were a substitute punished in place of the perpetrator.

Hence, there are circumstances in which penal substitution in human jurisprudence is deemed appropriate, while there are others—perhaps more precise analogues to our situation as condemned sinners before God—where it seems that it is not. What the defender of the theological application of penal substitution needs is some reason for thinking that it is just for God to punish Christ in place of the sinner. We need to know why the theological application of the doctrine is morally permissible, as with the case of pecuniary penal substitution outlined by Lewis. For whatever else the defender of penal substitution says, unlike pecuniary penal substitution, it certainly *looks* unjust that Christ, an innocent individual, should be punished in place of me, a sinful individual. This concern goes all the way back to the Socinians of the immediate post-Reformation period and can still be heard today.[22]

The Union Account of Atonement

Nevertheless, I think there is an argument that preserves many of the intuitions motivating penal substitution, yet with a different mechanism for atonement that gets around these difficulties. It is to that argument we now turn. A central plank of the reasoning I will set forth involves appropriating a theological concept called Augustinian realism, deriving from Augustine of Hippo's work on original sin.[23] It is this Augustinian realism that does much of the conceptual heavy lifting for the union account of atonement. Advocates of Augustinian realism claim that original sin includes both the state of moral corruption with which all post-Adam humans are born, which inevitably leads humans into acts of sin, and the culpability aspect of guilt that accrues from Adam's first sin.[24] Both the moral corruption engendered

---

22. Thus Vincent Brümmer: "A theory of penal substitution strikes many of us today as highly immoral since it claims that God punishes the innocent for the transgressions of the guilty" (Brümmer, *Atonement, Christology and the Trinity: Making Sense of Christian Doctrine* [Aldershot, UK: Ashgate, 2005], 75).

23. Despite the fact that this view is called "Augustinian realism," Augustine doesn't have a settled view on the matter. But in certain places in his works he seems to think that all humanity was somehow "seminally present" in Adam. See, e.g., Augustine, *City of God*, trans. Henry Bettenson (Harmondsworth, UK: Penguin, 1972), 13.14. For a theological recapitulation of this view, see Berkhof, *Systematic Theology*, 241–42.

24. A number of Augustinians distinguish between that aspect of guilt which is nontransferable—i.e., "that *Jones* was the one guilty of stabbing Smith"—and the aspect of guilt that

by Adam's primal sin and the culpability aspect of his guilt are transferred, on this way of thinking, from Adam to his progeny. This transfer of Adam's sin and guilt to me is just, provided God somehow organizes things such that Adam and his posterity are one metaphysical entity so that what the first part of that entity does has moral implications for later parts of the same entity.[25] Hence, Adam's sin and guilt, on this view, are (somehow) *really* mine. For this reason, the view is called Augustinian *realism*.

A number of theologians who have defended robust accounts of original sin, including the concept of original guilt, have thought that it makes much more sense to conceive of the transmission of original sin as a question of God imputing Adam's sin and guilt to me, treating me as if I was originally sinful and guilty of Adam's sin, though I am not, strictly speaking (which is, of course, another instance of a theological forensic fiction). But defenders of Augustinian realism usually object that treating someone *as if* they are guilty of a crime is not the same as being guilty of that crime. Moreover, being held culpable for the crime of another, especially another that is removed in time and space from me and whose course of action I did not and could not have approved or otherwise endorsed, is monumentally unjust. Thus, if God imputes the sin and guilt of Adam to me, he acts unjustly. But God cannot act unjustly. Scripture states that God does transmit the sin and guilt of Adam to his progeny (Rom. 5:12–19).[26] So there must be some other account of this transmission that does not have the morally unpalatable consequence of God imputing Adam's sin and guilt to me. And Augustinian realism is such an explanation.[27] (Augustine

---

is transferable, having to do with liability to punishment. As we shall see in a moment, the punishment for a crime might be transferred to a penal substitute, though the person who committed the crime is still the one guilty of perpetrating the crime.

25. In fact, as we shall see, one construal of Augustinian realism is stronger than this. On this stronger view, the transfer of Adam's sin and guilt to me is just, provided God somehow organizes things such that Adam and his posterity are one metaphysical entity *at the moment of primal sin* and only thereafter differentiated into distinct human natures.

26. Note, I am not *endorsing* the view that, according to Paul in Rom. 5:12–19, Adam's sin and guilt are transferred to me. I am just rehearsing a standard, oft-repeated argument. It is well known that this is not an adequate interpretation of the passage. I have dealt with this in passing in "On Original Sin," *International Journal of Systematic Theology* 17, no. 3 (2015): 252–66.

27. The idea that God imputes Adamic sin and/or guilt to Adam's progeny is found in much, though not all, Reformed theology. "Realism" is a somewhat plastic term, having a variety of different applications in the current philosophical literature. But, as I indicate here, Augustinian realism uses the term in a rather different way from current analytical discussions about realism vs. antirealism.

does not put it quite like that, but there are certainly later Augustinian realists who do think in these terms.)[28]

The central Augustinian realist notion that Adam and his progeny are somehow metaphysically united, so that original sin may be justly transmitted from Adam to his posterity, is often conflated with a particular theory about the manner of such transmission. But Augustinian realism is not a thesis that requires a particular account of the exact mechanism by which this transmission occurs. It is simply the theological notion that God ordains such an arrangement between Adam and his progeny. How such a metaphysical arrangement obtains is not the same issue as that it obtains (if it does obtain). Some Augustinian realists claim that the mechanism by which this arrangement obtains involves traducianism. Individual souls are produced by fission or parturition, being generated by the soul of one or both parents as part of the process of natural generation. The parent souls are produced in the same fashion from their parents, and so on, going all the way back through the generations to the first human pair. In which case my soul is literally, though mediately, a chip off the old (Adamic) block; my soul was part of the soul of Adam when he sinned, prior to its being individualized, so to speak, through a process of fission or parturition down through the generations from Adam to me.[29] According to the traducian, it is just for God to punish me for Adam's sin since my soul was part of Adam's soul when it sinned. But an Augustinian realist need not be a traducian, although, as a matter of historical fact, most have been. That is, an Augustinian realist need not be committed to a particular theory of *how* God brings about the distinction between Adam and his progeny while still making the idea of original unity plausible, in order for sin to be justly transmitted from one human being to the other.

Let us now attempt to apply this theologically "realist" thesis about the union of Adam and his progeny in the transmission of original sin to the atonement in order to help make sense of the union between Christ

---

28. A robust defense of the imputation view can be found in Murray, *Imputation of Adam's Sin*. An example of the Augustinian realist view can be found in William G. T. Shedd, *Dogmatic Theology*, 3rd ed., ed. Alan W. Gomes (Philipsburg, NJ: Presbyterian & Reformed, 2003), 434–82; 557–64; 630–31.

29. It would seem that traducians deny a doctrine of the simplicity of souls, according to which souls are, as Roderick Chisholm puts it, "simple substances"—that is, without more basic parts from which they are composed. See Chisholm, "On the Simplicity of the Soul."

and those human beings he saves through his work. In so doing I shall not be concerned with expounding Augustine or his followers, but merely with trying to make sense of a particular construal of Augustinian realism and its application to the work of Christ. This construal avoids the traducian version of Augustinian realism and opts instead for a different, four-dimensionalist account of the "realist" transmission of sin.

We begin with the idea that Adam and his progeny are (somehow) one metaphysical entity, such that God may justly pass on the moral consequences of Adam's sin to his heirs because they are all members of one persisting entity, or object, that we might call *Fallen Humanity*. To be clear, this object is composed only of Adam and his progeny, all of whom are parts or phases in the life of the whole entity.[30] On the sort of view of Fallen Humanity I have in mind, if the first part of the object sins, later parts of the same object (including all of humanity after Adam) have a vitiated moral nature as a result of the action of Adam. It is rather like an acorn that is infected with some disease that then affects all the later stages in the life of the sapling and tree into which it grows.[31]

Of course, it does not follow that just because Adam and his progeny are parts of one persisting object, Adam's progeny share the same morally vitiated condition as Adam. Nor does it follow that just because an acorn is infected with some disease, all the later stages in the life of the tree into which it grows will be affected by this disease. Some diseases might only affect the first phase of the life of the tree rather than all phases of its life. But the sort of reasoning I have in mind is offered as a possible explanation of how original sin is transmitted from one generation to the next from some first human parents. It is true that later phases of the life of a persisting entity may not be affected by what happens in an earlier

---

30. Note that although I am using the term "parts" here and in what follows, I am not concerned to assimilate the particular theological story concerning a realist account of penal substitution with the doctrine of temporal parts, which I take to be a particular metaphysical account of perduring objects. A doctrine of temporal parts is one possible means of underpinning this theological story. But it is not the only means, a matter to which we shall return.

31. On the traditional way of understanding matters, Fallen Humanity has parts that are not "fallen," since Adam prior to his primal sin was unfallen, and Christ does not possess a "fallen" human nature (i.e., a human nature that has original sin), though he is a "Son of Adam." Whether one subscribes to a literal fall or not, it seems that possession of original sin is a contingent property of almost all the parts or phases of the life of Fallen Humanity. Alternatively, Fallen Humanity comprises the phase of Adam's life from his primal sin onward and all other humans born after Adam, except Christ, whose human nature is miraculously preserved from being tainted with original sin.

phase of the same life. But the Augustinian realist story is concerned to make sense of the claim that just such an arrangement does obtain in the case of Adam and his progeny. All that needs to be granted here is that it is possible for a given entity to have phases of its life that are affected by earlier phases of its life, and that all phases of the life of a given persisting entity may be affected by what happens to one of the first parts or phases of that entity. This seems plausible, just as it seems plausible to think that an infected acorn may grow into a tree that is diseased in every subsequent phase of its existence. And this fits with the Augustinian realist story of original sin I am drawing upon.[32]

Still, even if there are diseases that affect the life of the tree in all its phases, the disease afflicting the life of the mature oak is not necessarily the same as the disease affecting the life of the sapling or the acorn. But suppose it is the same disease introduced to the acorn that affects all the later phases of the life of the oak into which it grows. Is the corruption affecting the oak the same as the corruption affecting the acorn? Much depends here on the ontology one adopts. If one thinks persisting objects are wholly present at each moment of their existence, then one might think that this is the same disease. But if one thinks that the acorn and oak are different temporal parts of one perduring four-dimensional whole object, then one has a reason for thinking the disease affecting the oak is not numerically the same as that affecting the acorn. For, presumably, any disease persisting through time has temporal parts, just as the tree it infects has. And the temporal parts of a given thing are said to be numerically distinct. So the fact that on this way of thinking the oak tree does not have numerically the same disease as the sapling does not pose any particular problem that defenders of temporal parts are not already familiar with.

Temporal parts theorists sometimes speak of "tokens" possessed by individual temporal parts of an object, and the property possessed by a whole object. On this way of thinking, the guilt-token of the temporal part of Jones existing now is numerically distinct from the guilt-token of Jones existing a moment ago. Yet both are tokens of the guilt of Jones, the four-dimensional entity who has these temporal parts. The Augustinian realist can claim that the original sin (and perhaps guilt) Jones has transmitted

---

32. Advocates of Augustinian realism often point to Heb. 7:9–10 as evidence that Levi was (somehow) in the loins of Abraham when Abraham paid a tithe to Melchizedek. But it seems to be consistent with other passages of Scripture too, including Rom. 5:12–19 and 1 Cor. 15:22.

to him from the first human is like the example of the guilt-token later temporal parts of Jones share with earlier temporal parts of Jones. God arranges things such that Adam and his progeny are a four-dimensional entity to whom such moral-tokens can be attributed, and the morally vitiated condition Adam incurs post-fall is one that is transmitted to all later phases of the life of this entity, Fallen Humanity.

But this may not be the only metaphysical story consistent with Augustinian realism. Perhaps one can say both that objects that persist through time are normally wholly present at each moment of their existence, and that, in the case of the transmission of original sin, the human species propagates sin through natural generation. Construed along the lines of traducianism, this means that I have Adam's sin (and guilt) because my soul is either a fraction of the soul Adam possessed (if souls are generated through fission) or the product of the soul of at least one of my parents, going all the way back to Adam (if souls are parturient). Though individualized or otherwise brought about through natural generation, I retain the property of original sin that has been passed on to me, as would be the case with inherited physical diseases. The important difference between inherited disease and original sin, on this way of thinking, is that my soul was present when Adam sinned as part of the unindividualized soul that Adam possessed. Or, perhaps, the "seed" of my soul was present in the soul of Adam, if souls are parturient rather than fissiparous (compare Heb. 7:10). So I am guilty of Adam's sin on account of possessing a fraction of Adam's soul, or "seed" thereof, that is now individualized through soul-fission or parturition. But it seems consistent with this theological account of the manner by which sin is transmitted to say that persisting objects are wholly present at each moment of their existence. If this is right, then an Augustinian realist account of the transmission of original sin can be underpinned by more than one metaphysical account of persisting objects, depending on what the Augustinian realist thinks about the mechanism by which sin is transmitted.

This reasoning about an Augustinian realist account of the doctrine of original sin can be applied, the relevant changes having been made, to Christ and those for whose sins he came to atone. Call them, with a nod to the tradition, the elect. Consider the possibility that Christ and the elect together compose one metaphysical entity that persists through time, just as, on the Augustinian realist way of thinking, Adam and his progeny do.

This object we shall dub *Redeemed Humanity*. Christ is in some sense the first member of this entity, and the elect are subsequent members.

But here the analogy between Adam and Christ begins to break down. For, according to the Augustinian realist account of the transmission of sin, Adam as the first human can affect the moral condition of all subsequent humans in a way that any later human being could not (because some earlier humans would already have perished, or be beyond the influence of this later person, or could not be in possession of the whole unindividualized soul that Adam had, or whatever). However, Christ's influence cannot just follow the arrow of time, moving from the moment his atonement is complete to include all those who are elect that exist after that time. Were this the case, then we would have no reason to think that anyone who lived temporally prior to Christ's act of atonement was among the elect. But, of course, Scripture says otherwise, with Hebrews 11 recounting a great cloud of witnesses for the faith in the Old Testament, and Paul in 1 Corinthians 10 speaking of the presence of Christ with the children of Israel wandering in the desert, who drank from the rock (at Meribah) that was Christ. So, a realist account of the atonement must also be able to include within the ambit of salvation those of the elect who lived prior to Christ.

One way of making sense of this[33] would involve co-opting Karl Barth's doctrine of election, or something very like it, as found in *Church Dogmatics* II/2.[34] According to Barth, Christ is the Elect One, and all those for whom Christ's work atones are somehow derivatively elect "in" Christ (which, for present purposes, we shall take to be functionally equivalent to Redeemed Humanity). This solves the problem of those who are derivatively elect and die before Christ by making Christ the "first" among the elect, or, perhaps better, the agent through whom election is derived. (Perhaps he has this place in virtue of being the prototypical image of God after which we are modeled, as we saw in the fourth chapter.) He would not be temporally first among all the derivatively elect, as Adam, on the Augustinian realist account, must be temporally the first human

---

33. Another way of making sense of this would involve using a doctrine of backwards causation. Then Christ's work could backwardsly cause the election of those who lived before him. But I do not really understand backwards causation, and it is a controversial idea anyway. So I shall not pursue this possibility here.

34. Karl Barth, *Church Dogmatics* II/2, ed. G. W. Bromiley and T. F. Torrance (Edinburgh: T&T Clark, 1957).

being for his sin to affect *all* those living after him. Instead, he would be somehow logically or metaphysically prior to the derivatively elect, whose derivative election depends, in some proleptic sense, on Christ's work as the Elect One. A realist version of a Barth-like doctrine of election would also go some way toward explaining the relation between Christ and the derivatively elect, Redeemed Humanity. They are all somehow members of one metaphysical entity, with Christ being metaphysically prior, as it were, to those elect in Christ. Each of the derivatively elect is a part of a larger whole, including Christ. But—and here the Augustinian realism comes to the fore—the punishment due for the sin of the derivatively elect is transferred to Christ, or to that part of Christ on the cross, such that he really does take upon himself the penal consequences of sin for humanity. Although he is not the one who has sinned, or the part of the mass of Redeemed Humanity that has sinned, because he is a member of this larger entity he may pay the consequences for the sin of other members of the same entity, by which I mean the derivatively elect, like you and me.

Conversely, the atoning work of Christ means that the derivatively elect are really united with Christ as parts of one whole entity (Redeemed Humanity). Notice that there is no imputation involved in this process, no forensic fiction, whereby God treats Christ as if he were the sinner for the purpose of bringing about atonement, as with many traditional accounts of penal substitution. The transference of the punishment for sin from Fallen Humanity to Christ and the union of those self-same humans with Christ are two aspects of Christ's atoning work that involve a real union between Christ and the human beings concerned. And, plausibly, this Barth-like doctrine of election could be conjoined with a construal of the nature of the atonement very similar to penal substitution: Christ suffering the penal consequences of my sin.[35] If what has been said so far sketches out how a Barth-like doctrine could tell an internally consistent story about the way in which the punishment due for human sin is transferred to Christ and how sinful human beings may be united to Christ in virtue of his act of atonement such that the nature of Christ's atonement is realist, then what remains to be explained is the manner in which his work brings about atonement.

---

35. Given that this doctrine is only *inspired* by Barth's account rather than being an exposition of it, it does not matter whether it tracks all that Barth himself believed about election and atonement. What matters is that these notions can be fitted together into a coherent whole.

The explanation goes like this. At the cross, Christ has transferred to himself the penal consequences of the sin of the derivatively elect—that is, the derivatively elect members of Redeemed Humanity. At that moment, he takes the penal consequences for which they are guilty, as one part of the larger metaphysical whole. As a result he suffers for that sin. Having made atonement by expiating human sin in his own person, Christ reconciles the members of Redeemed Humanity to God.

A variation on this Barth-like version of realist penal substitution that involves a more traditional Reformed account of election could be applied just as well (I do not suppose these are the only two ways of construing this doctrine).[36] As with the Barth-like version of the doctrine, the key problem is accounting for those among Redeemed Humanity who die prior to Christ's atoning act. A distinction must be maintained between the natural union of Adam and his progeny, in which Adam had to be the first human being in order that his sin might be transferred to the rest of humanity, and the forensic union of Christ and the elect. The forensic nature of the atonement does not require that Christ is chronologically the first human of a new, elect humanity. All it requires is that somehow his atonement is the catalyst by which human sin is atoned for. In this respect, as before, he is metaphysically or logically prior to the other parts of Redeemed Humanity, although many of those who make up Redeemed Humanity live chronologically prior to Christ.

The manner of atonement on this more traditional Reformed account is as follows. Christ on the cross has transferred to himself the penal consequences for the sins of the rest of Redeemed Humanity, and he atones for their sins on the cross. As a consequence of this act, the members of Redeemed Humanity other than Christ, including all those who lived and died prior to the atonement, are reconciled to God.[37] On this view, the important difference between Christ and the elect and Adam and his progeny is that because the relation between Christ on the cross and the

---

36. It may be possible to construct a version of the union account that factors in a doctrine of traducianism. Then Christ has a fraction of Adam's soul that is miraculously cleansed at the moment it is individualized, so to speak. But I shall not outline such a view here, since I am dubious about traducianism.

37. And lest we forget, the problem of Christ being temporally subsequent to some of the elect is a problem common to all accounts of Christ's work that suppose Christ's death is an atonement for sin. He lives before some of his elect and after others, but somehow his death has consequences for all the elect existing at many different moments in time.

elect is a forensic one, Christ is not a part of Redeemed Humanity that is guilty of sin. He is innocent. But he is able to take upon himself the penal consequences of the sin of the elect because he is a part of the same object.[38]

So we have at least two ways in which an Augustinian realist account of the atonement could be set forth, namely, the Barthian and the traditional Reformed versions of the doctrine. Note that although both the Barthian and more traditional Reformed realist versions of the union argument for atonement require that the penal consequences of the sin of the elect are transferred to Christ, they avoid the moral problems besetting standard arguments for penal substitution that require only that Christ acts on behalf of sinful humans as their representative. This is usually called *representationalism*, and it is this argument that requires a forensic fiction in order to make good on the act of atonement. It is this that has generated so many of the difficulties facing apologists for penal substitution. This problem is not so much overcome as circumvented by the realist aspect of the union account offered here, because Christ's act of atonement is not merely representationalist; he really takes upon himself the penal consequences for human sin—hence, a *union* account of atonement. This does not mean that the other members of Redeemed Humanity are no longer guilty of sinning. As many historic theologians have noted, there is a difference between *being the one guilty of committing a sin* and *being the one whose guilt requires punishment for that sin*. My sin can be atoned for, yet I remain the one who committed that sin. It is just that the penal consequences of it have been dealt with so that I am no longer liable to be punished for that sin. (The same is true according to representationalism, of course, *mutatis mutandis*.) But according to the realist element of the union account, these penal consequences of sin are transferable to Christ because he and I are members of one metaphysical whole, Redeemed Humanity.

Earlier, in outlining Augustinian realism, I pointed out that the central theological thesis of this model is consistent with more than one metaphysical story concerning the mechanism by which God transmits

---

38. This could be taken in a more radically realist direction, where Christ is really united with sinners and really becomes guilty for their sin. Then justice is truly being carried out at the cross, exacting punishment for one guilty of the sin of other temporal parts of the same Redeemed Humanity, not wrongfully afflicting the innocent. But this radically realist doctrine does also have the unwelcome consequence that Christ is truly guilty of sin. And that seems theologically untenable. So I shall not pursue this option here.

original sin from Adam to his progeny. But it is difficult to see how the same could be true of the several realist accounts of the union doctrine of atonement just offered. For it looks like the advocate of a version of the union doctrine is committed to some metaphysical story that includes a four-dimensionalist ontology since, as I have set out in the argument above, both Fallen Humanity and Redeemed Humanity are, in some sense, four-dimensional entities. But there are different ways in which one could extrapolate a four-dimensional ontology.[39] All I have said thus far concerning the realist component of the union account of atonement commits its advocates to this sort of ontology. But there is still plenty of scope to argue over how one makes sense of that ontology, and in particular, how it is that the parts or phases in the life of Fallen and Redeemed Humanity are related to one another and to the four-dimensional entity as a whole.

Objections

Now this, I will admit, is strong mead that may be difficult to swallow. But then the problems of the transmission of Adam's sin (and guilt, for those committed to the doctrine of original guilt as well as original sin) and of the transmission of the penal consequences of my sin to Christ are theological difficulties at the heart of the Christian faith that many of the greatest minds in Christendom have struggled to overcome. What I am suggesting is novel in some respects, although not without precedent (Tobias Crisp, John Owen, and even Eusebius of Caesarea use realist-sounding language of the atonement at times).[40] But even if there have been a small number of theologians in the past willing to consider something approaching a realist doctrine of the atonement, or who have made much of the language of "mystical union" between Christ and the believer via the atonement, no one, to my knowledge, has mounted this sort of argument.

---

39. I suppose one could offer a "fictionalist" account of Fallen and Redeemed Humanity, according to which these entities are not real but fictional, or entities that are in some sense merely conventional. But it is difficult to see how this would be an improvement on those forensic fiction accounts of the atonement, according to which Christ represents me and is treated as if he is the one culpable for my sin, though he is not, strictly speaking.

40. See Oliver D. Crisp, *An American Augustinian: Sin and Salvation in the Dogmatic Theology of William G. T. Shedd* (Milton Keynes, UK: Paternoster; Eugene, OR: Wipf & Stock, 2007), 102n7, for references.

One problem with this is that many Christian thinkers are somewhat suspicious of theological novelty, because any articulation of a particular doctrine must conform to Scripture and the tradition. I do not think the doctrine just outlined is contrary to Scripture. In fact, it seems to me to make good sense of Isaiah 53:6, Romans 5:12–19, and 2 Corinthians 5:21 in particular, where union with Christ and the notion of Christ "becoming sin for us" are stressed. But it is true to say that this is not a traditional argument, and that may be a problem. However, if this union account makes better sense of the atonement by offering a different metaphysical underpinning for that doctrine, and a different mechanism for reconciliation that avoids certain problems that beset other traditional models for the atoning work of Christ, then I think it is worthy of serious consideration. After all, our understanding of the truth of the gospel is sometimes mistaken.[41]

In addition to such theological concerns, there are objections of a more philosophical nature that could be raised. One of the most pressing concerns is how an apparently gerrymandered object like Redeemed Humanity can possess moral properties, such as "being sinful" or "having parts that are sinful." It makes sense to think that you or I can be thought of like this, because we are recognizably objects that persist through time (whatever that means). But Redeemed Humanity is not like that. It is an object cobbled together from real persisting or perduring objects—that is, human persons—that seems to lack the integrity and personhood requisite to have such moral properties.

One line of response might be to query whether Fallen and Redeemed Humanity really are the subjects of moral properties, like persons. "Being sinful" looks like a moral property, and one that does not apply to Fallen or Redeemed Humanity as a four-dimensional entity. But is, say, "having temporal parts that are sinful" the sort of property that requires the entity of which it is predicated to be a moral subject? Not obviously. I suggest that Fallen Humanity does not have any moral properties that would require it to be a moral subject, like a person. Though Fallen Humanity is a real object, according to the Barth-like and traditional Reformed versions of the union account, it is not a person, nor a moral subject. Some of its

---

41. Also, like the account of Tim Bayne and Greg Restall in "Participatory Account of the Atonement," the argument offered here does echo concerns about the recovery of language of participation and union that one can find in recent New Testament scholarship.

members have moral properties. But it does not have moral properties that are predicated of it over and above the moral properties of some of its members. And the same is true, *mutatis mutandis*, for Redeemed Humanity.

Still, if this means that some members of Fallen and Redeemed Humanity have moral properties, this might be problematic. Earlier, in explaining how an advocate of Augustinian realism might appropriate a temporal parts construal of a four-dimensionalist ontology, I said it could be that moral properties apply to certain sorts of four-dimensional wholes, like persons, the temporal parts of which have tokens of moral properties. Perhaps this component of a temporal parts doctrine can be applied here as well. Assume Fallen Humanity and Redeemed Humanity are objects that have temporal parts. Some of the temporal parts of these objects are themselves parts of other entities—distinct human agents that are themselves four-dimensional perduring objects that are moral subjects, whose temporal parts may only have tokens of moral properties. Now, Fallen and Redeemed Humanity have human agents as temporal parts, or, perhaps better, as phases (the term "stages" having already been co-opted by another sort of four-dimensionalist, about which more in a moment). But from this it does not necessarily follow that Fallen or Redeemed Humanity as an object has properties that only a moral subject may.

There is another way of understanding a four-dimensionalist ontology that is also of help to the theologian in making sense of the transference of sin from Adam to his progeny and of righteousness from Christ to his elect. This is stage theory.[42] According to the stage theorist, what we have been calling the temporal parts of four-dimensional wholes—but what they call "stages" of four-dimensional entities—*do* have moral properties, and it *does* make sense to say "this stage of a four-dimensional agent is guilty of sinning at such-and-such a time." Stage theorists need not posit entities like Fallen and Redeemed Humanity either. They can tell a story according to which God treats certain stages as one persisting (the technical term is "exduring") entity, or "makes" this the metaphysical truth of the matter. Or perhaps there are certain immanent causal relations between stages of Adam up to his moment of original sin and all his progeny, on the one hand, and of Christ on the cross and all the elect, on the other, which

---

42. For an excellent treatment of this, see Michael C. Rea, "The Metaphysics of Original Sin," in *Persons: Human and Divine*, ed. Peter van Inwagen and Dean Zimmerman (Oxford: Oxford University Press, 2007), 319–56.

corresponds to what I have been calling Fallen and Redeemed Humanity, respectively. But the argument I have offered thus far, which depends on the sort of organic connection between Adam and his progeny and Christ and his elect spoken of by a number of theologians, is not quite the same as this. Perhaps a stage-theoretic account of original sin and union with Christ is preferable to the perdurantist story. For present purposes, three issues need to be made clear: that the four-dimensional ontology assumed in the foregoing argument for the union account of atonement can be construed in at least two ways, namely, a doctrine of temporal parts or a stage theory account; that the temporal parts construal of Fallen and Redeemed Humanity need not end up requiring that these two four-dimensional objects are moral agents of some kind; and that one could take a stage-theoretic account rather than a temporal parts account of these things, making use of the same ontology understood rather differently. Either way, the problem of attributing moral properties to gerrymandered four-dimensional wholes may be avoided.

I have already hinted that the four-dimensional ontology (however this is construed) might be thought to depend on a divine conventionalism, which seems consistent with scriptures such as Romans 9, Malachi 1, and other biblical passages that suggest there is no partiality with God, and even that God's choice does not depend on creaturely actions (e.g., 2 Chron. 19:7; Job 34:19; Luke 20:21; Gal. 2:6; Col. 3:25; etc.). But then it looks like divine convention is doing all the work, which is yet another sort of philosophical objection to a union account of the atonement conjoined with some doctrine of divine conventionalism with respect to God bringing about certain four-dimensional objects. In fact, there are two parts to this objection, which might be put like this: Couldn't God bring about something like the union account of atonement, or an Augustinian realist account of the transfer of original sin from Adam to his progeny, by divine convention and without a doctrine of temporal parts or stage theory? And couldn't something much more like the commonsense view I mentioned earlier have purchase here if God simply ordains that a realist atonement and/or a realist account of the transfer of original sin obtains?

We have already answered the first of these questions in the affirmative: there are several ways of construing the four-dimensional ontology that underpins the versions of the union account we have set forth. The argument will need to be tweaked depending on which construal of this ontology one opts for. But I am much more dubious about using a different ontology to make sense of the union account, such as that presupposed by the commonsense position, according to which persisting objects are wholly present at each moment of their existence. The obvious way forward for a commonsense way of thinking about these things is to say that God imputes Adam's sin to me and my sin to Christ. But it should be clear that such a way of thinking about these matters is mired in real moral difficulties, having to do with the very idea of imputing sin from one person to another, which implies a sort of moral and/or legal fiction that appears unjust. If it is said that divine conventionalism means God may treat any two persons or their parts as related in certain sorts of ways—even certain sorts of moral ways—as he sees fit, this seems to me to be divine conventionalism run amok. It is no part of the version of the union account outlined thus far that there are no morally relevant similarities between the temporal parts that make up Fallen or Redeemed Humanity. Nor is it any part of this doctrine that God may simply gerrymander temporal parts willy-nilly.[43] For I suppose that God acts in accordance with his divine character, doing that which seems to him most fitting.

There is much more to be said about the atonement. What I have set out here is one theological story that connects the atonement with the doctrine of original sin in a way that involves a somewhat novel use of Augustinian realism but remains faithful, I think, to those passages in Scripture wherein the union between Adam and his progeny, on the one hand, and Christ and his elect, on the other, are treated. I have tried to indicate some of its virtues, not the least of which is that on this view we can say with the apostle that "as by one man's disobedience many were *made* sinners, so also by one man's obedience many will be *made* righteous" (Rom. 5:19 NKJV, emphasis added).

---

43. This worry is not idle. Jonathan Edwards seems to suggest God may do exactly this in *Original Sin*, vol. 3 of *The Works of Jonathan Edwards*, ed. Clyde A. Holbrook (New Haven: Yale University Press, 1970), §IV.III.

8

The Spirit's Role in Union with Christ

> This is the wonderful exchange which, out of his measureless benevolence, he has made with us; that, becoming Son of man with us, he has made us sons of God with him; that, by his descent to earth, he has prepared an ascent to heaven for us; that, by taking on our mortality, he has conferred his immortality upon us; that, by accepting our weakness, he has strengthened us by his power; that, receiving our poverty into himself, he has transferred his wealth to us; that, taking the weight of our iniquity upon himself (which oppressed us), he has clothed us with his righteousness.
>
> —John Calvin[1]

Following on from the union account of atonement set forth in the previous chapter, this chapter offers a dogmatic sketch of the Holy Spirit's role in uniting us to Christ that draws on the Reformed tradition in particular. If the question that framed the previous chapter was "How does the atonement bring about human salvation?," the question that frames this chapter is "How does the Holy Spirit unite us to Christ in a way commensurate with the union account of atonement set out in the previous chapter?" To begin with, we shall set out some important preliminary issues pertaining

---

1. Calvin, *Institutes* 4.17.2.

to the doctrine of the person and work of the Holy Spirit. Then we shall focus on the notion of union with Christ.

Pneumatological Preliminaries

Usually, doctrinal discussion of the Holy Spirit divides the topic into two halves. There is discussion of the person of the Spirit as a member of the Holy Trinity, and an account is usually also given of the work of the Holy Spirit in the economy of creation and salvation. However, this division of pneumatology may also go some way to explaining why it is that the Reformed contribution to this dogma has often been regarded as rather thin. For, on the one hand, discussion of the person of the Holy Spirit properly belongs to the dogma of the Holy Trinity. But, on the other hand, discussion of the work of the Spirit is parceled out to several different doctrinal *loci*, including the doctrines of creation, providence, and salvation (soteriology), as well as (for some theologians) Christology. In fact, if we were to look closely, we could find aspects of the work of the Spirit scattered across almost every topic in Reformed theology. The reason is not hard to find: the Spirit is that member of the Trinity whose work has to do with the execution of various divine functions in the economy of creation and salvation. But he does this without drawing attention to himself. He is, as has often been observed, the quiet member of the Trinity that goes about his work of creation, conservation, salvation, and consummation without fanfare and sometimes without us even noticing his presence in the creation or in the life of the church.

So the first thing to say about a Reformed account of pneumatology relevant to the topic of this chapter is that we should not mistake the absence of an elaborate discussion of the person and work of the Spirit as a distinct theological topic in systematic theology with the absence of a serious theological engagement with pneumatology. This is not a new insight. In his Warfield Lectures on pneumatology in 1964, the Dutch Reformed theologian Hendrikus Berkhof noted that "the Spirit constantly leads our attention away from himself to Jesus Christ. So he hides himself, on the one hand, in Christ; and, on the other hand, he hides himself in his operations in the life of the church and the lives of individuals."[2] We

---

2. Hendrikus Berkhof, *The Doctrine of the Holy Spirit*, The Annie Kinkead Warfield Lectures 1963–1964 (Richmond: John Knox, 1964), 10.

shall see that this is certainly true of Reformed accounts of the work of the Spirit.

A second preliminary comment follows on the heels of the foregoing. Discussion of the person and work of the Spirit involves drawing out issues connected to other doctrines, locating his work within the larger context of other theological topics. So, discussion of the person of the Spirit must be drawn from the broader attempt to give account of the Holy Trinity as part of the doctrine of God. The work of the Spirit must be gleaned from his activity in creation, providence, soteriology, and eschatology. The same is not true of, say, the person and work of Christ. Christology is a separate topic in systematic theology, and for good reason. The person of Christ is God the Son, and his work is the redemption of fallen humanity. We encounter the flesh-and-blood Jesus of Nazareth in the canonical Gospels and extrapolate from these accounts views about who Jesus is and what he was about. We do not have to look hard to find questions about who Jesus is and what it is that he accomplished; these are matters that lie, as it were, close to the surface of the text. We do have to look harder to find a developed pneumatology, just as we have to look harder to find a doctrine of the Trinity. At least part of the reason for this is that these two dogmas are not as *immediately* apparent to readers of the New Testament.

The Person of the Holy Spirit

Let us begin with consideration of the person of the Spirit. The catholic creeds provide us with the basic dogmatic framework. The Nicene-Constantinopolitan Creed says, "I believe in the Holy Ghost, the Lord and Giver of Life; who proceeds from the Father and the Son; who with the Father and the Son together is worshiped and glorified; who spoke by the prophets." As is well known, the *filioque* clause expressed in the words "who proceeds from the Father *and the Son [ex patre et filioque procedit]*" was added unilaterally to the Nicene symbol by the Western church and was a cause of the Great Schism in AD 1054. I do not intend to comment on this, except to say that what is dogmatically nonnegotiable here: that the *filioque* was intended to underscore (whether rightly or wrongly) the full divinity of the Third Person of the Trinity. This was reinforced by the Second Council of Constantinople in AD 553, whose canons include the following solemn anathema:

If anyone does not confess that the Father and the Son and the Holy Spirit are one nature or essence, one power or authority, worshipped as a Trinity of the same essence, one deity in three hypostases or persons, let him be anathema. For there is one God and Father, of whom are all things, and one Lord Jesus Christ, through whom are all things, and one Holy Spirit, in whom are all things.[3]

This statement of Nicene trinitarianism is reiterated by the Reformed confessions. Take, for instance, the Heidelberg Catechism (1563). It says this:

Question 53. What do you believe concerning the "Holy Spirit"?
Answer: First, that, with the Father and the Son, he is equally eternal God; second, that God's Spirit is also given to me, preparing me through a true faith to share in Christ and all his benefits, that he comforts me and will abide with me forever.[4]

Similarly, Article 11 of the Belgic Confession of 1561 states,

We believe and confess also that the Holy Spirit proceeds eternally from the Father and the Son—neither made, nor created, nor begotten, but only proceeding from the two of them. In regard to order, the Spirit is the third person of the Trinity—of one and the same essence, and majesty, and glory, with the Father and the Son, being true and eternal God, as the Holy Scriptures teach us.[5]

The Second Helvetic Confession (1566) provides a sophisticated account of the Trinity, including an endorsement of the *filioque* in the following terms:

Notwithstanding we believe and teach that the same immense, one and indivisible God is in person inseparably and without confusion distinguished as Father, Son and Holy Spirit so, as the Father has begotten the Son from eternity, the Son is begotten by an ineffable generation, and the Holy Spirit

---

3. The text of this first canon can be found in Leith, *Creeds of the Churches*, 46.
4. The entire text of the Catechism can be found in *The Constitution of the Presbyterian Church (U.S.A.), Part I: The Book of Confessions* (Louisville: Office of the General Assembly, 2004), ch. 3, 5.016, p. 56.
5. This translation by the Christian Reformed Church is available online at http://www.crcna.org/sites/default/files/BelgicConfession_2.pdf.

truly proceeds from them both, and the same from eternity and is to be worshipped with both.[6]

Similar words can be found in the second chapter of the Westminster Confession:

> In the unity of the Godhead there be three Persons of one substance, power, and eternity: God the Father, God the Son, and God the Holy Ghost. The Father is of none, neither begotten nor proceeding; the Son is eternally begotten of the Father; the Holy Ghost eternally proceeding from the Father and the Son.[7]

The upshot of this sampling of symbolic material is clear enough: the Reformed confessions uphold and elaborate upon a basically Western, catholic view of the Godhead, in which the Holy Spirit is regarded as a constituent member, fully divine, personal, and proceeding from the Father and the Son. He is the comforter and the divine agent that unites us to Christ.

For present purposes I have little to add to this dogmatic deposit about the person of the Holy Spirit. This is not because I think this unimportant, but because I think that we are not in a position to say a great deal about the divine nature beyond what we find set forth for us in the catholic creeds and Reformed confessions, as they reflect the teaching of Scripture. God's inner life is hidden from us (Exod. 33:18–23; Deut. 29:29; 1 John 4:12). We do not have access to it because God has revealed very little about himself (that is, about his divine nature) to us. This is true even if we take the incarnation into account, as any adequate Christian theology must (John 1:18). So what we can say with confidence about the divine life is rather slim. The psalmist says that "He parted the heavens and came down; dark clouds were under his feet." What is more, "He made darkness his covering, his canopy around him—the dark rain clouds of the sky. Out of the brightness of his presence clouds advanced, with hailstones and bolts of lightning" (Ps. 18:9–12 NIV). The correlation of God's activity with various meteorological phenomena is obvious. Yet surely there is something here suggestive of what Pseudo-Dionysius the Areopagite called "the brilliant

---

6. This translation of the text of the Second Helvetic Confession can be found in *The Book of Confessions*, ch. 3, 5.016, p. 56.

7. Ibid., 6.013, p. 124.

darkness of God."[8] We cannot penetrate the darkness of God's mysterious presence in order to ascertain the intricacies of his divine life. This is because we stand on the creaturely side of the great chasm that separates God from everything else; without divine revelation we can know little about our Creator, and almost nothing salvific. Nevertheless, God reveals himself to us in Scripture and the economy of salvation. We can glean from these economic functions something of the life of God—that is, something of the immanent relations that exist between the divine persons. But our grasp of such things is piecemeal, fragmentary, partial, and fallible and is not something into which (as Calvin would put it) we should pry.

A dim analogy: We cannot know the inner workings of the mind of anyone but ourselves. Yet we can glean from what we are able to see of a person, in what they communicate to us of themselves, in their gestures and expressions, something of their inner life. Nevertheless, our understanding of such things is bound to be piecemeal, fragmentary, partial, and fallible—even in the case of a person we know well. *Mutatis mutandis*, we have only our fallible and fallen experience, and the testimony of those who committed into words the revelation of Scripture, to guide us in our understanding of the divine nature.

Well, what *can* we say about the person of the Spirit then? That he is fully divine, being the Third Person of the Trinity; that he is to be worshiped together with the Father and the Son; that he is the Lord, the Giver of Life, the Comforter, the Paraclete—in short, that he has a special responsibility for the application of salvation to creatures.

Some modern Reformed thinkers have argued that the classical, orthodox dogma of the Holy Spirit is erroneous because he is not a distinct divine person in the Godhead. On this view, the ascription of personhood to the Spirit of God is a later dogmatic development that does not reflect the earliest apostolic witness. Biblical passages cited in support of this include the farewell discourse in the Fourth Gospel:

> And I will ask the Father, and he will give you another advocate to help you and be with you forever—the Spirit of truth. The world cannot accept him, because it neither sees him nor knows him. But you know him, for he lives with you and will be in you. *I will not leave you as orphans; I will come to*

---

8. Pseudo-Dionysius, *The Mystical Theology*, ch. 1, in *Pseudo-Dionysius: The Complete Works*, trans. Colm Luibheid (Mahwah, NJ: Paulist Press, 1987), 135.

you. Before long, the world will not see me anymore, but you will see me. (John 14:16–19a NIV, emphasis added)

Similar ideas can be found in the theology of the apostle Paul. In 2 Corinthians 3:17–18 he writes, "Now *the Lord is the Spirit*, and where the Spirit of the Lord is, there is freedom. And we all, who with unveiled faces contemplate the Lord's glory, are being transformed into his image with ever-increasing glory, which comes from *the Lord, who is the Spirit*" (NIV, emphasis added). Passages like these are said to imply Christ *becomes* the Spirit upon his ascension; or, alternatively, they are evidence that the Spirit is not a distinct divine person at all, but merely a mode of the presence of God in the creation. A clear example of this view in modern Reformed theology is the aforementioned Hendrikus Berkhof, who writes, "Christ and the Spirit are identical . . . the Spirit is Christ in action." He goes on to say, "The Spirit in Scripture is not an autonomous substance, but a predicate to the substance God and to the substance Christ. It describes the fact and the way of functioning of both."[9]

But this is hopeless. For one thing, it involves biblical cherry-picking, so to speak. The beginning of the Johannine passage just quoted clearly states that God will give the disciples "*another* advocate" to help and be with them forever, which Christ calls "the Spirit of truth." Only by strangling the text could you make of this "other" a predicate of a divine person. But, second, in making this sort of appeal, Berkhof sets himself against his own tradition. He becomes a latter-day disciple of the patristic *pneumatomachoi*, the "fighters against the Spirit" that denied the deity of the Third Person of the Trinity and subordinated, or even assimilated, the Holy Spirit to Christ. In his later work on the subject, Berkhof goes beyond this, claiming that there is one event in God that pertains to two persons, the divine Father and his human representative, the Son, between whom the Spirit acts as a bond—yet not as a divine person: he is God's action in history, who creates Jesus and is in turn sent by Jesus in order to bring about salvation.[10]

---

9. Berkhof, *Doctrine of the Holy Spirit*, 25–26 and 28, respectively.

10. See Hendrikus Berkhof, *The Christian Faith: An Introduction to the Study of the Faith*, trans. Sierd Woudstra (Grand Rapids: Eerdmans, 1979), 326 and 331. In the latter passage he writes, "The Father is the divine partner, the Son the human representative, the Spirit the bond between them and therefore the bond between the Son and the sons whom he draws to the Father." He goes on to say, "May we then call the Spirit a person? No, if thereby we put

In repudiating the catholic doctrine of the person of the Spirit, Berkhof thinks he is able to appeal to both the New Testament authors and the early patristic witness, against which the later symbolic material is pitted. Traditions may be wrong, of course. But the claim to be a Reformed theologian surely implies a positive and constructive relationship to that theological tradition and its confessions, even if it is not a slavish one. (Reformed theology does pride itself on being reformed and always reforming itself according to the Word of God, after all.) Yet in this fundamental dogmatic matter at least, Berkhof sets himself against both the Reformed confessionalism of his forebears as well as the catholic faith more generally. For if the Spirit is a predicate of Christ, or merely a mode of the presence of God in history, not a divine person at all, one is left without an orthodox doctrine of the Trinity.[11] That is an uncomfortable place in which to practice dogmatic theology. It is also, I think, an untenable position for someone who self-identifies with the Reformed tradition, given its essentially confessional nature. One cannot claim to stand within a particular theological tradition while repudiating fundamental tenets of the tradition.[12]

The Work of the Holy Spirit

With this in mind, we segue from the person of the Spirit to his work. Here, two theological principles will guide us. The first of these is that

---

him separately beside the person of God. Yes, if we understand that this name expresses the personhood of God in its outward action." As Moltmann observes, this is tantamount to unitarianism (see Jürgen Moltmann, *The Spirit of Life: A Universal Affirmation*, trans. Margaret Kohl [Minneapolis: Fortress, 1993], 13).

11. At the beginning of his treatment of pneumatology, Moltmann says that the Holy Spirit "is not a characteristic of God's being. It is a *mode of his presence* in his creation and in human history" (*Spirit of Life*, 11 [emphasis original]). It is unfortunate that he chooses "mode" here, given its associations with less-than-personal views of the members of the Godhead. I take it that by "mode" he does not mean to connote the modality or manner of God's presence (as per Berkhof, whom he criticizes on this point) but rather his way of being as a third divine person. God has three "ways of being," three "modes" (to borrow the phrase used by Karl Rahner and Barth, with which Moltmann is decidedly unhappy!), and these are to be identified with divine persons, not predicates.

12. Objection: Isn't the union account of atonement just such a rejection of much traditional teaching on the atonement? Answer: yes and no. Yes, it is novel in some respects; but no, it does not attempt to introduce ideas that are not found in much traditional atonement theology. What it does is supply a novel mechanism for atonement and a novel metaphysical story in which the doctrine of atonement is embedded. But the mechanism and story can be found piecemeal in the work of other theologians.

"the external works of the Trinity are indivisible, the distinction and order of the persons being preserved" (*opera trinitatis ad extra sunt indivisa servato discrimine et ordine personarum*). The second is that "what is first in intention is last in application."[13]

As to the first of these, which we shall call *the Trinitarian Appropriation Principle* (TAP), it safeguards two important theological claims relevant to our discussion of pneumatology. The first is that the external works of God—that is, his works in creation and the economy of salvation—are all works of the Trinity. The twentieth-century Swiss Reformed divine Emil Brunner denies this. He claims, "There are works of the Father, which are most certainly not the works of the Son. For the Scriptures never speak of the 'works of wrath' of Christ, but only of the wrath of God."[14] For this reason, he says, caution should be exercised in using the TAP without what he calls the "Augustinian Clause," namely, the latter part of the principle, which speaks of "the distinction and order of the persons being preserved."[15]

There are divine works that are the preserve of particular divine persons—that much is surely right. The Father creates; the Son redeems; the Spirit regenerates. But if Brunner means to suggest that there are external works of the Trinity that belong to one, and only one, of the divine persons, *all things considered*, then that seems to be mistaken. In fact, the TAP can only be construed along the lines he suggests if one misunderstands its import. For the TAP is actually a means by which we can hold onto the indivisibility of the Trinity while also making room, so to speak, for the particular works of the divine persons in the economy of creation and salvation. We can put it like this: all the external works of God are indivisible. All his external works are triune works involving all three divine persons. Yet for the most part these works devolve upon a particular member of the Trinity (which is the second theological claim derived from the TAP that is relevant to pneumatology). Thus, for instance, creation is often thought of as the work of the Father. However, Genesis 1:2 has traditionally been

---

13. This can be found in Aquinas, e.g., *Summa Theologiae* I-II, q. 1, a. 1, ad. 1: "Ad primum ergo dicendum quod finis, etsi sit postremus in executione, est tamen primus in intentione agentis. Et hoc modo habet rationem causae." Kathryn Tanner makes good use of the principle in her account of Barth's doctrine of creation. See Tanner, "Creation and Providence," in *The Cambridge Companion to Karl Barth*, ed. John Webster (Cambridge: Cambridge University Press, 2000), 114.

14. Emil Brunner, *Dogmatics, Vol. 1: The Christian Doctrine of God*, trans. Olive Wyon (London: Lutterworth, 1949), 234.

15. Ibid.

thought to connote the Spirit's role of brooding over the deep,[16] and the Prologue to the Fourth Gospel tells us that through the Word of God all things were made and that nothing was made without his agency (John 1:3). So it transpires that the work of creation is triune, even though it is traditionally thought to be God (the Father) who says in the beginning, "Let there be light!" The same goes for all other divine works in creation, the relevant changes having been made. Even the incarnation, which is the work of the Son, is commanded by the Father and brought about by the agency of the Spirit in the virginal conception and in his empowering of Christ in his ministry from his baptism onwards.

Applied to pneumatology, we can say this: the Spirit is at work everywhere, at all times, in all places, and in particular ways in the action of creation, conservation, redemption, and the consummation of all things. He is at work in this way as a member of the Godhead because all the divine persons are at work in this manner, though their particular roles in any given work may differ. What is more, there are works that terminate upon the Spirit in particular, or are associated with him, such as the virginal conception of Christ and the application of redemption to the believer. However, one of the reasons the universality of the Spirit's work is sometimes overlooked is that the TAP is not taken with sufficient metaphysical seriousness. He is not merely at work in certain divine actions and not others. Necessarily, he is involved in every divine action in creation.

What, then, of our second principle? Let us call it *the Intention-Application Principle* (IAP). It is related to the TAP in the following way. What God ordains must surely come to pass according to his good pleasure and will, as the writer of Ephesians reminds us (Eph. 1:5). Nevertheless, there is an order to what God ordains. Even if this is not a temporal ordering, it is a conceptual or logical ordering. I may make a "to do" list and put down one thing after another, one thing at a time. We do not suppose God does that. He does not *take time* to ponder his options—at least not according to the traditional, confessional Reformed theology, which is our focus here. Instead, God eternally ordains all that takes place in the created order, from beginning to end. But what he first intends, what is logically or conceptually first in his ordered list, is what will obtain last in time. Suppose you go on a journey. Your ultimate goal (your final destination)

---

16. Assuming one translates *ruach* in Gen. 1:2 as connoting a divine person, the Spirit, rather than as an impersonal breath or wind.

is your first intention. But it is the last thing your action brings about because it can only be reached once the other components of the event have been successfully executed, such as the distance that must be traversed in order to reach the destination.

The IAP makes the claim that God intends his ultimate goal in creation first as well. This ultimate end is variously described, depending on the theologian you are reading. However, in common with several Reformed theologians and with a number of theologians in other Christian traditions, I want to suggest that the ultimate end of God in creation is union with his creatures.[17] This is a peculiar work of the Holy Spirit. For it is the Spirit who is particularly responsible for the regeneration of fallen human beings, the union of believers to Christ, and the transformation of the creation at the end of the age (Rom. 8:22–27), all of which are subordinate ends to the ultimate end of union with God. Although this IAP is a triune work, as TAP would lead us to expect, it is also a work that has an important, indeed fundamental, pneumatological dimension.

Union with God in Christ

It is to this fundamental pneumatological work of uniting creatures to God that I want to turn in the final constructive phase of this chapter, building upon the work of the previous chapter in elucidating the atonement. In the course of this reasoning, I will offer a brief account of the union in question here. There are two things to say about this union by way of preamble. The first is that there is a renewed interest among theologians, including Reformed theologians, in the notion of union with Christ. This is the recovery of a doctrine that had to some extent dropped out of discussion, but the recovery is most welcome, not least because of its ecumenical implications. What I say here builds on much of this recent work, although my particular account is slightly different from many others, for reasons I shall go into in a moment.[18] The second thing to say

---

17. This candidate for the ultimate end of God in creation does not necessarily instrumentalize creatures as, arguably, Jonathan Edwards does in his great work on the subject, "Concerning the End for Which God Created the World," which can be found in *Ethical Writings*.

18. Recent important treatments of union with Christ from Reformed theologians that are germane to my argument here include J. Todd Billings, *Calvin, Participation, and the Gift: The Activity of Believers in Union with Christ*, Changing Paradigms in Historical and Systematic Theology (Oxford: Oxford University Press, 2007); Billings, *Union with Christ: Reframing*

about this doctrine is that although it is only one of several important external works of the Trinity traditionally associated with the agency of the Spirit, this is, I think, the fundamental motif by means of which we can explain almost all the other activities particularly associated with him that fall under the topic of the economy of salvation. By this I mean that other aspects of the Spirit's work in the redemption and reconciliation of fallen creatures can be understood as in some way connected to or implied by this more fundamental theological motif. Although I won't be able to fully demonstrate this in a short chapter like this one, I will offer some indication of what I mean by this at the conclusion of my argument. In particular, I will intimate how this notion of union makes sense of one of the practical, liturgical works of the Spirit—namely, his work in the sacraments.[19]

Union with Christ is an important doctrine in much historic Reformed theology. For example, in his *Institutes of the Christian Religion*, Calvin says, "First, we must understand that as long as Christ remains outside of us, and we are separated from him, all that he has suffered and done for the salvation of the human race remains useless and of no value for us." Moreover, "the Holy Spirit is the bond by which Christ effectually unites us to himself." He goes on to say, "By the grace and power of the same Spirit we are made his members"—that is, the members of Christ with whom we are mystically united.[20]

Theology and Ministry for the Church (Grand Rapids: Baker Academic, 2011); Julie Canlis, *Calvin's Ladder: A Spiritual Theology of Ascent and Ascension* (Grand Rapids: Eerdmans, 2010); William B. Evans, *Imputation and Impartation: Union with Christ in American Reformed Theology*, Studies in Christian History and Thought (Milton Keynes, UK: Paternoster; Eugene, OR: Wipf & Stock, 2007); Mark A. Garcia, *Life in Christ: Union with Christ and Twofold Grace in Calvin's Theology*, Studies in Christian History and Thought (Milton Keynes, UK: Paternoster; Eugene, OR: Wipf & Stock, 2008); Myk Habets and Robert Grow, eds., *Evangelical Calvinism: Essays Resourcing the Continuing Reformation of the Church* (Eugene, OR: Pickwick, 2012); Michael S. Horton, *Covenant and Salvation: Union with Christ* (Louisville: Westminster John Knox, 2007); Marcus Peter Johnson, *One with Christ: An Evangelical Theology of Salvation* (Wheaton: Crossway, 2013); Robert Letham, *Union with Christ: In Scripture, History, and Theology* (Phillipsburg, NJ: Presbyterian and Reformed, 2011); and Carl Mosser, "The Greatest Possible Blessing: Calvin on Deification," *Scottish Journal of Theology* 55, no. 1 (2002): 36–57. The wider literature on the topic is growing apace.

19. We have already seen how the motif of union has implications for the doctrines of original sin and the atonement. An argument that has interesting parallels to that offered here can be found in Marcus Peter Johnson, "'The Highest Degree of Importance': Union with Christ and Soteriology," in *Evangelical Calvinism: Essays Resourcing the Continuing Reformation of the Church*, ed. Myk Habets and Robert Grow (Eugene, OR: Pickwick, 2012).

20. Calvin, *Institutes* 3.1.1 and 3.1.3, respectively.

Yet union with Christ is also a very broad doctrine, one that bundles together a number of discrete components, including but not comprising the work of the Spirit. The Scottish Reformed divine John Murray, in his classic treatment of the atonement, writes,

> Union with Christ is really the central truth of the whole doctrine of salvation not only in its application but also in its once-for-all accomplishment in the finished work of Christ. Indeed the whole process of salvation has its origins in the one phase of union with Christ and salvation has in view the realization of other phases of union with Christ.[21]

Although the doctrine bears the name union with *Christ*, it should be tolerably clear that the agent who brings about this union is the Third Person of the Trinity. Thus, uniting us to Christ is part of the larger trinitarian work of union with God that terminates upon the Holy Spirit.

Recall that what is first in divine intention is last in application—our second theological principle, the IAP. Suppose that God's first intention is union with his creatures. Not long ago this would have been thought an Orthodox, not a Reformed, doctrine. However, one of the most interesting developments in recent work on soteriology has been the recovery of "Western" forms of theosis,[22] including that of the great evangelical theologian Jonathan Edwards. He speaks of our union with God in Christ in the following terms: "If strictness of union to God be viewed as thus infinitely exalted; then the creature must be regarded as infinitely, nearly and closely united to God."[23] What is more,

> If by reason of the strictness of the union of a man and his family, their interest may be looked upon as one, how much more one is the interest of

---

21. John Murray, *Redemption Accomplished and Applied* (Edinburgh: Banner of Truth, 1965), 161.
22. For a helpful treatment of the convergence between Reformed and Orthodox accounts of theosis, see Horton, *Covenant and Salvation*, ch. 12.
23. Edwards, "Concerning the End for Which God Created the World," in *Ethical Writings*, 535. Edwards is not the only Reformed theologian who held to a version of theosis. But his doctrine is one of the more pronounced versions of it in the Reformed tradition. This is true, although he never uses the term "theosis" in his writings. See, e.g., Oliver D. Crisp, *Jonathan Edwards on God and Creation* (New York: Oxford University Press, 2012), ch. 8; Kyle Strobel, "Jonathan Edwards and the Polemics of *Theosis*," *Harvard Theological Review* 105, no. 3 (2012): 259–79; and Michael J. McClymond, "Salvation as Divinization: Jonathan Edwards, Gregory Palamas, and the Theological Uses of Neoplatonism," in *Jonathan Edwards: Philosophical Theologian*, ed. Paul Helm and Oliver D. Crisp (Aldershot, UK: Ashgate, 2003), 139–60.

Christ and his church (whose first union in heaven is unspeakably more perfect and exalted, than that of an earthly father and his family), if they be considered with regard to their eternal and increasing union! Doubtless it may justly be esteemed as so much one that it may be supposed to be aimed at and sought, not with a distinct and separate, but an undivided respect.[24]

If the ultimate end of God's work in creation is an "infinitely strict" union with his creatures, as Edwards puts it, then this is a work that is everlasting. For, as he goes on to point out, there will never come a time, either in this world or the next, at which we can say that we have become completely united to God through Christ. No, this is a work that, like a mathematical asymptote, continues on into eternity. We are to be ever more closely united to God in Christ by the power of the Holy Spirit, yet without ever losing ourselves in God, without ever (as Edwards puts it) being "godded with God."[25] Thus, our union with God in Christ that the Spirit brings about is a journey into God that has no end; it is an ever-closer participation in the divine life.[26] The Spirit unites us to God in Christ in "infinite strictness," yet not so that we lose our identity, becoming "part" of God as a drop of water becomes part of the ocean into which it is poured. To use a distinction Edwards does not (but that is consistent with what he does say), in theosis we creatures are invited to participate in the divine life but not the divine essence. Union does not imply fusion.

Now, God ordains this world. He ordains a world where human beings fall into sin and Christ is required to bring about human reconciliation with an estranged God. Does God ordain union with himself, as the destiny of his creatures, logically prior to his decision to create this world? That is, is the work of the Spirit in uniting us to Christ contingent upon his decision to create a world where human beings rebel against God and need to be reunited to him by means of the work of Christ? In short, does the Spirit's work depend on the need for an incarnation? My own view is that even if

---

24. Ibid.
25. Jonathan Edwards, *Religious Affections*, vol. 2 of *The Works of Jonathan Edwards*, ed. Paul Ramsey (New Haven: Yale University Press, 1959), 203.
26. Johnson claims that "deification" has unhelpful connotations of losing oneself in the divine that "theosis" does not (*One with Christ*, 50–51). However, I am not clear that this is a sustainable distinction. In their helpful work on the topic, Stephen Finlan and Vladimir Kharlamov argue that the terms "deification," "divinization," and "theosis" are synonyms and should be treated accordingly. See the introduction to Finlan and Kharlamov, eds., *Theosis: Deification in Christian Theology* (Eugene, OR: Pickwick, 2006).

God had created a world where sin never occurred, the unfallen creatures that inhabited it would still need the work of the Spirit to unite them to God. Such a union is not natural to us; it requires a special divine action. The nearest analogue in the New Testament is that of marriage. But even when discussing the sexual union of a man and woman as a correlate to the union between Christ and the church, the author of Ephesians has to admit that the comparison is inadequate. The union between us and Christ, brought about by the agency of the Spirit, is deeper and closer than even the most intimate physical union here on earth, though we know not how to express it (Eph. 5:25–32). I also think that our union with God would require an incarnation independent of any putative fall of human beings.[27] As we saw in chapter 4, Christ, the God-man, is the image of the invisible God and the one in whose image we are formed as image-bearers. We image God as we image Christ. And we image Christ as we are conformed to his image by the work of the Holy Spirit uniting us to him.

How then does the Spirit unite believers to Christ? This is where things get interesting. Often at this juncture, Reformed theologians gesture toward the mystical union between Christ and the believer. This is a real union, perhaps, but not one that we can really fathom—rather like the doctrine of a real but noncorporeal presence of Christ in the Eucharist proposed by Calvin, who frankly admits that he has no notion of exactly how the Spirit unites the believer to Christ in partaking of the elements.[28] The English Puritan John Owen is a good example of a defender of this mystical union with Christ. He writes, "Although they [Christ and his church] are not one in respect of personal unity, they are, however, one—that is, one body in mystical union, yea, one mystical Christ—namely, the surety is the head, those represented by him the members."[29]

---

27. I argue this at greater length in Crisp, "Incarnation without the Fall," forthcoming in *Journal of Reformed Theology* (2016).

28. "Now, should any one ask me as to the mode, I will not be ashamed to confess that it is too high a mystery either for my mind to comprehend or my words to express; and to speak more plainly, I rather feel than understand it. The truth of God, therefore, in which I can safely rest, I here embrace without controversy. He declares that his flesh is the meat, his blood the drink, of my soul; I give my soul to him to be fed with such food. In his sacred Supper he bids me take, eat, and drink his body and blood under the symbols of bread and wine. I have no doubt that he will truly give and I receive. Only, I reject the absurdities which appear to be unworthy of the heavenly majesty of Christ, and are inconsistent with the reality of his human nature" (Calvin, *Institutes* 4.17.31).

29. John Owen, *A Dissertation on Divine Justice*, in *The Works of John Owen, Vol. X*, ed. William H. Goold (Edinburgh: Banner of Truth, 1967), 598.

However, what if we take the notion of a real union between Christ and the church, brought about by the work of the Spirit, with full metaphysical seriousness, as we did when examining the atonement? That is, what if the Spirit really and truly unites us to Christ so that we are, in some carefully circumscribed sense, one entity with him? Other Reformed thinkers have wondered the same thing in the past. Take the Mercersburg divine John Williamson Nevin. At one point in his work *The Mystical Presence*, he writes, "Strange, that any who hold to the Augustinian view of Adam's organic union with his posterity, as the only basis that can properly support the doctrine of original sin, should not feel the necessity of a like organic union with Christ, as the indispensable condition of an interest in his salvation."[30] Perhaps we can sketch an answer to Nevin's suggestive question, drawing on organic analogies similar to those used in the previous chapter, when the atonement was the focus of attention.

Suppose, then, that we think of the church on analogy with an organism once again—say, a great oak tree. It is a living, growing thing that can be damaged and stunted and that can flourish and develop. The church grows from a seed, namely, Christ. He is that principle without which the church would not exist. The church is an outgrowth of the work of Christ; it is the product of Christ's redemptive action. As more are added to the church, so the organism that Christ has founded enlarges. Some parts of the organism may be in better shape than others. And at some points in the life of the organism, it may have suffered setbacks, periods of slow or no growth, even events that led to the withering or removal of certain branches. But it continues to grow nonetheless under the watchful eye of the gardener. To be a member of this organism or body is to be joined to it, to be a part of it, a constituent. Just as a tree has a lifespan, different phases to that life, different stages of growth and development, so does the church. But unlike the organism, our union with Christ does not mean that the redeemed are numerically identical with Christ.

Again, Edwards comes to our aid. He conceives of the union between Christ and his elect as the union between the parts of a whole, rather like the union account of atonement set forth in the last chapter.[31] We are parts

---

30. John Williamson Nevin, *The Mystical Presence: A Vindication of the Reformed or Calvinistic Doctrine of the Holy Eucharist* (Philadelphia: J. B. Lippincott and Co., 1846), 212.

31. Here I am thinking of his famous discussion of four-dimensionalism in *Original Sin*, IV.III. For a fascinating discussion of this in relation to his doctrine of atonement, see S. Mark

of Christ rather like the stages in the life of the tree are parts of the one whole lifespan across time, from its planting to its withering. As the tree has different physical parts (trunk, branches, leaves, and so on) and different phases to its life (shoot, sapling, mature tree), so also we are "parts" of Christ scattered across space and time—one four-dimensional entity with Christ as its head. The Spirit's work on this way of thinking is vital. It is as if the Spirit acts as a kind of adhesive, preparing and enabling the human subject to be joined to the body of Christ. Like the glue that holds together a composite object that is made up of different parts, such as a piece of furniture or some other artifact, so the Spirit "glues" us to Christ. We become part of his body really and truly—as really and truly as the foam, wood, tacks, fabric, and glue form the one composite object that is an armchair.[32] But, of course, the union he brings about is much more than the gluing together of disparate parts into a composite whole. His work is personal, intimate, the real union of one organism with another, the bringing about of a new whole that is the body of Christ. We might say that just as the Holy Spirit generates and prepares Christ's human body at the incarnation, so he generates and prepares Christ's bride, his ecclesiastical body, which in one sense will be complete at the inauguration of the eschaton, when God's ultimate end in creation will be accomplished and creaturely participation in the divine life begins in earnest.

I said I would indicate at the end of my argument how this fundamental soteriological work of union with God, with which the Spirit is particularly associated, has implications for other areas of doctrine that depend upon it in some sense. Let me close the constructive section of this chapter by

---

Hamilton, "Jonathan Edwards on the Atonement," *International Journal of Systematic Theology* 15, no. 4 (2013): 394–415. For discussion of the metaphysics of Edwards's position, see Oliver D. Crisp, *Jonathan Edwards and the Metaphysics of Sin* (Aldershot, UK: Ashgate, 2005), and Rea, "Metaphysics of Original Sin."

32. Cf. the great Puritan divine William Ames. He writes,
> The relationship is so intimate that not only is Christ the church's and the church Christ's, Song of Solomon 2:16, but Christ is *in* the church and the church *in* him, John 15:4; 1 John 3:24. Therefore, the church is *mystically* called Christ, 1 Corinthians 12:12, and the Fullness of Christ, Ephesians 1:23. The church is metaphorically called the bride and Christ the bridegroom; the church a city and Christ the king; the church a house and Christ the householder; the church the branches and Christ the vine; and finally the church a body and Christ the head. But these comparisons signify not only the union and communion between Christ and the church but also the relation showing Christ to be the beginning of all honor, life, power, and perfection in the church. *This church is mystically one*, not in a generic sense, but *as a unique species or individual*—for it has no species in the true sense. (*The Marrow of Theology*, trans. John Dykstra Eusden [Grand Rapids: Baker, 1968], 176–77)

doing that. (Here, I have in mind doctrines other than those included in previous chapters of this study, such as the image of God and the atonement.) A leitmotif in Calvin's theology is the distinction between what is offered and what is received.[33] The Spirit is offered to us in salvation. By his agency we may be united to God through Christ. But much depends on whether we receive that which is offered. Something similar obtains in the eucharistic teaching of those Reformed theologians who look to Geneva rather than to Zurich for their sacramental theology. The Spirit unites us to Christ so that in the Lord's Supper we may be nourished by the real presence of Christ in the bread and wine. On this way of thinking, eucharistic presence is not a corporeal presence. It is a real, mystical presence nonetheless. Not only does the Spirit act in this manner in the Eucharist, thereby ensuring that believers commune with Christ. His sacramental action divides those who truly receive that which is offered in the eucharistic elements from those that do not. In other words, we understand what goes on in the Eucharist, that central liturgical Christian mystery, by reference to the more fundamental work of union the Spirit brings about, not vice versa. When we understand something of the Spirit's action in uniting us to God in Christ, and when we see its eschatological import (being the first fruits, as it were, of that final union of "infinite strictness" with Christ), then the Eucharist makes sense. It is a means by which the believer who is already united to Christ by the Spirit is inwardly nourished in her faith by the same Spirit, in anticipation of the stricter union between believer and Christ that will obtain at the end of the age. Here too participation in the divine life is what is in view. The Eucharist becomes a sort of foretaste and reminder of the union that awaits us in Christ, a union that is generated, fostered, and sustained by the agency of the Holy Spirit.

The Upshot

This completes the constructive pneumatological argument of this chapter; it is time to take stock. First, I reasoned that by adopting two widely

---

33. See, e.g., David Steinmetz, "Calvin and the Natural Knowledge of God," in *Calvin in Context* (New York: Oxford University Press, 1995), 32. There he writes, "In short, Calvin draws a distinction between what is offered and received that becomes a guiding principle of his thought, even outside the context of natural theology." In particular, Steinmetz notes the application of this principle to his eucharistic theology.

accepted theological principles, we see that (a) the external work of the Spirit is always in concert with the other members of the Godhead, and (b) that his peculiar work is bound up with God's first intention to be united to his creatures. The charisms of the Spirit (including the so-called charismata, which are not the only charisms known in Scripture or tradition) are, it seems to me, yet another indication of this work of the Spirit. We might say that they are visible indications of his secret work in the hearts of fallen humans as he reconciles them to God through Christ. But, as Jonathan Edwards has pointed out at length and in detail, these and other extraordinary physical manifestations in liturgical contexts are no reliable indication of a true work of the Spirit of God.[34] That must be sought elsewhere. Indeed, that must be sought in the place that we have located them—namely, in the heart, where a person is united by the Spirit to God through Christ.

If chapter 7 is right, then in one important sense those who are numbered among the elect are already united to Christ as parts of one metaphysical whole ordained by God. Nevertheless, the secret work of the Spirit brings those numbered among Redeemed Humanity into what we might call a union of hearts with Christ,[35] which is a union that is grounded in Christ's objective work for us and made epistemically real to us by the inward working of the Holy Spirit. It is this role that the Spirit plays in reconciliation, one that is of a piece with the union account of atonement. Yet this raises a question about the nature and scope of union with Christ. This is the subject of the next, and last, chapter.

---

34. Edwards, *Religious Affections*.
35. The notion of a "union of hearts" is stolen from S. Mark Hamilton's recent discussion of Jonathan Edwards's doctrine of atonement in "Jonathan Edwards on the Atonement," 405.

9

The Nature and Scope of Union with Christ

Are the elect "in Christ" simply by virtue of being human (ontology) or because they have somehow become beneficiaries of his life and work (soteriology)?

—Kevin J. Vanhoozer[1]

Hitherto, our discussion about union with Christ has generated the following sort of account: Christ is the eternally begotten Son Incarnate, the Word enfleshed, an essentially incorporeal being that has assumed a human nature that includes a corporeal body. He is also the prototypical human being in whose image we are all created. He is the one entity in whom humanity and divinity are united *personally* as parts of one composite whole that comprises Christ. Because he unites a human and a divine nature in one person, human beings are in principle capable

---

1. Kevin J. Vanhoozer, "The Origin of Paul's Soteriology: Election, Incarnation, and Union with Christ in Ephesians 1:4 (with Special Reference to Evangelical Calvinism)," in *Reconsidering the Relationship between Biblical and Systematic Theology in the New Testament: Essays by Theologians and New Testament Scholars*, ed. Benjamin E. Reynolds, Brian Lugioyo, and Kevin J. Vanhoozer (Tübingen: Mohr Siebeck, 2014), 182.

of being united to God in Christ by means of the secret working of the Holy Spirit, who joins believers to Christ. Those so united are members of Christ in a real, metaphysical sense; they are "parts" of Redeemed Humanity.

However, perceptive readers will have noticed a potential ambiguity in this account, which reflects a debate in recent Reformed theology about the scope and nature of union with Christ. The ambiguity can be expressed in this way: Is union with Christ something that obtains *in virtue of Christ's work—that is, his incarnation and atonement*—or is it something that obtains *in virtue of faith in Christ*?[2] It might be thought that the argument about the divine image in the fourth chapter, coupled with the union account of atonement outlined in the seventh chapter, favor the first of these options. Although the final chapter on union with Christ via the secret working of the Holy Spirit suggests that any union of hearts (as I put it there) requires the work of the Spirit, it looks like this is a *merely* epistemological requirement. The elect—that is, those who are members of Redeemed Humanity—are in one sense already united to Christ, who has acted in their place in atonement. In which case it appears that the work of the Spirit is a matter of making those that are already members of Redeemed Humanity aware of that membership. This too points in the direction of the notion that union with Christ obtains in virtue of his work in incarnation and atonement, not in virtue of faith.

However, although the work of the Spirit in uniting the elect to Christ is indeed a matter of making those who are members of Redeemed Humanity aware of the fact that Christ has atoned for their sin, this is not the whole of the Spirit's remit in this matter. To put this less gnomically, God ordains the salvation of Redeemed Humanity in eternity and then brings about the reconciliation of Redeemed Humanity by Christ's atoning work, a work that is then effectually applied to the elect in time by the secret work of the Holy Spirit. In a previous study I argued that God may ordain the justification of the elect eternally via the work of Christ, though this is actualized, as it were, at particular moments in history through the secret work of the Holy Spirit. This view I designated *justification from eternity*, the view according to which

---

2. Vanhoozer is asking a similar question in his pointed critique of Evangelical Calvinism, "Origin of Paul's Soteriology," 182.

the act of eternal justification is in one sense incomplete at the moment God ordains the justification of the elect in eternity. Although God has decreed that certain persons will be elect and justified in and through the work of Christ, this must be actualized in time through the secret work of the Holy Spirit in the hearts of the elect. As the Westminster Confession puts it, the Spirit must "apply Christ unto them" that are elect, in due time so that there appear to be two phases or aspects to the eternal decision of God to justify the elect. The first aspect is the eternal decree (the eternal "moment" of formal justification); the second aspect is the bringing about of God's eternal purpose in the justification of the elect at a particular moment in time (the temporal moment of material justification).[3]

This justification from eternity view can be elaborated in numbered propositions, as follows:

1. God eternally decrees the number of the elect (that is, Redeemed Humanity).
2. God eternally decrees that Christ is the mediator of salvation.
3. Christ is the ground of election (given that God the Son, the divine person who voluntarily assumes human nature, is a member of the divine Trinity) and the means by which election is brought about as the Elect One and mediator of our election.
4. God knows all those who are elect (that is, all the members of Redeemed Humanity).
5. God knows that all the elect (that is, members of Redeemed Humanity, other than Christ) will be saved through the work of Christ as mediator.
6. God knows that all the elect will be justified through the work of Christ by God's divine grace alone, according to God's divine will and purpose (Eph. 1:5).
7. It is eternally true that the members of Redeemed Humanity (other than Christ) are justified by Christ's meritorious work alone (not by their own merit).

3. Oliver D. Crisp, *Deviant Calvinism: Broadening Reformed Theology* (Minneapolis: Fortress, 2014), 45. I refer interested readers to the elaboration of justification from eternity in ch. 2 of *Deviant Calvinism*.

8. The secret work of the Holy Spirit applies the benefits of Christ's work to each individual member of the elect.
9. This application normally obtains by means of the gift of faith, bestowed on the elect individual by the Holy Spirit, uniting that individual to Christ.[4]
10. The application of faith to the elect individual completes the eternal act of justification; justification is an eternal act of divine grace that obtains in time at the very moment in which the Holy Spirit applies the benefits of Christ to the individual.
11. The application of faith to the elect individual enables that person to understand that she is included within the ambit of divine election and that she is justified.
12. The application of faith to the elect individual brings about an epistemic change to the person concerned.
13. The application of faith also brings about a moral and (perhaps) a legal change in the elect individual.[5]

Now, this doctrine of justification from eternity should not be conflated with union with Christ, though there is considerable conceptual overlap between them. We might say that justification from eternity concerns the God's-eye view of salvation from the perspective of the eternal decrees of God, whereas union with Christ concerns the particular outworking of God's plan of salvation in history, through the work of Christ and the Holy Spirit in atonement and salvation, respectively. However, if we augment what has been said in the foregoing chapters about union with Christ in atonement and its application by the work of the Spirit with the understanding of justification from eternity outlined here,[6] then I think we can avoid the worry that the doctrine of union with Christ elaborated upon in the pages of this study collapses union with Christ brought about by means of his work with the union brought about by the agency of the Spirit. (We might call this *Vanhoozer's Worry*, since it is a variation on a theme brought to my attention by Vanhoozer's essay, cited as the epigraph to this chapter.)

---

4. The caveat "normally" provides some wiggle room for those who may be elect and members of Redeemed Humanity, but who are incapable of exercising faith, e.g., the severely mentally impaired and infants who die before the age of maturity.

5. Adapted from *Deviant Calvinism*, 51–53.

6. And given in more detail in *Deviant Calvinism*, ch. 2.

Why should we be exercised about this apparently rather arcane theological distinction? Because it has rather far-reaching theological consequences that have been the subject of some dispute in recent Reformed theology. According to the Evangelical Calvinists, who take their cue from the work of the great twentieth-century Scottish theologian Thomas Torrance, union with Christ is an ontological matter.[7] We are united to Christ because of the incarnation. More specifically, all human beings (other than Christ) are united to Christ in virtue of his act of assuming human nature. By taking on human nature, God the Son unites himself to a particular entity (a human being), but in so doing brings about the healing of humanity in general. Torrance refers to this as Christ's "vicarious humanity." There appear to be patristic roots to this sort of view. As Benjamin Myers has recently observed, "The view that humanity is essentially one—that there is a universal human nature in which individuals participate—is so widely taken for granted in early Christianity that it is seldom discussed or defended."[8] Torrance takes up this theme when he says, "In the incarnation the eternal Son assumed human nature into oneness with himself but in that assumption Jesus Christ is not only real man but *a* man. He is at once the *One* and the *Many*."[9]

However, as Vanhoozer points out (and he is not alone in making this distinction), if union with Christ obtains via the incarnation, then it looks like all humanity is united to Christ ontologically. The idea is something like this: Christ's assumption of human nature is both particular (i.e., the assumption of the particular human nature of Jesus of Nazareth) and universal (i.e., the assumption of the universal human nature common to all humanity). Because of this, Christ can (somehow) heal all human natures (other than his own) by means of his incarnation. Union with Christ is said to obtain *because* of this assumption of human nature in Christ.[10] As Vanhoozer puts it, "Classical Calvinists associate being chosen in Christ with the Spirit's uniting people to Christ

---

7. See, e.g., the essays in Habets and Grow, *Evangelical Calvinism*.
8. Myers, "Patristic Atonement Model," 94.
9. T. F. Torrance, *The Christian Doctrine of God: One Being, Three Persons* (London: T&T Clark, 1996), 161.
10. Admittedly, the means by which the act of incarnation brings about the healing of human nature in general (i.e., the human natures of all human beings) is still not terribly clear on this characterization, though I think it does represent the sort of reasoning to be found among these Evangelical Calvinist writers indebted to Torrance.

through faith, whereas Evangelical Calvinists [following Torrance's lead] associate being chosen in Christ with the Son's assumption of humanity in the Incarnation."[11]

As should be apparent from the foregoing, this study owes an important debt to the Barth-inspired trajectory in modern theology that finds its apogee in the theology of Torrance. However, whatever the merits or shortcomings of the Evangelical Calvinist account of union with Christ, it should now also be clear that the account set forth here is similar to much traditional Reformed thought, and different from Evangelical Calvinism in important respects. We have seen that, in the case of the divine image, human beings are made so that *in principle* they may participate in life with God by being united to Christ. However, since this image is marred through sin, it must be restored through the secret work of the Holy Spirit in reconciled human beings. Then we noted that in the atonement, Redeemed Humanity together with Christ are "parts" of one four-dimensional whole, so that by means of their incorporation into Christ, he may act in their place, bringing about reconciliation with God. But this atoning act is only efficacious for the elect. Finally, there is the union that obtains through the secret work of the Holy Spirit in the members of Redeemed Humanity, awakening them to their salvation and bringing about in history (so to speak) the actualization of God's purposes in election and justification ordained before the foundation of the world, in what I have called justification from eternity. However, this change brought about by the Spirit's agency is more than a merely epistemological change; it is a moral and legal change too. We might say that it is the means by which the members of Redeemed Humanity are brought into the fullness of salvation that has been obtained by the work of Christ, supremely in his atonement. Like a royal pardon that is issued earlier than the time at which it is served upon the subject in prison, on this way of thinking the Spirit's work applies the action of Christ in the incarnation and atonement to the individual. Whereas the subject was pardoned *in principle* by means of Christ's work, that must be applied *in fact* and in time. This is the work of the Spirit, and this is why his work in uniting us to Christ is so important.[12]

---

11. Vanhoozer, "Origin of Paul's Soteriology," 191.
12. See my *Deviant Calvinism*, 53. Note that in the analogy of the royal pardon, the change that obtains when the pardon is received by the subject is more than merely epistemic: he is only

For these reasons it should be clear that, whatever other shortcomings it may have, the argument set forth in these pages does not fall foul of Vanhoozer's Worry. Union with Christ is brought about by the work of Christ and actualized in history via the agency of the Holy Spirit.

---

released from prison at that moment, though he was in principle pardoned from the moment it was issued. My point is that the same is true, the relevant changes having been made, with respect to the work of Christ and the application of that work by the Spirit.

Bibliography

Adams, Marilyn McCord. *Christ and Horrors*. Cambridge: Cambridge University Press, 2006.

———. *What Sort of Human Nature? Medieval Philosophy and the Systematics of Christology*. The Aquinas Lecture of 1999. Milwaukee: Marquette University Press, 1999.

Allen, Michael, and Scott R. Swain. *Reformed Catholicity: The Promise of Retrieval for Theology and Biblical Interpretation*. Grand Rapids: Baker Academic, 2015.

Ames, William. *The Marrow of Theology*. Translated by John Dykstra Eusden. Grand Rapids: Baker, 1968.

Anderson, James. *Paradox in Christian Theology: An Analysis of Its Presence, Character, and Epistemic Status*. Milton Keynes, UK: Paternoster, 2007.

Anselm of Canterbury. *Anselm: Basic Writings*. Translated by Thomas Williams. Indianapolis: Hackett, 2007.

———. *Anselm of Canterbury: The Major Works*. Edited by Brian Davies and Gillian Evans. Oxford: Oxford University Press, 1998.

———. *The Complete Philosophical and Theological Treatises of Anselm of Canterbury*. Translated by Jasper Hopkins and Herbert Richardson. Minneapolis: Banning, 2000.

Aquinas, Thomas. *Summa Contra Gentiles Book IV: Salvation*. Translated by Charles J. O'Neil. Notre Dame, IN: University of Notre Dame Press, 1975.

———. *Summa Theologica*. Translated by Brothers of the English Dominican Province. New York: Benziger Brothers, 1948.

Athanasius. *De Synodis*. Edited by Philip Schaff and Henry Wace. *Nicene and Post-Nicene Fathers*, Second Series, Vol. 4. Peabody, MA: Hendrickson, 1994.

———. *On the Incarnation*. Translated by A Religious of C.S.M.V. Crestwood, NY: St. Vladimir's Seminary Press, 2003.

Augustine. *City of God*. Translated by Henry Bettenson. Harmondsworth, UK: Penguin, 1972.

———. *Confessions*. Translated by Henry Chadwick. Oxford: Oxford University Press, 1992.

Aulén, Gustav. *Christus Victor*. London: SPCK, 1931.

Ayres, Lewis. *Nicaea and Its Legacy: An Approach to Fourth-Century Trinitarian Theology*. Oxford: Oxford University Press, 2004.

Baker, Mark D., and Joel B. Green. *Recovering the Scandal of the Cross: Atonement in New Testament and Contemporary Contexts*. 2nd ed. Downers Grove, IL: IVP Academic, 2011.

Barth, Karl. *Church Dogmatics* II/2. Edited by G. W. Bromiley and T. F. Torrance. Edinburgh: T&T Clark, 1957.

Bauckham, Richard. *Jesus and the God of Israel: God Crucified and Other Studies on the New Testament's Christology of Divine Identity*. Grand Rapids: Eerdmans, 2008.

Bayne, Tim, and Greg Restall. "A Participatory Account of the Atonement." In *New Waves in Philosophy of Religion*, edited by Yujin Nagasawa and Eric J. Wielenberg, 150–66. Houndmills, UK: Palgrave Macmillan, 2009.

Berkhof, Hendrikus. *The Christian Faith: An Introduction to the Study of the Faith*. Translated by Sierd Woudstra. Grand Rapids: Eerdmans, 1979.

———. *The Doctrine of the Holy Spirit*. The Annie Kinkead Warfield Lectures 1963–1964. Richmond: John Knox, 1964.

Berkhof, Louis. *Systematic Theology*. Edinburgh: Banner of Truth, 1988.

Billings, J. Todd. *Calvin, Participation, and the Gift: The Activity of Believers in Union with Christ*. Changing Paradigms in Historical and Systematic Theology. Oxford: Oxford University Press, 2007.

———. *Union with Christ: Reframing Theology and Ministry for the Church*. Grand Rapids: Baker Academic, 2011.

Brinks, C. L. "On Nails, Scissors, and Toothbrushes: Responding to the Philosophers' Critiques of Historical Biblical Criticism." *Religious Studies* 48, no. 1 (2013): 1–20.

Brümmer, Vincent. *Atonement, Christology and the Trinity: Making Sense of Christian Doctrine*. Aldershot, UK: Ashgate, 2005.

Brunner, Emil. *Dogmatics, Vol. 1: The Christian Doctrine of God*. Translated by Olive Wyon. London: Lutterworth, 1949.

Bultmann, Rudolf. "New Testament and Mythology." Reprinted in *New Testament and Mythology and Other Basic Writings*, edited and translated by Schubert M. Ogden, 1–43. Minneapolis: Fortress, 1984.

Buschart, W. David, and Kent D. Eilers. *Theology as Retrieval: Retrieving the Past, Renewing the Church*. Downers Grove, IL: IVP Academic, 2015.

Bynum, Caroline Walker. "The Power in the Blood: Sacrifice, Satisfaction, and Substitution in Late Medieval Soteriology." In *The Redemption*, edited by Stephen T. Davis, Daniel Kendall, and Gerald O'Collins, 177–86. Oxford: Oxford University Press, 2004.

Calvin, John. *Institutes of the Christian Religion*. Edited by John T. McNeill. Translated by Ford Lewis Battles. Philadelphia: Westminster, 1960.

Campbell, Constantine R. *Paul and Union with Christ*. Grand Rapids: Zondervan, 2012.

Canlis, Julie. *Calvin's Ladder: A Spiritual Theology of Ascent and Ascension*. Grand Rapids: Eerdmans, 2010.

The Catechism of the Catholic Church. http://www.vatican.va/archive/ccc_css/archive/catechism/p3s1c1a1.htm.

Chisholm, Roderick W. "On the Simplicity of the Soul." In *Philosophical Perspectives*. Vol. 5, *Philosophy of Religion*, edited by James Tomberlin, 157–81. Aterscadero, CA: Ridgeview, 1991.

Christensen, Michael J., and Jeffrey A. Wittung, eds. *Partakers of the Divine Nature: The History and Development of Deification in the Christian Traditions*. Grand Rapids: Baker Academic, 2008.

Coakley, Sarah. "What Does Chalcedon Solve and What Does It Not? Some Reflections on the Status and Meaning of the Chalcedonian 'Definition.'" In Davis, Kendall, and O'Collins, *The Incarnation*, 143–63.

The Constitution of the Presbyterian Church (U.S.A.), Part I: The Book of Confessions. Louisville: Office of the General Assembly, 2004.

Cooper, John W. *Panentheism: The Other God of the Philosophers; From Plato to the Present*. Grand Rapids: Baker Academic, 2006.

Corcoran, Kevin. *Rethinking Human Nature: A Christian Materialist Alternative to the Soul*. Grand Rapids: Baker Academic, 2006.

Crisp, Oliver D. *An American Augustinian: Sin and Salvation in the Dogmatic Theology of William G. T. Shedd*. Milton Keynes, UK: Paternoster; Eugene, OR: Wipf & Stock, 2007.

———. *Deviant Calvinism: Broadening Reformed Theology*. Minneapolis: Fortress, 2014.

———. "Divine Retribution: A Defense." *Sophia* 42 (2003): 35–52.

———. *Divinity and Humanity: The Incarnation Reconsidered*. Cambridge: Cambridge University Press, 2007.

———. *God Incarnate: Explorations in Christology*. London: T&T Clark, 2009.

———. "Incarnation without the Fall." *Journal of Reformed Theology* (forthcoming, 2016).

———. "Is Ransom Enough?" *Journal of Analytic Theology* 3 (2015): 1–11.

———. *Jonathan Edwards and the Metaphysics of Sin*. Aldershot, UK: Ashgate, 2005.

———. *Jonathan Edwards on God and Creation*. New York: Oxford University Press, 2012.

———. "On Original Sin." *International Journal of Systematic Theology* 17, no. 3 (2015): 252–66.

———. "On the Orthodoxy of Jonathan Edwards." *Scottish Journal of Theology* 67, no. 3 (2014): 304–22.

———. *Revisioning Christology: Theology in the Reformed Tradition*. Aldershot, UK: Ashgate, 2011.

Crisp, Oliver D., and Fred Sanders, eds. *Locating Atonement: Explorations in Constructive Dogmatics*. Grand Rapids: Zondervan, 2015.

Cross, F. L., and E. A. Livingstone, eds. *The Oxford Dictionary of the Christian Church*. 3rd ed. New York: Oxford University Press, 1997.

Cross, Richard. "The Incarnation." In *The Oxford Handbook to Philosophical Theology*, edited by Thomas P. Flint and Michael C. Rea, 452–75. Oxford: Oxford University Press, 2009.

———. *The Metaphysics of the Incarnation: Thomas Aquinas to Duns Scotus*. Oxford: Oxford University Press, 2002.

———. "Two Models of the Trinity?" *Heythrop Journal* 43, no. 3 (2002): 275–94.

Daley, Brian. "Nature and the 'Mode of Union': Late Patristic Models for the Personal Unity of Christ." In Davis, Kendall, and O'Collins, *The Incarnation*, 164–96.

Davis, Stephen T., Daniel Kendall, and Gerald O'Collins, eds. *The Incarnation*. Oxford: Oxford University Press, 2002.

DeWeese, Garrett J. "One Person, Two Natures: Two Metaphysical Models of the Incarnation." In Sanders and Issler, *Jesus in Trinitarian Perspective*, 114–53.

Dyrness, William. "The *Imago Dei* and Christian Aesthetics." *Journal of the Evangelical Theological Society* 15, no. 3 (1972): 161–72.

Edwards, Jonathan. "Concerning the End for Which God Created the World." In *Ethical Writings*. Vol. 8 of *The Works of Jonathan Edwards*. Edited by Paul Ramsey. New Haven: Yale University Press, 1989.

———. *Original Sin*. Vol. 3 of *The Works of Jonathan Edwards*. Edited by Clyde A. Holbrook. New Haven: Yale University Press, 1970.

———. *Religious Affections*. Vol. 2 of *The Works of Jonathan Edwards*. Edited by Paul Ramsey. New Haven: Yale University Press, 1959.

———. *Sermons and Discourses, 1734–1738*. Vol. 19 of *The Works of Jonathan Edwards*. Edited by M. X. Lesser. New Haven: Yale University Press, 2001.

Emory, Gilles. *The Trinitarian Theology of Thomas Aquinas*. Translated by Francesca Murphy. Oxford: Oxford University Press, 2007.

Enns, Peter. *The Evolution of Adam: What the Bible Does and Doesn't Say about Human Origins*. Grand Rapids: Brazos, 2012.

Evans, William B. *Imputation and Impartation: Union with Christ in American Reformed Theology*. Studies in Christian History and Thought. Milton Keynes, UK: Paternoster; Eugene, OR: Wipf & Stock, 2007.

Farris, Joshua R. "An Immaterial Substance View: Imago Dei in Creation and Redemption." *Heythrop Journal* (forthcoming).

Farris, Joshua R., S. Mark Hamilton, and James S. Spiegel, eds. *Idealism and Christian Theology*. Idealism and Christianity 1. London: Bloomsbury, 2016.

Fergusson, David. "Creation." In *The Oxford Handbook of Systematic Theology*, edited by John Webster, Kathryn Tanner, and Iain Torrance, 72–90. Oxford: Oxford University Press, 2009.

Finlan, Stephen, and Vladimir Kharlamov, eds. *Theosis: Deification in Christian Theology*. Eugene, OR: Pickwick, 2006.

Flint, Thomas P. "A Puzzle concerning the Mereological Model of the Incarnation." Unpublished manuscript.

Franks, R. S. *The Work of Christ*. Edinburgh: Thomas Nelson and Sons, 1962.

Freddoso, Alfred J. "Human Nature, Potency and the Incarnation." *Faith and Philosophy* 3, no. 1 (1986): 27–53.

Garcia, Mark A. *Life in Christ: Union with Christ and Twofold Grace in Calvin's Theology*. Studies in Christian History and Thought. Milton Keynes, UK: Paternoster; Eugene, OR: Wipf & Stock, 2008.

Geach, Peter. *Reference and Generality*. 3rd ed. Ithaca, NY: Cornell University Press, 1980.

Giles, Kevin. *The Eternal Generation of the Son: Maintaining Orthodoxy in Trinitarian Theology*. Downers Grove, IL: IVP Academic, 2012.

Gomes, Alan W. "*De Jesu Christo Servatore:* Faustus Socinus on the Satisfaction of Christ." *Westminster Theological Journal* 55 (1993): 209–31.

Gorman, Michael. "Christological Consistency and the Reduplicative Qua." *Journal of Analytic Theology* 2 (2014): 86–100.

Gorman, Michael J. *The Death of the Messiah and the Birth of the New Covenant: A (Not So) New Model of the Atonement.* Eugene, OR: Cascade, 2014.

Gunton, Colin E. *The Actuality of Atonement: A Study of Metaphor, Rationality, and the Christian Tradition.* London: T&T Clark, 1988.

Habets, Myk, and Robert Grow, eds. *Evangelical Calvinism: Essays Resourcing the Continuing Reformation of the Church.* Eugene, OR: Pickwick, 2012.

Hamilton, S. Mark. "Jonathan Edwards, Anselmic Satisfaction and Moral Government." *International Journal of Systematic Theology* 17, no. 1 (2015): 46–67.

———. "Jonathan Edwards on the Atonement." *International Journal of Systematic Theology* 15, no. 4 (2013): 394–415.

Harrison, Mark McLeod. "On Being the Literal Image of God." *Journal of Analytic Theology* 2 (2014): 140–59.

Harrison, Nonna Verna. "The Human Person as Image and Likeness of God." In *The Cambridge Companion to Orthodox Christian Theology*, edited by Mary B. Cunningham and Elizabeth Theokritoff, 78–92. Cambridge: Cambridge University Press, 2008.

Hector, Kevin. *Theology without Metaphysics: God, Language, and the Spirit of Recognition.* Cambridge: Cambridge University Press, 2011.

Helm, Paul. "Eternal Creation." *Tyndale Bulletin* 45, no. 2 (1994): 321–38.

———. *Eternal God: A Study of God without Time.* 2nd ed. Oxford: Oxford University Press, 2010.

———. "Eternity." *Stanford Encyclopedia of Philosophy*, http://plato.stanford.edu/entries/eternity/.

———. *Faith and Understanding.* Edinburgh: Edinburgh University Press, 1997.

———. "Of God, and of the Holy Trinity." *Churchman* 115, no. 4 (2001): 350–57.

Hick, John. *The Metaphor of God Incarnate: Christology in a Pluralist Age.* London: SCM, 1993.

Hight, Marc A., and Joshua Bohannon. "The Son More Visible: Immaterialism and the Incarnation." *Modern Theology* 26, no. 1 (2010): 120–48.

Hill, Jonathan. "Aquinas and the Unity of Christ: A Defense of Compositionalism." *International Journal of Philosophy of Religion* 71, no. 2 (2012): 117–35.

Hobbes, Thomas. *Computatio sive Logica.* Translated by A. P. Martinich. New York: Abaris, 1981.

———. *Elementorum philosophiae sectio prima "De corpore."* London: Andrew Crook, 1655.

Hodge, Charles. *Systematic Theology*. Vol. 2. Grand Rapids: Eerdmans, 1940.

Hoekema, Anthony A. *Created in God's Image*. Grand Rapids: Eerdmans, 1994.

Horton, Michael S. *Covenant and Salvation: Union with Christ*. Louisville: Westminster John Knox, 2007.

Irenaeus. *Against Heresies*. In *Ante-Nicene Fathers*. Vol. 1, *The Apostolic Fathers, Justin Martyr, Irenaeus*. Edited and translated by Alexander Roberts and James Donaldson. Peabody, MA: Hendrickson, 1994.

Jedwab, Joseph. "Against Mereological Christological Concretism." Unpublished manuscript.

Jenson, Robert W. "*Ipse Pater Non Est Impassibilis*." In Keating and White, *Divine Impassibility and the Mystery of Human Suffering*, 117–26.

———. "Once More the *Logos asarkos*." *International Journal of Systematic Theology* 13, no. 2 (2011): 130–33.

———. *Systematic Theology*. Vol. 1, *The Triune God*. New York: Oxford University Press, 1991.

———. *Systematic Theology*. Vol. 2, *The Works of God*. New York: Oxford University Press, 1999.

John of Damascus. *Three Treatises on the Divine Images*. Translated by Andrew Louth. Crestwood, NY: St. Vladimir's Seminary Press, 2003.

Johnson, Marcus Peter. "'The Highest Degree of Importance': Union with Christ and Soteriology." In Habets and Grow, *Evangelical Calvinism*, 222–52.

———. *One with Christ: An Evangelical Theology of Salvation*. Wheaton: Crossway, 2013.

Jowers, Dennis W., and H. Wayne House, eds. *The New Evangelical Subordinationism? Perspectives on the Equality of God the Father and God the Son*. Eugene, OR: Pickwick, 2012.

Kaufman, Gordon D. *Systematic Theology: A Historicist Perspective*. New York: Scribner's Sons, 1968.

Keating, James F., and Thomas Joseph White. *Divine Impassibility and the Mystery of Human Suffering*. Grand Rapids: Eerdmans, 2009.

Leftow, Brian. *Time and Eternity*. Ithaca, NY: Cornell University Press, 1991.

———. "A Timeless God Incarnate." In Davis, Kendall, and O'Collins, *The Incarnation*, 273–99.

Leith, John H. *Creeds of the Churches: A Reader in Christian Doctrine from the Bible to the Present*. 3rd ed. Louisville: John Knox, 1982.

Le Poidevin, Robin. "Identity and the Composite Christ: An Incarnational Dilemma." *Religious Studies* 45, no. 2 (2009): 167–86.

———. "Incarnation: Metaphysical Issues." *Philosophy Compass* 4, no. 4 (2009): 703–14.

Letham, Robert. *Union with Christ: In Scripture, History, and Theology*. Phillipsburg, NJ: Presbyterian and Reformed, 2011.

Lewis, David. "Do We Believe in Penal Substitution?" *Philosophical Papers* 26 (1997): 203–9.

Lombard, Peter. *The Sentences Book 3: On the Incarnation of the Word*. Translated by Giulio Silano. Toronto: Pontifical Institute of Medieval Studies, 2008.

Macquarrie, John. *Jesus Christ in Modern Thought*. London: SCM, 1990.

Marmadoro, Anna, and Jonathan Hill, eds. *The Metaphysics of the Incarnation*. Oxford: Oxford University Press, 2011.

McCall, Thomas H. *An Invitation to Analytic Christian Theology*. Downers Grove, IL: IVP Academic, 2015.

———. *Which Trinity? Whose Monotheism? Philosophical and Systematic Theologians on the Metaphysics of Trinitarian Theology*. Grand Rapids: Eerdmans, 2008.

McClymond, Michael J. "Salvation as Divinization: Jonathan Edwards, Gregory Palamas, and the Theological Uses of Neoplatonism." In *Jonathan Edwards: Philosophical Theologian*, edited by Paul Helm and Oliver D. Crisp, 139–60. Aldershot, UK: Ashgate, 2003.

McCormack, Bruce L. "The Person of Christ." In *Mapping Modern Theology: A Thematic and Historical Introduction*, edited by Kelly M. Kapic and Bruce L. McCormack, 149–74. Grand Rapids: Baker Academic, 2012.

Merricks, Trenton. "The Word Made Flesh: Dualism, Physicalism, and the Incarnation." In van Inwagen and Zimmerman, *Persons: Human and Divine*, 281–300.

Middleton, J. Richard. *The Liberating Image: The* Imago Dei *in Genesis 1*. Grand Rapids: Brazos, 2005.

Moberly, R. W. L. *The Theology of the Book of Genesis*. Old Testament Theology. Cambridge: Cambridge University Press, 2009.

Moltmann, Jürgen. *The Spirit of Life: A Universal Affirmation*. Translated by Margaret Kohl. Minneapolis: Fortress, 1993.

———. *The Way of Jesus Christ: Christology in Messianic Dimension*. Translated by Margaret Kohl. London: SCM, 1990.

Moreland, J. P. *The Recalcitrant* Imago Dei*: Human Persons and the Failure of Naturalism*. London: SCM, 2009.

Mosser, Carl. "The Greatest Possible Blessing: Calvin on Deification." *Scottish Journal of Theology* 55, no. 1 (2002): 36–57.

Muller, Richard A. *Post-Reformation Reformed Dogmatics*. Vol. 4, *The Triunity of God*. Grand Rapids: Baker Academic, 2003.

Murray, John. *The Imputation of Adam's Sin*. Grand Rapids: Eerdmans, 1959.

———. *Redemption Accomplished and Applied*. Edinburgh: Banner of Truth, 1965.

Myers, Benjamin. "The Patristic Atonement Model." In *Locating Atonement: Explorations in Constructive Dogmatics*, edited by Oliver D. Crisp and Fred Sanders, 71–88. Grand Rapids: Zondervan, 2015.

Nevin, John Williamson. *The Mystical Presence: A Vindication of the Reformed or Calvinistic Doctrine of the Holy Eucharist*. Philadelphia: J. B. Lippincott and Co., 1846.

Oberman, Heiko. *The Harvest of Medieval Theology: Gabriel Biel and Late Medieval Nominalism*. Cambridge, MA: Harvard University Press, 1963.

Oden, Thomas. *Classic Christianity: A Systematic Theology*. San Francisco: HarperOne, 2009.

Ott, Ludwig. *Fundamentals of Catholic Dogma*. Translated by Patrick Lynch. Rockford, IL: Tan Books, 1955.

Owen, John. *The Works of John Owen, Vol. X*. Edited by William H. Goold. Edinburgh: Banner of Truth, 1967.

Packer, J. I. "What Did the Cross Achieve? The Logic of Penal Substitution." In *The J. I. Packer Collection*, edited by Alister McGrath, 94–136. Downers Grove, IL: InterVarsity, 1999.

Pannenberg, Wolfhart. *Systematic Theology, Vol. 2*. Translated by Geoffrey Bromiley. Grand Rapids: Eerdmans; Edinburgh: T&T Clark, 1995.

Pawl, Timothy. "A Solution to the Fundamental Philosophical Problem for Christology." *Journal of Analytic Theology* 2 (2014): 61–85.

Peacocke, Arthur. *All That Is: A Naturalistic Faith for the Twenty-First Century*. Edited by Philip Clayton. Minneapolis: Fortress, 2007.

Plantinga, Richard J., Thomas R. Thompson, and Matthew D. Lundberg. *An Introduction to Christian Theology*. Cambridge: Cambridge University Press, 2010.

Plotinus. *Ennead VI.6–9*. Translated by A. H. Armstrong. Cambridge, MA: Harvard University Press, 1988.

Pseudo-Dionysius. *Pseudo-Dionysius: The Complete Works*. Translated by Colm Luibheid. Mahwah, NJ: Paulist Press, 1987.

Quinn, Phillip L. "Abelard on Atonement: 'Nothing Unintelligible, Arbitrary, Illogical, or Immoral about It.'" In Stump, *Reasoned Faith*, 281–300.

Rad, Gerhard von. *Genesis*. Philadelphia: Westminster, 1961.

Rashdall, Hastings. *The Idea of Atonement in Christian Theology*. London: Macmillan, 1919.

Rea, Michael C. "The Metaphysics of Original Sin." In van Inwagen and Zimmerman, *Persons: Human and Divine*, 319–56.

Richards, Jay Wesley. *The Untamed God: A Philosophical Exploration of Divine Perfection, Immutability, and Simplicity*. Downers Grove, IL: InterVarsity, 2003.

Sanders, Fred. "Introduction to Christology: Chalcedonian Categories for the Gospel Narrative." In Sanders and Issler, *Jesus in Trinitarian Perspective*, 1–41.

Sanders, Fred, and Klaus Issler, eds. *Jesus in Trinitarian Perspective: An Introductory Christology*. Nashville: B&H Academic, 2007.

Schleiermacher, Friedrich. *The Christian Faith*. Translated by H. R. MacIntosh and J. S. Stewart. Edinburgh: T&T Clark, 1999.

Senor, Thomas. "The Compositional Account of the Incarnation." *Faith and Philosophy* 24, no. 1 (2007): 52–71.

Shedd, William G. T. *Dogmatic Theology*. 3rd ed. Edited by Alan W. Gomes. Philipsburg, NJ: Presbyterian & Reformed, 2003.

Socinus, Faustus. *De Jesu Christo Servatore, hoc est, cur & qua ratione Jesus Christus noster servator sit, Fausti Socini Senensis disputatio*. . . . Kraków, 1594.

Steinmetz, David. *Calvin in Context*. New York: Oxford University Press, 1995.

Strobel, Kyle. "Jonathan Edwards and the Polemics of *Theosis*." *Harvard Theological Review* 105, no. 3 (2012): 259–79.

Stump, Eleonore. "Aquinas' Metaphysics of the Incarnation." In Davis, Kendall, and O'Collins, *The Incarnation*, 197–218.

———, ed. *Reasoned Faith*. Ithaca, NY: Cornell University Press, 1993.

Stump, Eleonore, and Norman Kretzmann. "Eternity." *Journal of Philosophy* 78, no. 8 (1981): 429–58.

Sturch, Richard. *The Word and the Christ: An Essay in Analytic Christology*. Oxford: Oxford University Press, 1991.

Swain, Scott R. *The God of the Gospel: Robert Jenson's Trinitarian Theology*. Downers Grove, IL: IVP Academic, 2013.

Swinburne, Richard. *The Christian God*. Oxford: Oxford University Press, 1994.

———. *The Evolution of the Soul*. Oxford: Oxford University Press, 1986.

———. "God and Time." In Stump, *Reasoned Faith*, 204–22.

———. *Mind, Brain, and Free Will*. Oxford: Oxford University Press, 2013.

———. *Responsibility and Atonement*. Oxford: Oxford University Press, 1989.

———. "Tensed Facts." *American Philosophical Quarterly* 27 (1990): 117–30.

Taliaferro, Charles. "Incorporeality." In *A Companion to Philosophy of Religion*, edited by Philip L. Quinn and Charles Taliaferro, 271–78. Oxford: Blackwell, 1997.

Tanner, Kathryn. *Christ the Key*. Cambridge: Cambridge University Press, 2009.

———. "Creation and Providence." In *The Cambridge Companion to Karl Barth*, edited by John Webster, 111–26. Cambridge: Cambridge University Press, 2000.

Tanner, Norman P., ed. *Decrees of the Ecumenical Councils*. Vol. 1, *Nicaea I–Lateran V*. London: Sheed & Ward; Washington, DC: Georgetown University Press, 1990.

Tertullian. *Treatise on the Incarnation*. Translated by Ernest Evans. London: SPCK, 1956.

Torrance, Thomas F. *The Christian Doctrine of God: One Being, Three Persons*. London: T&T Clark, 1996.

Vanhoozer, Kevin J. "The Origin of Paul's Soteriology: Election, Incarnation, and Union with Christ in Ephesians 1:4 (with Special Reference to Evangelical Calvinism)." In *Reconsidering the Relationship between Biblical and Systematic Theology in the New Testament: Essays by Theologians and New Testament Scholars*, edited by Benjamin E. Reynolds, Brian Lugioyo, and Kevin J. Vanhoozer, 177–212. Tübingen: Mohr Siebeck, 2014.

van Inwagen, Peter, and Dean Zimmerman, eds. *Persons: Human and Divine*. Oxford: Oxford University Press, 2007.

Weaver, J. Denny. *The Nonviolent Atonement*. 2nd ed. Grand Rapids: Eerdmans, 2011.

Weinandy, Thomas. "God and Human Suffering: His Act of Creation and His Acts in History." In Keating and White, *Divine Impassibility and the Mystery of Human Suffering*, 99–116.

West, J. L. A. "Aquinas on Peter Lombard and the Metaphysical Status of Christ's Human Nature." *Gregorianum* 88 (2007): 557–86.

Williams, C. J. F. "A Programme for Christology." *Religious Studies* 3, no. 2 (1968): 513–24.

Williams, Rowan. *Arius*. 2nd ed. London: SCM, 2001.

Young, Frances. *God's Presence: A Contemporary Recapitulation of Early Christianity*. Cambridge: Cambridge University Press, 2013.

Index

Abelard, Peter, 126–27. *See also* atonement: moral exemplar account of
accountability, age of. *See* theological anthropology: incapacity for faith-rationality
Adam (biblical figure), 54–55, 61–62, 70, 120, 130–44. *See also* theological anthropology
Adams, Marilyn McCord, 87n25, 97–99, 116n39
adoptionism. *See* christological heresies: adoptionism
advocate, another. *See* pneumatology: and the Person of the Holy Spirit
Ames, William, 161n32
analytic theology. *See* theological method: analytic theology
anathema. *See* christological heresies; ecumenical creeds
angels, 53, 55, 58, 124
Anselm of Canterbury, 9, 13–14, 44, 123–26
anthropology. *See* theological anthropology
Aquinas. *See* Thomas Aquinas
archetype-ectype, or Christ-humanity relation. *See* atonement: union account of
Arianism. *See* christological heresies: Arianism
a se (contra *per aliud*). *See* attributes of God: aseity
atemporalist (eternalist) view of God. *See* attributes of God: eternality
Athanasius of Alexandria, 3, 14, 53–54, 60–62, 76n8, 93, 121n3
atonement, x–xiii, 124n9, 166–71
  christological doctrine of. *See* atonement: union account of
  governmental account of, 123n7
  moral exemplar account of, 126–28
  nonviolent account of, 122n5, 128n18. *See also* atonement: ransom account of
  penal substitutionary account of, 128–30, 140, 143
  ransom account of, 121–23, 125, 126, 128
  realist penal substitutionary account of, 133–44
  reparative substitutionary account of, 125n11
  satisfaction account of, 119–23, 123–28, 131n24, 133n30, 136–40, 143–44, 167–68
  union account of, xi–xiii, 52, 56n11, 60–70, 119–20, 130–44, 152n12, 155–63, 166, 170–71. *See also* theosis
attributes of God
  aseity, 4–6, 13, 16–17, 41, 112–15
  eternality, 1–31, 36–37, 57–58, 74, 83–84, 100–101, 111–12, 147–49. *See also* Trinity: eternal (ontological) generation of the Son
  immutability, 21, 27–31, 108–16. *See also* incarnation
  impeccability, 61–64, 122–25. *See also* atonement
  incorporeality, xi, 33–50, 55–56, 61–65, 98n5, 101n12, 105n20, 108–9, 114–16. *See also* Christology: *Logos asarkos*; image of God: substantive account of
  oneness, 2–4, 9, 25–31, 35–36, 43–46, 92, 101, 108–14. *See also* theological method: Trinitarian Appropriation Principle for
  providence, 76, 146–47, 154–55, 157, 166–68. *See also* justification from eternity
  simplicity, 43, 61–64, 122–25. *See also* Trinity
  See also hypostatic union: *communicatio idiomatum*
Augustine of Hippo, 5, 124n9, 130–33
  influence of, 9, 12–16, 30–31, 43, 44n13
Augustinian realism, 130–44. *See also* Melchizedek; theological anthropology: and the soul: traducianism
Aulén, Gustav, 121–22. *See also* atonement: ransom account of
Ayres, Lewis, 2, 174

185

Index

Barth, Karl, 19, 57n12, 136–44, 152n11, 153n13, 170–71
Batman, 11–12, 14
Bauckham, Richard, 74
Bavinck, Herman, 56n11
Berkeley, George (bishop of Cloyne), 37–38
Berkhof, Hendrikus, 146, 151–52
Berkhof, Louis, 12n22, 130n23
Boethius, Anicius Manlius Severinus, 87–88, 94–95
Brümmer, Vincent, 130n22
Brunner, Emil, 153
Bultmann, Rudolf, 72, 175

Calvin, John, 54–56, 64, 145, 156–63
Calvinism. *See* historical theological traditions: evangelical theology: Evangelical Calvinism; historical theological traditions: Reformed theology
Cartesianism, 98n5, 104–5, 115–18
Catechism of the Catholic Church, 54–55, 61
Chalcedonian Christology. *See* Cyril of Alexandria; ecumenical creeds: Chalcedonian definition
charisms of the Holy Spirit. *See* sacramentology
Chisholm, Roderick, 132n29
christological compositionalism. *See* Christology: person (*hypostasis*) of Christ
christological heresies
  adoptionism, 23. *See also* Socinianism
  Apollinarianism, 98
  Arianism, 2–6, 15–17, 20, 74
  monothelitism, 83, 91–94
  Nestorianism, 23–24, 27, 88–92, 99, 102–18
Christology, x, 16–17, 27, 44–49, 72–99, 103n17, 112, 147
  degree Christology. *See* Hick, John
  historical Jesus, 72–76, 83–84, 111, 147, 169–70
  Logos asarkos, xi–xiii, 20–26, 31, 52–54, 93n32, 107, 152–54
  person (*hypostasis*) of Christ, xi–xii, 20–37, 45–47, 90–92, 97–118, 115. *See also* hypostatic union
  representationalism in. *See* atonement: realist penal substitutionary account of
  theories for
    compositional model. *See* Christology: person (*hypostasis*) of Christ
    joined-up account. *See* atonement: union account of
    mereological model. *See* Christology: person (*hypostasis*) of Christ
  time in relation to, x, 5, 66–68, 105–8, 138, 154. *See also* functions of the Triune God: Son
  vicarious humanity of Christ. *See* Torrance, Thomas F.
  work of Christ. *See* atonement
Christus Victor. *See* atonement: ransom account of
church, life of the. *See* ecclesiology
Coakley, Sarah, 80–81, 175
Comforter, the. *See* pneumatology: and the Person of the Holy Spirit
commercial (sacrificial) theory of atonement. *See* atonement: satisfaction account of
communication of (divine/human) attributes in Christ. *See* hypostatic union: *communicatio idiomatum*
consensus view in theology. *See* theological method: consensual Christianity
constructive theology. *See* theological method
creation. *See* functions of the Triune God: Father
Cross, Richard, 22, 88n26, 102n14, 103n17, 106n24, 113–14
Cyril of Alexandria, 30, 92

Daley, Brian, 86–87
death, 7n10, 36n4, 136–39, 168n4
  of Christ, 28, 120–21, 126–29, 139n37
definition of Chalcedon. *See* ecumenical creeds: Chalcedonian definition
deification. *See* theosis
denominationalism. *See* ecumenism; historical theological traditions
Descartes, René. *See* Cartesianism
Devil, the, 121–24, 125n9
DeWeese, Garrett J., 85n20, 92. *See also* theological method: Chalcedonian Axiom
dignity, human. *See* theological anthropology: incapacity for faith-rationality
disability. *See* theological anthropology: incapacity for faith-rationality
divine election. *See* justification from eternity
divine pardon. *See* justification from eternity
divinization. *See* theosis
dualism (human body/soul). *See* Cartesianism; theological anthropology: concrete nature view of body-soul composite for
dyophysitism. *See* Christology: person (*hypostasis*) of Christ; hypostatic union: two-natures doctrine of
dyothelitism. *See* hypostatic union: two wills in

Index

ecclesiology, 139–40, 142–47, 159–62
economic functions of God. *See* functions of the Triune God
ecumenical councils, 74–76
  Chalcedon (451), 73, 79–85, 92–95, 118. *See also* ecumenical creeds: Chalcedonian definition
  Constantinople I (381), 83n17. *See also* ecumenical creeds: Nicene-Constantinopolitan Creed
  Constantinople II (553), 82–91, 95, 107–10, 118, 147–48. *See also* hypostatic union: two-natures doctrine of
  Constantinople III (681), 82–89, 91–95. *See also* hypostatic union: two-natures doctrine of; hypostatic union: two wills in
  Ephesus (431), 83n17
  Nicaea I (325), 5. *See also* ecumenical creeds: Nicene Creed
  Nicaea II (787), 92–93
ecumenical creeds
  Athanasian Creed. *See* Athanasius of Alexandria
  Chalcedonian definition (451), 74, 79–95, 102, 105–10. *See also* ecumenical councils: Chalcedon
  Nicene Creed (325), 15. *See also* ecumenical councils: Nicaea I
  Nicene-Constantinopolitan Creed (381), 1, 5, 15, 92–93, 147
  See also ecumenical councils
ecumenism, 70, 155–56
Edwards, Jonathan, ix, 37–43, 119, 144n43, 155n17, 157–63
eikōn of God. *See* image of God: Christ as
elect, the, 65–66, 68n22, 135–44, 161–63, 165–71
  infants. *See* theological anthropology: incapacity for faith-rationality
election (doctrine). *See* atonement; Barth, Karl
emergent monism. *See* Peacocke, Arthur
Enns, Peter, 64–65
eschatology, 7n10, 66, 147, 161–62
eternalist (atemporalist) view of God. *See* attributes of God: eternity
evangelicalism. *See* historical theological traditions: evangelical theology
evolutionary theory. *See* theological anthropology: and evolutionary theory

faith in Christ. *See* functions of the Triune God: Spirit: epistemological realism
Farris, Joshua, xvi–xvii, 37n6, 60n15, 177

Fergusson, David, 57–58, 177
filioque. *See* pneumatology: and *filioque*
Flint, Thomas P., 99n6, 103n16, 104n18
forgiveness, divine. *See* justification from eternity
Franks, R. S., 121n2, 127n16
functions of the Triune God, 11–15, 146, 150–51. *See also* Christology; pneumatology
  Father, xi, 1–17, 20–29, 147–58. *See also* protology
  Son, ix, 2–7, 11–17, 31, 120–28, 138–41, 146, 156–58, 163–71. *See also* atonement
  Spirit, xii–xiii, 55, 61, 64–66, 70, 145–47, 152–63, 165–71. *See also* sacramentology
  epistemological realism, 163, 166, 170–71. *See also* theological method: human experience as (secondarily) authoritative for; revelation, divine

global monism, 37–50
global immaterialism, 37–38, 47–50
global materialism, 38–47, 56–57
God-consciousness. *See* Hick, John
Gregory of Nyssa, 121n3

hamartiology. *See* sin
Harrison, Mark McLeod, 62–63, 70n23
Heidegger, Martin, 77
Helm, Paul, xvi, 1, 3n3, 4n6, 5n8, 7–15, 158n23, 178, 180
heretical doctrines. *See* christological heresies
Hick, John, 48–49, 127
historical biblical criticism. *See* theological method
historical theological traditions
  evangelical theology, xi, 6–7, 16–17, 92–93, 156–57
    Evangelical Calvinism, 169–71. *See also* Torrance, Thomas F.
  Lutheran theology, 8n13, 20, 59. *See also* Jenson, Robert W.; Protestant confessions of faith
  medieval theology, xiii–xiv, 45–46, 87–100, 111, 118, 127. *See also* theological method: and Aristotelian metaphysics
  patristic theology, 3, 52–54, 55n10, 60, 70, 74, 76n8, 86, 121–22
  Puritan theology, ix, 159, 161n32. *See also* Edwards, Jonathan
  Reformed theology, xi–xiii, 8–9, 56, 129n20, 132n27, 138–63, 166–71. *See also* Protestant confessions of faith
Hobbes, Thomas, 39–40, 44, 47
Hodge, Charles, 41n8, 129n20

187

Hoekema, Anthony A., 55n8, 56n11, 60n14
Holy Spirit. *See* pneumatology
honor, divine. *See* atonement: ransom account of
human person. *See* theological anthropology
hylomorphism. *See* theological method: and Aristotelian metaphysics
hypostatic union, xii–xiii, 21–31, 33–50, 63–69, 71–95, 97–118, 119
 anhypostatic-enhypostatic distinction for, 82–95
 archetype-ectype distinction for, 52–54, 61–68
 communicatio idiomatum, 114–18
 three-part compositional model of, 98–118
 two-natures doctrine of, ix, 24, 30, 49, 79–95, 103n17, 105–16
 two wills in, 73, 83–85, 89–95

iconography. *See* ecumenical councils: Nicaea II
image of God, xi–xiii, 8–9, 52–70, 120. *See also* theological anthropology
 Christ as, 53, 60, 61, 64–65, 70n23. *See also* atonement: union account of
 relational account of, xi–xii, 21–22, 24n14, 25–27, 57–70, 136–37. *See also* Trinity: social (or relational) model of
 substantive account of, 54–65, 69–70. *See also* hypostatic union: archetype-ectype distinction for
imago Dei. *See* image of God
immaterialism. *See* attributes of God: incorporeality; global monism: global immaterialism
impassibility of God. *See* attributes of God: immutability
incarnation, 20, 23, 166–71
 and metaphysics, ix, 7–12, 23–31, 45–49, 63, 74, 77–95, 98–118. *See also* attributes of God: incorporeality
 transformational model of, 24–25
infinite strictness of union with Christ. *See* theosis
invisible God. *See* attributes of God: incorporeality; image of God: Christ as
Irenaeus of Lyons, 53, 60–62

Jedwab, Joseph, 105n21
Jenson, Robert W., xvi, 19–31, 44, 59, 179
Jesus of Nazareth. *See* Christology
John of Damascus, 86n21, 93n33
justice, 54n7, 128–30, 139n38, 142–44, 145
justification from eternity, ix, 66–68, 154–55, 166–71

Leftow, Brian, 10n18, 24n15, 99–102, 106–13
Lewis, David, 129–30
Logos Christology. *See* Christology: *Logos asarkos*
Lombard, Peter, xviii, 4n5, 88n26
Lord and Life-Giver. *See* pneumatology: and the Person of the Holy Spirit
Lutheranism. *See* historical theological traditions: Lutheran theology

materialism. *See* global monism: global materialism; Hobbes, Thomas
Maximus the Confessor, 83, 86n21
McCormack, Bruce, 77–79
Melchizedek (biblical figure), 134n32
mental impairment. *See* theological anthropology: incapacity for faith-rationality
meritorious act (supererogation) of Christ. *See* atonement: satisfaction account of
Merricks, Trenton, 104–5, 180
Middleton, J. Richard, 65n19
mind, human. *See* theological anthropology: and human rationality
missio Dei. *See* functions of the Triune God
Moltmann, Jürgen, 57n12, 83–84, 89–91, 151n10
monarchianism. *See* christological heresies: adoptionism
monism
 emergent. *See* Peacocke, Arthur
 global. *See* global monism
monothelitism. *See* christological heresies: monothelitism
moral law, divine. *See* atonement: ransom account of
Moreland, J. P., 55n7, 59–60
Murray, John, 129n20, 132n28, 157
Myers, Benjamin, 121n3, 169
mystical union. *See* atonement: union account of

natures (divine and human) of Christ. *See* hypostatic union: two-natures doctrine of
Neoplatonism. *See* Plotinus
Nestorianism. *See* christological heresies: Nestorianism
Nevin, John Williamson, xiv, 160, 181

Oden, Thomas. *See* theological method: consensual Christianity
ontological functions of God. *See* attributes of God
ontology, human. *See* theological anthropology: four-dimensional ontology for

original guilt and/or sin. *See* sin: transmission (imputation) from Adam
orthodoxy (doctrinal normativity). *See* ecumenical creeds
Owen, John, xiv, 140, 159–60, 181

Packer, J. I., 128n19
panentheism, 34, 41–42, 47–49
Pannenberg, Wolfhart, 54n7, 57n12, 61n16, 66
pantheism, 34, 40–41, 44
Paraclete. *See* pneumatology: and the Person of the Holy Spirit
Peacocke, Arthur, 47–49. *See also* panentheism
penance. *See* sin: repentance (penitence) for
perichoresis, 42, 48, 57–58
physicalism. *See* global monism; global materialism
Plantinga, Alvin, 72n2
Plantinga, Richard J., 53n3, 181
Plotinus, 42–44
pluralism, religious. *See* Hick, John
pneumatology, 145–63
  and *filioque*, 11, 14, 147–49
  and the Person of the Holy Spirit, 147–52
  secret work of the Holy Spirit. *See* functions of the Triune God: Spirit
prayer, 59, 63–64. *See also* image of God; theological anthropology
predestination. *See* justification from eternity
Protestant confessions of faith, 8, 16–17, 54n7, 93–94, 148–49, 167. *See also* ecumenical councils
protology, xi–xiii, 2–5, 14–15, 36, 41–50, 52–69, 146–62. *See also* Trinity: eternal (ontological) generation of the Son
Pseudo-Dionysius the Areopagite, 149–50
Puritanism. *See* historical theological traditions: Puritan theology

Quinn, Philip L., 126–27

Rahner, Karl, 152n11
Rashdall, Hastings, 127n17, 182
rationality, human. *See* theological anthropology: and human rationality
Rea, Michael C. *See* theological anthropology: stage theory view of
realist penal substitutionary atonement. *See* atonement: realist penal substitutionary account of
reconciliation. *See* theosis
Redeemed Humanity. *See* elect, the

regeneration. *See* functions of the Triune God: Spirit
relational account of *imago Dei*. *See* image of God: relational account of
revelation, divine, 73, 149–50
righteousness. *See* justice
Roman Catholic Councils (selected)
  Lateran IV (1215), 4, 35
  Vatican I (1869–70), 35

sacramentology, 93, 155–63. *See also* ecumenical councils: Nicaea II; theosis
sanctification. *See* functions of the Triune God: Spirit
Sanders, Fred, xvi, 83n17, 85n20, 121n3, 176, 181, 182
Satan. *See* atonement: ransom account of; Devil, the
Schleiermacher, Friedrich, 66n21, 84, 91–92, 182
Scholasticism. *See* historical theological traditions: medieval theology
Scotus, Duns, 88n26, 98, 114n37, 176
sensus fidei. *See* theological method: consensual Christianity
sin, 46, 61–65, 120–44, 156n19, 158–60, 166–71
  divine conventionalism for human guilt of, 143–44. *See also* sin: transmission (imputation) from Adam
  Fallen Humanity, 55, 64, 122–24, 133–47, 163
  legal fiction view of. *See* theological method: forensic fiction approach to
  moral fiction view of. *See* theological method: forensic fiction approach to
  repentance (penitence) for, 126
  transfer (imputation) to Christ. *See* atonement: realist penal substitutionary account of
  transmission (imputation) from Adam, 70, 129–44, 155n19, 160
social trinitarianism. *See* Trinity: social (or relational) model of
Socinianism, 126–30
soul. *See* theological anthropology: and the soul
  fissiparous. *See* theological anthropology: and the soul: traducianism
  parturient. *See* theological anthropology: and the soul: parturition
Spirit of God. *See* pneumatology
Steinmetz, David, 162n33, 182
structural view of *imago Dei*. *See* image of God: substantive account of
Stump, Eleonore, 3n3, 10n18, 72n2, 99n6, 105n20, 110n31, 127n15, 181

Sturch, Richard, 79–80, 182
substantive account of *imago Dei*. *See* image of God: substantive account of
Swinburne, Richard, 3–5, 88n25, 117–18, 125–28, 182
symbol (*symbolum*) of faith. *See* ecumenical creeds
systematic theology. *See* theological method

Taliaferro, Charles, xvi, 36–37, 183
Tanner, Kathryn, xiii–xiv, 51, 57n12, 76n8, 153n13, 177
temporal parts (doctrine). *See* theological anthropology: four-dimensional ontology for
temporalist view of God. *See* attributes of God: eternality
Tertullian, 71, 183
theistic naturalism. *See* Peacocke, Arthur
theological anthropology, 51–54, 61–65, 119–20
  concrete nature view of body-soul composite for, 24–25, 45–47, 67, 77–78, 86–110, 117–18
  distinction of perdurantist-exdurantist metaphysics for. *See* theological anthropology: four-dimensional ontology for
  and evolutionary theory, 68–69
  four-dimensional ontology for, 133–35, 140–44, 161, 170–71
  and human rationality, 55–69, 87–89, 94–95, 111
  incapacity for faith-rationality, 56, 59, 61, 69, 91–92, 168n4
  and the soul, 24–30, 31n26, 35–38, 43–49, 54–65, 98nn4–5
    parturition, 132, 135
    traducianism, 132–38
  stage theory view of, 142–43. *See also* theological anthropology: four-dimensional ontology for
theological method, ix–x, 7–10, 54–61, 72–81, 120, 121n2, 136n33, 147
  analytic theology, x–xii, 1–7, 17, 35–37, 61–65, 79–95, 102–18, 121n3, 132n27, 157n23
  and Aristotelian metaphysics, 36n4, 79, 87–88, 105n20
  Chalcedonian Axiom, 85–95
  consensual Christianity, 22n8, 64–65, 73, 75, 79–81, 95. *See also* ecumenical councils
  dogmatic minimalism, 80–95
  forensic fiction approach to, 37, 129–41, 144. *See also* atonement
  human experience as (secondarily) authoritative for, 150

Intention-Application Principle for. *See* attributes of God: providence
novelty vis-à-vis orthodoxy in, 140–44, 152n12
Scripture and tradition (together) as authoritative for, 37, 72–75, 80, 141, 150
Trinitarian Appropriation Principle for, 153–55. *See also* functions of the Triune God; Trinity
theosis, ix–x, xiii n5, 120–40, 141, 156–63, 166, 170–71. *See also* functions of the Triune God: Spirit
Thomas Aquinas, 6n9, 13–15, 21, 26, 36n4, 45n14, 87. *See also* theological method: and Aristotelian metaphysics
three-part compositional model of hypostatic union. *See* hypostatic union: three-part compositional model of
Torrance, Thomas F., xiv, 76n8, 153n13, 169–71, 174
Trinity
  economic. *See* functions of the Triune God
  eternal (ontological) generation of the Son, xi, 1–17, 21–27, 52, 67
  functional subordination of the Son. *See* functions of the Triune God: Son
  immanent, xii–xiii, 1–3, 10, 14–17, 20–30, 44–49, 58, 149–50
  Latin trinitarianism, 22–25, 27, 31. *See also* attributes of God: simplicity
  mereological model of, 10, 35–45. *See also* perichoresis
  ontological. *See* Trinity: immanent
  procession of the Son. *See* Trinity: eternal (ontological) generation of the Son
  social (or relational) model of, 22–25, 57–58. *See also* perichoresis
  trinitarian law. *See* attributes of God: oneness
  See also attributes of God; functions of the Triune God

union of hearts. *See* functions of the Triune God: Spirit
unitarianism, 151n10. *See also* Socinianism

Vanhoozer, Kevin J., 165–71
virginal conception and birth of Jesus. *See* Christology: time in relation to
visio Dei. *See* eschatology

will(s) of Christ. *See* hypostatic union: two wills in
Word of God. *See* Christology: *Logos asarkos*

www.ingramcontent.com/pod-product-compliance
Lightning Source LLC
Chambersburg PA
CBHW021810220426
43662CB00006B/248